The Higher Education System

D0209765

The Higher Education System

Academic Organization in Cross-National Perspective

BURTON R. CLARK

UNIVERSITY OF CALIFORNIA PRESS

BERKELEY   LOS ANGELES   LONDON

University of California Press
Berkeley and Los Angeles, California
University of California Press, Ltd.
London, England
Copyright © 1983 by The Regents of the University of California
Library of Congress Cataloging in Publication Data

Clark, Burton R.
    The higher education system.

    Bibliography
    Includes index.
    1. Education, Higher.   2. Comparative education.
I. Title.
LB2322.C57   1983   378   82-13521
ISBN 0-520-04841-5

        Printed in the United States of America
              1 2 3 4 5 6 7 8 9

To Adele Halitsky Clark

For all our days, through the flow of time

CONTENTS

ACKNOWLEDGMENTS

My preparation for the writing of this book extends back over a decade and entails a debt of gratitude to scholars and officials in many countries. In the late 1960s, Sergio Bruno, Pier Paulo Giglioli, and other Italian colleagues helped me fathom the Italian variant of Continental systems of higher education, an eye-opening experience for an American. In the years that followed, I was similarly instructed by colleagues at home and abroad on other important national systems: in particular, John H. Van de Graaff and Dietrich Goldschmidt on the Federal Republic of Germany; Roger Geiger, R. R. Palmer, and Dorotea Furth on France; Rune Premfors, Bertil Östergren, and Olof Ruin on Sweden; Geoffrey Giles on the German Democratic Republic and Yugoslavia; Robert O. Berdahl, David Jones, Maurice Kogan, Graeme C. Moodie, Naomi McIntosh, and Harold Perkin on Great Britain; Edward Sheffield on Canada; Ikuo Amano, William Cummings, Kazuyuki Kitamura, Morikazu Ushiogi, and Donald F. Wheeler on Japan; Daniel C. Levy on Mexico and other Latin American countries; and John Whitehead, Jon McKenna, and Peter Hall on the American system. I have also learned more than is acknowledged in the following pages from the comparative writings of Lord Eric Ashby, Joseph Ben-David, Barbara Burn, Clark Kerr, James A. Perkins, and Martin A. Trow.

I was encouraged to write this comparative volume by my experience, between 1973–1974 and 1979–1980, as chairman of the Higher Education Research Group in the Institution for Social and Policy Studies, Yale University, a congenial research setting in which a good share of the individuals named above participated as postdoctoral researchers or visiting scholars. With much satisfaction I recall how little we knew about how to analyze national systems of higher education in the group's first seminars of 1973–1974 and how much more empirical detail and comparative capacity we possessed a half-dozen years later. Essential support of the group was provided by John Perry Miller and Charles E. Lindblom as successive directors of the Institution. I am indebted to them and to the dozen members of the group who participated most actively during those years. I hope this volume will be seen as a basic statement that capitalizes on the many specific working papers and monographs that stemmed from the field investigations of my colleagues.

Beyond the support of Yale University, the funds that made possible extensive research and continuing seminars flowed from successive grants by the National Science Foundation, the National Institute of Education, the Lilly Endowment, the Mellon Foundation, and the Exxon Education Foundation. I wish to thank particularly Laura Bornholdt, Vice-President for Education in the Lilly Endowment, whose enthusiastic commitment supported the research through four crucial years. There is also much pleasure in remembering the month spent in the summer of 1980 as a resident scholar in the utopian setting of the Villa Serbelloni in Bellagio, Italy, supported by the Rockefeller Foundation, where revision of central chapters convinced me that an integrated volume could be fashioned. Finally, I am indebted to the University of California, Los Angeles, where stimulating conditions provided by the Graduate School of Education allowed me to complete the manuscript and prepare final copy. The freedom and support allocated scholars in modern research universities remains an amazing phenomenon.

Helpful critical reviews of the penultimate draft were offered by a number of colleagues, especially Barbara Burn, Ladislav Cerych, Roger Geiger, Maurice Kogan, Daniel Levy, John Meyer, Rune Premfors, and Gary Rhoades. Manuscript typing of the last two drafts was the handiwork of Carolyn Davis and Jeannie Abrams.

Adele Clark has contributed substantially to my work for over thirty years. An appropriate acknowledgment is understated in the dedication of this book to her.

Portions of the manuscript draw upon the following previously published articles: Burton R. Clark, "The Benefits of Disorder," *Change* 8 (Oct. 1976):31–37; "Problems of Access in the Context of Academic Structures," in *Access, Systems, Youth and Employment*, edited by Barbara B. Burn, pp. 39–52. New York: International

Council for Educational Development, 1977; "Academic Differentiation in National Systems of Higher Education," *Comparative Education Review* 22 (June 1978):242–258; "Coordination: Patterns and Processes," in Clark Kerr, John Millett, Burton R. Clark, Brian MacArthur, and Howard Bowen, *12 Systems of Higher Education: 6 Decisive Issues*, pp. 57–95. New York: International Council for Educational Development, 1978; "The Many Pathways of Academic Coordination," *Higher Education* 8 (1979):251–267; "The Insulated Americans: Five Lessons From Abroad," *Change* 10 (Nov. 1978): 24–30.

Burton R. Clark

Santa Monica, California
November 1981

It is rare to find an institution which is at once so uniform and so diverse; it is recognisable in all the guises which it takes, but in no one place is it identical with what it is in any other. This unity and diversity constitute the final proof of the extent to which the university was the spontaneous product of mediaeval life; for it is only living things which can in this way, while fully retaining their identity, bend and adapt themselves to a whole variety of circumstances and environments.

—*Emile Durkheim*, The Evolution of Educational Thought

INTRODUCTION

National systems of higher education gather together a good share of those individuals who develop and disseminate the intellectual heritage of the world. Important through the centuries in training professionals and political elites, these centers of knowledge, growing many times over and multiplying their activities, occupy an ever more crucial place in the twentieth century. Yet we fail to do them justice. For a long time scholars did not take seriously the province of their own commitment. While disciplined perspectives developed on the economy, the polity, and such realms as the social-class system, only occasional comments by professors or retired rectors were mustered on the workings of systems of higher learning. After 1960, problems of expansion and discontent elicited much public and scholarly attention, but in ways that were fragmented and fragile. The research agenda centered on immediate issues and episodes as government and other patrons sought answers to problems of the day. The dramatic events of student political action drew much comment but left behind little serious literature. Notable, as attention freshened, were the scholars with new perspectives who came into the study of higher education in many countries, but all too briefly and soon to wander away: organizational theorists to gaze awhile upon the odd ways of universities and then return to the business firm; political scientists to assemble some essays on government and higher education and then go back to traditional political institutions; economists to measure some inputs and outputs and speculate on benefits and costs and then find other topics for their tools; sociologists to absorb education in the study of stratification and forget about the rest. In addition, much research has been limited to a single country, but then freely used to assert what the

1

academic life is like everywhere. Continuing comparative analysis has been left to a few. Thus, while measurably richer in ideas and facts, the emerging serious literature on higher education leaves much to be desired.

My purpose is to improve the state of the art by detailing systematically how higher education is organized and governed. The approach is twofold: to set forth the basic elements of the higher education system, as seen from an organizational perspective; and to show how those features vary across nations, with fateful effects. To identify the elements is to create general categories. To fill the categories empirically is to draw upon descriptions and analyses of higher education in such countries as the United States, the United Kingdom, Sweden, Japan, Italy, and the Federal Republic of Germany, where the best research has been done, and to add, wherever possible, such diverse countries as Poland, Mexico, and Thailand when some reliable and relevant information is available. The one effort is necessary to the other. To define what is basic requires that we move among nations and confront their common and varied structures and procedures. To group descriptive facts about countries in other than a mere list requires an ordering framework. Cross-national comparison is particularly advantageous in uncovering the unique features and unconscious assumptions that possess our vision when we study only a single country, generally our own. The "hometown" view has been particularly damaging in the study of higher education, since a large share of the literature has been written by Americans, and the U.S. system, in its fundaments, is a deviant case. Then, too, the brute realities of national differences restrain normative dogma. It makes sense to know what is in place and how the future is thereby prefigured for others who are as rational as we, before applying judgments on what ought to be done in higher education at home and abroad.

To pursue basic features of the higher education system, is to concentrate on how the system itself determines action and change. Such an internal approach thereby avoids easy imputation of influence to "society." This approach also is increasingly compelling in social science as large sectors split off as major specialties with their own constraints and imperatives. Ralf Dahrendorf put it well when he remarked that "certain areas of human activity have evolved their own action patterns: the world of science, or of painting. There is, in other words, such a thing as sectoral hegemony."[1] Science, scholarship, and higher education, for example, have autonomies not to be imagined in elementary schooling or modern secondary education. They are freer of the family, community, and church, and, for the most part, of local public officials and local lay control. The last century has seen the higher education system mature as a relatively independent sector of modern societies.

Despite the widespread impression that higher education is increasingly interdependent with other parts of society, and thereby heavily dependent, there is gain in seeing this sector as one that has developed its own massive structure and bounded procedures that provide some insulation and strengthened hegemony over certain tasks and functions.[2] This institutional capacity includes not only the power of groups within the system to shape their immediate work environment but also the power to affect the world. Near the end of a century in which physicists have harnessed atomic energy, mathematicians and engineers have developed the computer, and biologists have made their own revolutionary advances in genetic engineering, this point hardly needs additional initial support. What is involved is a vast professionalization of academic activities, a fundamental trend that roots persons in the fields of work in which they have taken prolonged advanced training and from which they receive material and symbolic rewards. In the modern world, professionalized occupations settle in organizational sectors—foresters in forest agencies, tax experts in revenue agencies and related financial institutions—there to express themselves decisively in their "own" sector and to use their "own" organizations as tools for struggle against other interests. When professionalization converges with bureaucratization in fashioning large organizations and larger sectors, powerful social actors are thereby produced. And so it is in higher education.

The view from the inside also has the advantage of emphasizing institutional responses. In the study of higher education, observers frequently note "demands" that ostensibly are set in motion elsewhere and become forces that either move the system or are denied by passive immobility. But any identifiable demand is but the beginning of analysis. What is the response to it? How is it implemented and thereby shaped? In fact, how much did the system determine the demand in the first place? as when long-standing tough standards make it perfectly clear to ninety percent of secondary school students that they should not think about approaching the doors of the higher education system. Even the origination and early development of new forms requires much internal analysis if we are to grasp what separated the significant from the trivial.

The English historian A. B. Cobban has brilliantly analyzed the struggle of the earliest efforts to construct universities in medieval Europe, facing the central question of why Bologna and its imitators in northern Italy survived but an earlier and equally promising effort in Salerno died out. "The central weakness of Salerno," he noted, "was its failure to develop a protective and cohesive organization to sustain its intellectual advance." Cobban concluded that

> the history of medieval universities reinforces that institutional response must follow quickly upon academic achievement if the intellectual moment is not to be dissipated. The absence of regular organization may initially provide a fillup for free-ranging inquiry, but perpetuation and controlled development can only be gained through an institutional framework.[3]

I shall push hard an internalist perspective that concentrates on the institutional framework, the regular organization that supports, perpetuates, and indeed helps to create "the intellectual moment."

Lurking behind many difficulties in this and other studies in social science and education is the murky term *system*. It is an idea we can hardly do without even when plagued by its ambiguity and shifting meanings. When we use the term, we construct boundaries, arbitrary definitions of relevant actors and structures that fashion insiders and outsiders. An economic system is a body of actors engaged in exchange of goods and services, together with the institutional forms they use, but such actors are outside the system when they are otherwise occupied. A political system may include those who vote only occasionally as well as those who are attentive and active, but unless the term is made synonymous with existence in a polity, individuals are clearly not in the system when they tend to their nonpolitical activities. This is true also of *the higher education system*. I will sometimes use the term in a narrow, conventional sense to refer to an aggregate of formal entities, e.g., the French system of higher education seen as the sum of many individual universities, colleges, and institutes, together with such apparent formal machinery as the ministry of education. But, made clear by context, I shall at times switch to a broader approach that includes any of the population when engaged in postsecondary educational activities, either as controllers, organizers, workers, or consumers. For example, legislative educational committees, public executives when attending to higher educational issues, trustees when acting as trustees, as well as administrators, professors, and students, full or part time, would all fall under this broader usage.

This necessary looser definition of system means that boundaries expand and contract, zig and zag, across time and space. To do otherwise is to place outside "the system" some of its most important participants and institutions. If we appropriately conceive of university trustees as within the U.S. system, then we clearly mean that slice of their lives when they attend to the higher education business, though we realize that they spend most of their time and energy in other pursuits. It is then also appropriate to think of certain representatives of external interests as parts of the systems in other countries when, as in the Swedish corporatist pattern later discussed, they occupy regular places on various boards. When it aids analysis and conception, I will freely enlarge the boundaries of the system.

A relaxed approach to system also better accommodates the peculiarities of academic tasks and work. The ways in which teachers and researchers in disciplines and professional fields hook up with their counterparts in other universities and other national systems—connections at the center of our analysis—make boundaries naturally uneven and problematic. Also, professors in many countries are officially part time and are legitimately employed elsewhere, and hence wander in and out. En masse, they are loosely bounded. Thus, it pays analytically both to assign system boundaries flexibly and to worry less about whether there is a boundary at all, for the university or college itself and especially for the larger systems. The effort in organizational theory to conceptualize the relation of organizations to their environments has evolved to the point of suggesting that we dissolve "as far as possible the boundary between an organization and its environment" in order to "speak in terms of groups within and without the organization using it for their own purpose."[4] This perspective is even more appropriate for large sets of organizations. With boundaries of systems so problematic, especially in higher education, it makes sense to focus on the capacity of well-located groups to use parts of the system for their own purposes, examining them without much concern about where they sit on the two sides of an arbitrary line.

If higher education is composed everywhere of knowledge-bearing groups, then it is useful to begin in chapter 1 with an examination of the special nature of knowledge as the prime material around which activity is organized. As it is multiplied, refined, and segmented, knowledge indeed becomes a peculiarly slippery and even invisible substance. Notably, its modern texture makes a mockery of the stated ends of higher education. Perhaps nowhere else in society is the gap between nominal and real purposes greater, with statements of broad goals by philosophers and statesmen increasingly removed from the realities of daily practice. To start with an elementary consideration of knowledge materials and knowledge groups is to approach the notion of purpose concretely, emphasizing its genuine location in operating units of universities and colleges, and its natural and increasing ambiguity at the higher reaches.

From this starting point, the analysis moves to three basic elements of the organization of higher education systems, the first of which is the way tasks are conceived and arranged. Around knowledge specialties, each national system develops a division of labor that becomes traditional, strongly institutionalized, and heavily influential on the future. Everywhere higher education has its work organized in two basic crisscrossing modes: by discipline and by institution, with disciplines cutting across the boundaries of the local enterprises and the institutions, in turn, picking up subgroups of the disciplines and aggregating then locally. The meta-institutional nature of the disciplines and professional fields of study is a salient and distinctive part of the character of the higher education system, and to grasp this feature, common across systems, marks a major step forward. But, on the institutional side, national systems have evolved quite different structures, necessitating a scheme that allows us to systematize the alternatives of differentiation and to identify a handful of patterns into which countries fall. It is necessary to consider departments and chairs, undergraduate and graduate levels, university and nonuniversity sectors, and functional and status differences that produce hierarchies of institutions. And we must estimate the effects thereby produced.

The second basic element is belief, the primary norms and values of the many actors variously located in the system. There is an uncommonly potent symbolic side to academic organization, with beliefs generated in different locations and roles. Ideas have a powerful effect among "men of ideas," and we can systematically account for many of them: they do not float around loose, but adhere to the divisions of work identified in chapter 2, with structure and culture closely interlocked. But national systems vary in how, and to what extent, they generate academic ideologies, and we can specify some causes of that variation. The symbolic side is the least-understood part of modern organization, and there are not many studies on which we can rely. But enough is known to give some footing in several major countries and to project what occurs in others. It is possible also to identify the symbolic disintegration of the higher education system that is produced by academic specialization and to weigh against this fundamental trend the standardizations and surviving common beliefs that symbolically link together hundreds and thousands of thoroughly disparate parts.

The third primary element is authority, the distribution of legitimate power throughout the system. Many relations of power follow from the work organization and its attendant beliefs. Interest groups form around commitment to disciplines and enterprises: faculty members develop and use personal and collegial, essentially guildlike forms of authority; trustees and institutional administrators, in some systems, have much legitimate influence. In central locations, other equally legitimate bases of authority are possessed by politicians, ministerial bureaucrats, and national academic oligarchs. Charisma runs loose from time to time. The necessary analytical vocabulary soon runs to nine or ten forms of authority. But empirical observation allows us to squeeze much of the world into a small number of profiles of combinations of authority and to suggest their consequences. The nature of academic authority is one of the most fascinating aspects of the higher education system. Understanding this component removes one more veil of confusion, even as we emphasize its complexity.

If we understood authority, it would seem that we knew all we needed to know about the integration of national systems. But "coordination" in a large sector is not synonymous with administrative hierarchy, and the various authorities are part of what is linked together to compose a system. Chapter 5 pursues the notion of integration by examining how disciplines and institutions are concerted in ways that vary from tight bureaucracy to professional oligarchy to loose market. The system qua system is a mix of these, with coordination vastly more complicated than normally depicted, and with national systems offering different blends. Consumer markets are everywhere in higher education, for example, but are rather strictly guided in some cases and turned loose in others. Since the twentieth century has exhibited a strong trend toward state control, special attention is given to the shape of state forms. Various major groups struggle within the state machinery to have their hands on the levers of control. And what are the limits of state control? We can readily point to explanations, revealed in various types of states, of why regimes trip over higher learning. If ever political regimes need a sense of balance, and a capacity to see the long run, in the supervision of a public good, it is in relating to the academic system.

Chapter 6 turns to the challenging topic of change, first to emphasize how much change is conditioned by existing forms. To put change in context, to understand it realistically, is to study the constraints and imperatives that inhere in the ongoing structures of work, belief, and authority. The interest-group struggle, largely internal, is at the heart of the dynamics of the system. Seen in the large, that struggle is shaped by what we might call the underlying "academic forces of production," forces that steadily produce contradictions and, at the same time, aid certain interests more than others. Perhaps most basic is a steady process of differentiation that seemingly undergirds both the internal and the external forces of change. This process in the higher education sector is illuminated by classic sociological arguments, particularly those of Emile Durkheim, on why differentiation occurs as a virtually irresistible form of change. Change also flows across national boundaries, and the phenomenon of international transfer of academic patterns is pursued as a second major avenue of change, one fraught with problems of acceptance and adaptation of transplants. Change in academic systems occurs in many ways; it is uncommonly incremental, disjointed, contradictory, and opaque. A complex analysis concludes on the note that we will be less confused about the ways of higher education if we adjust our expectations to these realities.

The final section of the volume moves to a normative posture. Chapter 7 postulates a clash of broad societal values in higher education systems that find various supporters in locales of power and influence. There are no ultimate answers. Such primary values as equality and competence often contradict one another, necessitating tradeoffs; fanatical pursuit of any one value leads to an ineffectual system. Major assertions are offered on how systems best express each of these values and simultaneously allow for the others. These ideas seem warranted by cross-national observation, but at the same time they are undoubtedly colored by my definition of what is basic and what solutions to current problems are viable. It is then but a short step in chapter 8 to a full-blown set of personal preferences that have emerged from observation of higher education in many countries and from the comparisons set forth in this volume. What makes modern higher education viable, productive, and capable of progress? It is increasingly compelling that power be divided, variety supported, and ambiguity legitimated. These preferences are linked to the uniqueness of the higher education system, expanding and concluding on the note with which the study began.

The argument of the book thus confronts five generic questions about academic systems. How is work arranged? How are beliefs maintained? How is authority distributed? How are systems integrated? How does change take place? Answers to these questions are interesting in their own right. But they also lead toward systematic answers to "issue" questions that are normally treated in an ad hoc manner: What determines access? How can general education be supported? Can higher education be further "democratized"? Can the integration of teaching and research be maintained in systems of mass higher education? In a time of expanding state power, what is happening to institutional autonomy? Is "graduate unemployment" inevitable? All such matters are heavily conditioned by the structural bases pursued here. Each system has macro constraints and compulsions that affect action up and down the line: the European chair and the American department shape teaching roles into different molds; the U.S. structure of undergraduate and graduate levels makes undergraduate student life something different from what it is elsewhere; severe selection for entry into one or two extremely prestigious institutions, as in Japan, produces an "examination hell" and related test anxiety and student suicide. To excavate the basic structure of the system is not to avoid the issues that confront administrators, faculty, and students in their daily rounds. Rather it is to find the primary and enduring sources of these issues.

It helps to have a single idea to fall back on as we move through a variety of topics, trying simultaneously to be far-ranging in international coverage, reasonably true to reality in various national settings, conceptually parsimonious, and hence somewhat confusing and even contradictory. That underlying idea is *interest*.[5] The division of labor in the academic world, as elsewhere, is a division of human commitment. The work commitments have related orientations. Commitment and orientation, work and belief, compose interests, a composite of the material and the ideal.[6] The interest groups that are thereby generated attach authority to themselves and seek modes of integration that are congenial. In turn, the powered structure of interests becomes the primary determinant of change in the system. It also determines to a considerable degree how, and how much, the system comes to express certain broad social values.

In the modern period, higher education appropriates functions. More knowledge is included, a larger share of the relevant age groups participate, more occupational placement and individual life chances are affected. There are more rewards within; more people want in. With such incorporation, there is a natural multiplication of interests, the interests of those who occupy the key positions are made more central. He who says academic organization says interest groups. We shall see how they are composed and how they express themselves.

ONE

KNOWLEDGE

No matter where we search among societies, we find academic work organized around materials that are uncommonly intellectual in character. The substances of higher education are different in their totality from those found in industrial organizations, governmental bureaus, and the many agencies that dot the nonprofit sector. It is not that everything is unique: indeed, other milieus are becoming similar to higher education as they base themselves on knowledge, science, and profession. But academic activities have special features that push academic organizations into certain shapes and cause them to have peculiar problems of performance and power.

KNOWLEDGE MATERIALS AND GROUPS

For as long as higher education has been formally organized, it has been a social structure for the control of advanced knowledge and technique. Its basic materials or substances are the bodies of advanced ideas and related skills that comprise much of the more esoteric culture of nations. Academic personnel handle these materials in several ways. When they pore over, memorize, and critically review written and oral accounts handed down by generations, as they have done through the centuries, they conserve and refine. As they instruct students, they transmit to others in deliberate and wholesale fashion: the medieval university emerged as a means of organizing such transmission,[1] and teaching still predominates in the work of every national system of higher education. As academics use what they know in practical ways to help other parts of society, they engage in direct application. Increasingly during the last two centuries, as science and its research imperative entered the university in many countries, academics have been committed to discovering and fashioning new bodies of knowledge. In varying combinations of efforts to discover, conserve, refine, transmit, and apply it, the manipulation of knowledge is what we find in common in the many specific activities of professors and teachers. If it could be said that a carpenter goes around with a hammer looking for nails to hit, then a professor goes around with a bundle of knowledge, general or specific, looking for ways to augment it or to teach it to others. However broadly or narrowly we define it, knowledge is the material. Research and teaching are the main technologies.

It is impossible to define closely this largely invisible material. Knowledge is a concept central to the discussion of education at any level; curricula are definitions of forms of knowledge worth imparting.[2] Knowledge is a concept central also to analysis of modern societies, defined, for example, as the learning society, the knowledge society, or the postindustrial society.[3] In the generic sense intended here, the meaning is broad, to include related subject matters, styles of thought, and intellectual skills. It covers, for example, in one useful classification, "occupational knowledge"—particular factual information and skills for manipulating some specific aspect of the environment; "historical (general education) knowledge"—a theoretical understanding of the accumulated scientific, esthetic, and philosophical wisdom of the general culture; and "process and concept knowledge"—the acquisition of the processes by which knowledge is increased and the development of skills that produce critical thinking and evaluation.[4] Thus, broadly conceived, knowledge is the common medium used for a wide variety of purposes—for "mass" as much as for "elite" functions, for the work of the technological institute and the two-year program as much as for the research university and the Ph.D. Not that the handling of knowledge is everything that an academic institution does: if a university has a fire department, that particular unit, of course, has other primary concerns. And higher education may still be variously viewed: psychologists may see it as a place where people undergo personality development; sociologists as a central institution for status attainment or denial; political scientists as a locus of political recruitment; economists as a developer of human capital. But knowledge materials, and advanced ones at that, are at the core of any higher education system's purposes and essence. This holds true throughout history and across societies as well.[5]

Modern advanced knowledge has several distinguishing characteristics whose effects radiate throughout academic organizations. First, it has a specialized character, long composed of specialties that become ever more numerous. Growth has led to division. The earliest European universities grew out of the efforts of small bands of teachers and learners, in answer to both external demand and internal need, to separate and systematize developing bodies of thought in law, medicine, theology, and a few other fields. A relatively simple division sufficed for a long time, since the inclusive body of knowledge evolved only slowly and remained relatively unchanged. But with industrialization and the accelerating division of labor of the last two centuries, the separation of specialties developed at an increasing rate. By the early twentieth century, Max Weber noted that a deep strain between the generalist of old and a new "specialist type of man" underlaid a host of problems in education.[6] The specialist has won the contest, despite the urging of many that it should be otherwise. Even in the United States, which along with the United Kingdom has enduringly professed a commitment to general or "liberal" approaches to knowledge, the generalists have become a small minority permanently on the defensive. At the turn of the century, William James taught Americans how to curse "the Ph.D. octopus," with its tentacles of specialization. Statesmen attempting to revive general education some seventy years later bemoaned its condition in the U.S. system as "a disaster area."[7] Led by the rapid rate of change in the physical and biological sciences, specialties throughout the academic world multiply with increasing rapidity. They also become narrower and more internally sequential, requiring specific and longer tracks of training. Denser and ever changing, branches of specialized education increasingly demand repeated trips back to the classroom by groups other than engineers, technologists, and applied scientists, who already know in their daily lives the meaning of recurrent education.

If higher education in every country is expected to provide a supporting social structure for advanced knowledge, it is thus bound to a virtually unlimited aggregation of specialties. While national systems have somewhat different coverages, all hold themselves responsible for a greater range of fields of study and application than that found in other institutional sectors, including elementary and secondary education. In a major system, the basic disciplines and professional fields number at least 50. With all the major subjects subdivided into specialties, some—biology, economics, physics, psychology, law, medicine—into five or more, the specialties in a major university readily exceed 200. And there seems to be no end to the proliferation. In contrast, no business firm, church, army, hospital, or public bureau, in any country, stretches across so many "arts and sciences," let alone attempts to include architecture *and* engineering *and* teaching *and* social work. Large aggregates of organizations in the other domains do not cover so much of the territory of knowledge as do clusters of universities and colleges: the innumerable bureaus that constitute the executive branch of modern government come closest. The reason is simple: across all of the division of labor in society, occupations and their related bodies of ideas and technique are defined as advanced when their training component is located within higher education. Thus, all components of practical advanced knowledge must appear inside the academic system, together with the many humanistic and philosophical endeavors that are largely peculiar to it. The vast scope of the knowledge encompassed is a unique central characteristic of institutions and systems of higher education, one that presses for special forms that are not easily understood by those accustomed to organizational life in other sectors of society.

The second fundamental characteristic of academic substances is their increasing autonomy, a steady distancing of the specialties from one another and from the general knowledge imparted in elementary and secondary education. An increasing number of knowledge fields are intrinsically esoteric and inherently autonomous. We might wish it otherwise, but the harsh fact is that those who handle the materials of microbiology and those who deal in medieval history do not need one another to get on with the work, either in teaching or research or service. Likewise for high-energy physicists and urban sociologists, professors of marketing and teachers of child psychology, instructors in criminal law and investigators of cosmology. Naturally, each field borders some others, and a few—clearly mathematics, for one—are preparatory to and heavily used in other subjects. But the linkages do not run through the array of fields in continuous chains; and even within the linked fields, specialists go down their separate tunnels, focusing narrowly in order to master and exploit a single complicated body of thought and technique. In arguing that universities as organizations are relatively disintegrated, one observer has noted appropriately:

> Mathematics will, to an extent, mesh its gears with phys-
> ics, chemistry, and engineering but care nothing what-
> ever about what goes on in history, romance languages,
> or in the schools of business, agriculture, or medicine.
> Each of these will strive to go its own way, and the admin-
> istrative task of maintaining a smoothly running opera-
> tion is made one of the most formidable in all of
> management.[8]

The increasingly disparate specialties range across the alphabetical spectrum from archeology and art to Western European studies and zoology, with dozens of others in between.

Third, the discovery of knowledge is an open-ended task. It is an assignment to the unknown, the uncertain, and as such, it is difficult to systematize through normal organizational structures that are ostensibly erected as rational means of attaining already known and defined ends. This peculiar mandate—known in other societal sectors in minor components—holds for each field within the vast range of subjects. Each specialty is expected to improve itself by going beyond its own frontier onto currently unchartered ground. As discovery, a major function of the system, comes to the fore in certain academic locales, its open quality is reflected in the ways academic organizations are put together and operate. For example, if professors are to think on their own and be free to originate, there is no reason why they must assemble in particular places at particular times. Hence, professors in "research universities" have an unusual degree of personal control over the use of time, compared even to such leading professionals as doctors and lawyers, including the privilege to stay at home to think and write instead of going to the office.[9]

Fourth, knowledge has weighty legacies. Subjects come down through time, expanding along the way and acquiring differential prestige.[10] There is an enormous amount of knowledge inheritance suggested in such expressions as "the cultural heritage" and "the best of mankind." The notion that certain ideas are the best and survive because they deserve to last forever is a powerful sustaining myth, especially in the humanities. But inheritance runs deep even in the sciences: seminal ideas are often centuries old; elaboration of a subject is the work of many past generations; what was thought previously is the patrimony that endows what is thought today. The term *scholarship* rings with overtones of uncommon historical linkage.

In sum, an academic system works with materials that are increasingly specialized and numerous, knowledge-intensive and knowledge-extensive, with a momentum of autonomy. This characterization applies most strongly to advanced systems, but even the most retarded systems will be based on a half-dozen or more distinct bundles of knowledge that have their own internal logics and an inherent bent toward autonomy. And such underdeveloped systems are tugged by the more advanced ones toward research and further refinement. No one has yet found a way to slow the division of labor in society. No one is about to find a way to stop the division of *knowledge* in *academic* society.

From the substance follows certain basic aspects of form: tasks and workers are grouped according to bundles of knowledge. The basic tasks, teaching and research, are both divided and linked by specialty; professors are similarly divided. This is so evident in all structures of higher education—medieval or modern, developed or developing—and so compellingly necessary, that we can hardly imagine it otherwise. The law professor does not combine teaching in law with research in medicine—unless he or she is developing a new specialty in legal medicine. Even in the relatively simple structure of the medieval university, professors conserved, refined, and taught not knowledge in general but the particular bodies in which they had become known as experts. Thus, a first principle: tasks and workers integrate around the many groupings of knowledge; the knowledge specialties are the fundaments on which all else is constructed. This principle holds for the research university, the teachers' college, the technological institute, the community college, or any other type of institution within postsecondary education. Of course, the groupings may be broad or narrow, organized around general or specialized sets of knowledge. In effecting such commitments, national systems as well as subsectors and institutions vary greatly. But broad or specific, subjects are the most important bases of organization.

What does it mean to group tasks and workers by fields of knowledge? The effects radiate throughout academic systems. For example, analysts who compare academic organization with that found in other sectors of society note that the hierarchy of work arrangements is unusually flat and loosely joined in the academic world.[11] A university-type organization is one in which there are many cells of specialization side by side and loosely connected at the operating level, together with only a small number of higher levels of coordination. How much this stems from the very nature of academic activities, rather than from accidental creations, is indicated by the fact that everywhere the degree of organizational hierarchy is more pronounced in the "business side" of academic organization—the domain of buildings, supplies, and finance—in comparison with the "academic side"—the domain of teaching and research. The business side often approximates the pyramid of accountability found in other major types of organization upon which classic organizational theory has concentrated, public interest in organizational life has centered, and models of organization have developed. A relatively clear chain of command radiates downward from an "administrative director," or a "vice-president for business and finance," to subdirectors and heads of bureaus—registrars, personnel directors, finance managers—whose offices are full of clerks, people understood to be "employees" in all senses, including subordination by rank.

On the academic side, from the beginning to the present, things have been different. A flat structure of loosely coupled parts has been the predominant form, and this has required a conception of the academic organization operationally like that of a federation, or perhaps even a coalition, rather than a kind of unitary system commonly known as a bureaucracy. Particularly in the modes of academic organization long dominant on the European continent and in Latin America, but also to a lesser degree in the British and the American modes, the major building blocks of organization— the Faculty (of Law), the Department (of Physics), the Chair (of Classical Literature)—have generally been sufficiently autonomous

and unlinked in work performance to say that the entire organization is actually a sort of holding company for groups involved in the
various strands of expertise. This also means that academic work is
rooted in the evolution of disciplines and professions, each possessing its own bodies of ideas, styles of inquiry, and traditions that set
directions of effort. The chapters that follow on work and belief will
pursue these matters in some detail.

In comparison with business firms and other organizations, the
configuration of control is therefore roughly similar to the configuration of the work structure. Academic organization exhibits a
relative diffusion of control, even in nationalized systems and ones
under authoritarian regimes. Why must this be? Organized settings
characterized by knowledge-intensive expertise at the point of production pull decision-making power toward the operating level. If
that level is fragmented into numerous bodies, then the power
diffused downward will also be extensively fragmented. The later
chapters on authority and integration will further explore such
characteristics and identify special features of institutional and system coordination.

THE NATURAL AMBIGUITY OF PURPOSE

With the tasks of higher education being both knowledge-intensive and knowledge-extensive, it is difficult for those involved to
state the purpose of comprehensive universities and colleges, and
especially of a state or national system. What sort of institution could
subsume classical literature and social work, knit together physics
and sociology, integrate archeology and zoology? For a long time,
large academic configurations have had, at best, vaguely formulated
goals. The twentieth century has seen a leap in ambiguity, making it
extremely difficult for those who attempt to clarify purpose.[12] In
present-day Britain, for example, astute observers, trying hard to be
faithful to reality, must nevertheless use such vague expressions as
"to diminish ignorance," in attempting to explain the tasks of the
higher education system. Such observers explain that the system has
something to do with "scholarship and education," but then note
that such expressions do not say very much about why or who or
how: Is scholarship and education for its own sake or for the

nation's? Should it produce rulers or train common people? Should it follow student demands or the needs of manpower planning, or neither? Should it teach sociology, technology, hairdressing, or none of these things? and with what priority should it do these things?[13] In the United States, for some decades, pragmatic observers have been reduced to speaking of "teaching, research, and service" as a trinity of purposes, only to leave limitless scope to *what* can be taught and *what* can be researched and *what* can be applied as a service. Efforts in the 1970s to clarify the statement of goals simply lengthened the list of unanalyzed abstractions. For example, the Carnegie Commission on Higher Education put forth five goals of higher education, such as "the advancement of human capability in society at large."[14] In Sweden, the "U68" national commission put forth such objectives as "democracy," "personality development," and "social change."[15] Japan, Canada, France, Germany—none seem to have clearer objectives.[16] Communist countries seem no better: e.g., Poland's 1958 Higher Education Act came up with a laundry list that ranged from "instruction of qualified personnel for all jobs in the economy, culture, and all sectors of social life requiring credentials of higher education" to "education for self-fulfillment."[17]

Unfortunately, there is little that exhortation can do to change this natural ambiguity of purpose. As stated by Michael D. Cohen and James G. March:

> Almost any educated person could deliver a lecture entitled "The Goal of the University." Almost no one will listen to the lecture voluntarily. For the most part, such lectures and their companion essays are well-intentioned exercises in social rhetoric, with little operational content. Efforts to generate normative statements of the goals of the university tend to produce goals that are meaningless or dubious.[18]

Goals are so broad and ambiguous that the university or system is left no chance to accomplish the goals—or to fail to accomplish them. There is no way that anyone can assess the degree of goal achievement. No one even knows if any or all the stated goals are accepted by significant groups within the system, and with what priority.[19]

The dilemma is clear and cruel. In every era, those who would speak for higher education are urged to, and feel the need to, clarify purpose by stating it simply. Surely, outsiders say, you can tell me what your enterprise is about, why, in sum, you are doing what you are doing. And as knowledge materials expand and fragment, academics themselves seek reassurance in formulations that promise to pull things together again and provide some overarching meaning. Thus, we witness a steady stream of purportedly new statements that, in their small alteration of phrases, become like old "whines" in new bottles: manpower training and/or cultural transmission and/or individual development, and always back to scholarship and research and public service. The statements are ineffective for directing effort, except that they serve to indicate, in rough-and-ready form, that higher education is not primarily responsible for the production of material goods, the defense of the realm, the provision of welfare services, the saving of souls, or the maintenance of law and order—even though, on second thought, it does have some bearing on each.[20]

A severe effect of simplified definitions of purpose is that they mislead those who believe them, raising expectations that will be dashed and promoting quarrels that cannot be resolved. Such outcomes especially follow when a vision of what ought to be is intermingled with purported observation of what exists. Thus, the prototypic American statesman of clear purpose, Robert Maynard Hutchins, argues that "a university is an intellectual community of people . . . who are trying to understand major issues that confront and are likely to confront mankind."[21] With this normative statement posing as a description of the university, Hutchins goes on to argue that specific professional training and specialized disciplinary research are inappropriate, since they are neither intellectual in a general sense nor sufficiently linked together to form an integrated community. But the practices denied by his pure vision are the realities of the modern American university, as they have been the realities of modern universities in other countries.

Specific professional training in law and medicine goes back to the beginnings of the Western universities: the need for such training generated the innovative response of new clusters of masters and students in academic guilds and guild federations, which became known as universities. As put by A. B. Cobban:

The medieval universities were largely vocational schools. They trained students in the mastery of areas of knowledge that could be utilized in one of the secular professions of law, medicine or teaching or in the service of the Church. Theology, Madame la Haute Science, was very much a minority discipline, the pursuit of some of the ablest spirits in the universities but too rarefied and time-consuming for the student mass. . . . The normal student ambition was to gain lucrative employment within the safety of the established order.[22]

On this ambition, we might add that the more things change the more they remain the same. After eight centuries, it seems time to accept the idea that disciplines and professional fields are inherent in academic life.

The effort to clarify purpose by forceful assertion of a specific vision has had long appeal. In the United States, before Hutchins, Abraham Flexner enunciated a vision different in content but similar in purity: the essence of the university is the cultivation of pure scholarship.[23] This cultivation is centered in specialized research that leads to discovery of the new, quite the opposite of the Hutchins assertion of general intellectuality. In Great Britain, in the mid-nineteenth century, Cardinal Newman boldly established the claim that the university is a place for conserving and teaching universal knowledge, that its "object" cannot be discovery or utility but rather the diffusion of eternal truths.[24] In Germany, in the early part of the nineteenth century, Wilhelm von Humboldt helped to establish the setting for the modern German university by stressing the centrality of discovery of knowledge.[25] Such definitions have sometimes served effectively as visions that led and rationalized reforms (Humboldt's did), but more often, it turns out, they represented memories of an idealized past, a nostalgic statement that could not stop reality from going the other way.

The antiresearch doctrine of Cardinal Newman, written and published in the 1850s, reflected the Oxford of his day, and, as Clark Kerr has pointed out, it even sought to fight "the ghost of Bacon," whose philosophy of utility had, for Newman, "aimed low."[26] But the evolution of the research-centered university was already well under way, and the following half-century saw the triumph of the German university as *the* foremost model internationally. The doctrine of Flexner, published in 1930, praised the ostensible concentration of the German model on pure scholarship—"the German ministers and the German faculties not only value education, but know what it is"—and disparaged the English university for its concentration on teaching and the American university for engaging in a "host of inconsequential things."[27] But the U.S. model was already well on its way to its future eminence, and the German model, even if fascism had not intervened, was neither the wave of the future nor *the* expression of *the* modern university.

The point is clear: broad statements of purpose and goal, essence and true nature, have served poorly as accounts of reality and are inappropriate when used as possible guides to the present. With the growing complexity of twentieth-century systems, efforts to specify in clear and limited terms the purposes of "higher education," and even of "the university" alone, are irrelevant to a true understanding of the situation. There is nothing more pointless than the debates that have now lasted for centuries about the ideal nature of higher education—indeed, as Margaret S. Archer has pointed out, the same can be said of education generally.[28] The debates will remain sterile until they are based upon an understanding of how higher education operates and how it changes.

How, then, do we grapple analytically with the relation of purpose to practice in universities, colleges, and larger academic systems, except than to say that it is confused? Modern theorists of decision making have contributed a rich set of metaphors to describe the nature of managerial choices in situations of ambiguity. With specific reference to universities and colleges, they speak of: "organized anarchies," in which ends and means are ill defined and poorly connected; "garbage-can situations," in which projects, issues, and solutions come together in a mess; "fields of action" that can be likened to soccer fields lined with goals on all sides; and a "technology of foolishness," as opposed to a traditional one of "rationality," in which it is assumed that purposes often do not precede action, that actions need be neither purpose-serving nor consistent, and that intuition, tradition, and faith are important bases of choice. "Individuals and organizations sometimes need ways of doing things for which they have no good reason. They need to act before they think."[29]

Institutions of higher education are seen as preeminent examples of loosely coupled organized systems in which ambiguity results from soft technologies, fragmented work, and participants who wander in and out, as well as from vague goals. This perspective has been valuable in pointing out the great gap that exists between traditional models of decision making and the realities of academic organizations. And this perspective has offered several pungent observations: for example, that one elementary tactic of administrative action is to use high-sounding supergoals as receptacles into which can be dumped a wide variety of problems and objectives. Here they can be disposed of safely and isolated from concrete problems and objectives.

> On a grand scale, discussions of overall organizational objectives or overall organizational long-term plans are classic first-class cans. They are general enough to accommodate anything. They are socially defined as being important. They attract enough different kinds of issues to reinforce their importance. An activist will push for discussions of grand plans (in part) in order to draw the garbage away from the day-to-day arenas of his concrete objectives.[30]

It is even better to insist that purpose is generated by the forming of academic groups around bodies of knowledge, that functioning objectives emerge from the relation between the organization of people and the organization of knowledge. It is fundamental to recognize that constituent factions have their own objectives, which are, in turn, in a cumulative fashion, the operating goals of the larger systems. The members of the physics department, putting first things first, collectively may have the goals of carrying out teaching and research in physics as effectively as possible, helping their own discipline to progress, and improving the standing of their department in their discipline and in their institution. Likewise for economics and for history, and for each of the other disciplines and represented professions. These are the kinds of objectives we discover when we concentrate on what academics actually do, rather than on philosophical statements of what they ought to be doing or on highly general characterizations that can encompass all academic activity. There is less mystery when we start from the operating levels; ambiguity and anarchy become less appropriate descriptors. In the department, chair, or institute, key actors generally have a well-grounded sense of why they are doing what they are doing. But, like everyone else, they scratch their heads and revert to trivial statements when asked to enunciate, in a sentence or two, the meaning and purpose of the entire institution.

If the many operationally separate groups interlock meaningfully to form larger clusters, then operationally they can effect larger purposes that are interdisciplinary in nature, perhaps even constituting liberal or general education. Thus, a group of disciplines within an American faculty of arts and sciences may cooperate to effect a divisional major for students. All the departments of a small American liberal arts college may combine their powers and efforts to construct a general set of required courses that can decently be proclaimed as a liberal education. Such grounded purpose is to be found not in the minds of statesmen but in what people do in the many operational parts, whether in splendid isolation or in linked sets. Shrewd administrators surely have always been aware of the difference between nominal and operational purpose; organizational theorists caught up with that distinction around 1960 and soon made it a shop-worn idea.[31] How odd that professors as much as legislators should continue to confuse the two! Perhaps the invisibility of knowledge, its intangibility, generates so much uncertainty that the urge to enunciate a principle is irresistible. Even in the old days, e.g., in the German university of the nineteenth century, the enunciated doctrines of the system's essence were undoubtedly pretenses to unities that never existed. In the twentieth century, the proliferation of materials and groups has stretched beyond credibility the usual global statements of essence.

If the objectives of the parts are primary, then the stated "goals" of the whole organization, and those of the state and national systems at large, must be like the "purposes" of massive institutional complexes rather than those of unitary organizations. Stated goals become more like the broadly worded objectives of such major entities as national government, rather than those of a specific business firm. And they must continue their slide into ambiguity in order to encompass the wider range of operating factions. Stated global purposes then simply help legitimate the host of specific objectives by placing them within a larger acceptable world view—and that, of course, is why we keep insisting upon them. Everyone can use them. "Teaching, research, and community service" is perhaps the best example of stated doctrine that has usefully served in this federative fashion. And one can always construct a new preferred statement— for example, that the university or college is a knowledge center, a place where many different thinkers think—thereby to sense that a higher education system is preeminently a place for intellectual virtues and vices. But no one can expect such statements to guide choices and steer behavior. Formal goals may help give meaning to the general character of the system, for insiders and outsiders alike. As integrating myths, they can be good for morale and can help keep external groups pacified.[32] But they hardly give you a clue about what to do.

Meanwhile, back down in the classroom and laboratory, the constituent groups get on with the work.

As a wise person once said: "You have to start thinking from the right end." Those who enunciate purpose and otherwise attempt to characterize higher education in a global fashion typically start, twice over, from the wrong end. They start from the top of the system, whereas the better end in higher education is the bottom. They work deductively from broad sweeping statements, instead of inductively from the many actions and interests of the many groups that operate the system. In an effort to begin at the bottom and work inductively, this chapter has observed, against a backdrop of organized effort in other realms, that: knowledge is the basic substance upon which and with which people work in academic systems; teaching and research are the basic activities for fashioning and manipulating this material; these tasks divide into autonomous specialties within which they are closely linked; the task divisions encourage a flat and loosely linked arrangement of work units; this structure promotes a diffusion of control; and, finally, purpose is necessarily ambiguous, with broadly worded goals serving as legitimating doctrine for the specific goals of operating parts. With much to follow on these features, we have begun to interrelate characteristics that are, in their combination, distinctive of the realm of higher education. Our initial discussion also serves as a first answer to the simple question so often posed: What *is* higher education all about? The insistent singular verb in the question requires a plural and indirect answer. Higher education is a conglomeration, in the dual sense that its missions are multifarious and its organizations composed of numerous disparate elements.

While providing some footing for later explanations of why academic organizations assume such odd shapes in every country, this initial characterization does not predict closely or well what those specific configurations will be. By uncontrolled evolution as well as by conscious design, by internal momentum as well as by external control, the academic systems of different countries have arrived at various patterns of organization. Hence, we next turn to an examination of those patterns. In so doing, we will necessarily become more realistic about the interaction between knowledge and organization. We have thus far come close to saying that knowledge is an actor, that it determines tasks and groups. But naturally it is not: persons and groups act on its behalf, and the ways in which educational groups are composed and controlled shape the ways in which knowledge is bundled. As educational institutions in general evolve, they develop categories of knowledge and thereby determine that certain types of knowledge exist and are authoritative.[33] They also define categories of persons privileged to possess the bodies of knowledge and to exercise the authority that comes from knowledge. Educational structures, in effect, are a theory of knowledge, in that they help define what currently counts as knowledge. Such specific structures in higher education as departments also help hold disciplines together and thereby give coherence to these organized carriers of academic subjects and the "cores of knowledge" they contain. Professional schools and interdisciplinary programs combine courses, and experts from several disciplines, thereby structuring "knowledge mixtures."

So now we turn to the actors, the knowers, in an effort to perceive the sizes and the shapes of their organizational clothing. As we identify the limited if complex styles in which they appear, we will continue to see that knowledge is the invisible material around which action takes place.

I
The Elements of Organization

TWO

WORK

In the beginning there is work, for if we reduce a knowledge-bearing system to its primordial elements we find first a division of labor, a structure of organized effort within which many people individually and collectively take different actions. The division of labor is a definition and delegation of tasks. It puts people in special roles and assigns particular duties to them. It thereby generates many different commitments, turning the whole into a plurality of well-rooted interests.

How then is the work divided? We first turn to the primary modes.

The Discipline and the Enterprise

Academic activities are divided and grouped in two basic ways: by discipline and by enterprise. The enterprise, or individual institution, is commonly a comprehensive grouping, in that it links together such disparate specialists as chemists, psychologists, and historians, specialists and nonspecialists, professors and students and administrators. Its wide coverage typically expands as it grows older. Occasionally, its scope is limited to a small set of fields, as in technological universities. Another variant, seen in Italy, are such abbreviated odd-lot groupings as law and teaching, or science and pharmacy, that happen to accumulate in a particular locale or are allocated to a city or region as part of the division of a formal national system.[1] Notably, nearly all enterprises specialize by locality, normally existing in whole or in large part in one geographic place rather than in many, and hence dividing a larger system into geographic blocs. With this comes a set of buildings, contiguous or locally scattered, which make the individual university or college a definite and sizable physical entity, something that can be seen and touched, even if we have to wander around a city (as in Europe and Latin America) to find it all. As a way of organizing knowledge groups, the enterprise catches everyone's eye and is well known. A state, provincial, or national system is commonly "seen" as a set of such institutions. Basic data about the system are gathered primarily on this basis, with national reports and international data books listing the enterprises and summing their students, faculties, and resources. Enterprise is the organizing mode that preempts attention.

The discipline is clearly a specialized form of organization in that it knits together chemists and chemists, psychologists and psychologists, historians and historians. It specializes by subject, that is, by knowledge domain. The profession follows a similar principle, putting together similar specialists. But the discipline (or profession) is also comprehensive in that it does not specialize by locality but rather pulls together a craftlike community of interest that reaches across large territories. Notably, it cuts across enterprises, linking parts of one with similar parts in another. Thus, a national system of higher education is also a set of disciplines and professions, even though we do not normally perceive larger systems in these terms. In addition, the reach of the discipline need not stop at the boundaries of the national system. Academic scientists, in particular, find it natural to practice world community. Their disciplinary perspectives and interests readily extend across nations, much as people in specialized lines of industry, commerce, and banking find more in common with counterpart specialists abroad who "speak the language" than with others outside the specialty at home. Faculty members also specialize within disciplines, teaching specific subjects not shared with many, if any, local colleagues but rather with scholars elsewhere at home and abroad. This point was less true in the past than it is in the present, less true in underdeveloped than in developed countries. But it is the discipline mode of organization that has rendered higher education, over time and space, basically meta-national and international, much more than elementary or secondary education.

Lacking work commitments that so strongly cut across institutions
and systems, the lower levels are more bounded by local and national
structures and cultures.

Despite the common tendency to overlook the importance of the
discipline, it can readily be seen as the primary mode. A simple test
suggests its power: give the academic worker the choice of leaving
the discipline or the institution and he or she will typically leave the
institution. It is more costly to leave one's field of expertise than to
leave one's university or college, since the higher the level of one's
advanced education, the greater the import of one's specialty in
determining commitment. Not only are most academics trained to
the highest levels available but they also serve as the trainers of all
others in their respective specialties, including those who will replace them. To be sure, as seen in chapter 3, institutions can sometimes provide an imposing counterweight in the form of attachment
to the enterprise as a whole. And differentiated systems of higher
education contain segments in which the bonds of specialty are
weakened, as when a U.S. community college instructor teaches
sociology *and* anthropology *and* psychology. Then, too, in times of
personnel stagnation, some enterprises may even attempt to retrain
surplus professors and shift them within the organization to another
field. But such possibilities are marginal in importance compared to
the commitment to specialized fields that academics acquire as they
go through advanced training and the stages of a working career.

For example, a "faculty development" movement that received
much attention in the U.S. system during the 1970s focused on
instructional skills and job shifting across specialties, to the exclusion
of content specialization. But research at the end of the decade on
the results found that within every segment of the system, faculty
overwhelmingly asserted the importance of knowing their discipline.[2] Of all the ways to improve themselves—workshops, courses,
consultants, etc.—the clear favorites were sabbatical leaves and
study or research grants. Faculty expressed concern about their
teaching but saw the problem as one of keeping abreast of one's
discipline rather than of pedagogy. Having a field and knowing a
discipline remained central.

In short, the discipline rather than the institution tends to become
the dominant force in the working lives of academics. To stress the
primacy of the discipline is to change our perception of enterprises

and systems: we see the university or college as a collection of local chapters of national and international disciplines, chapters that import and implant the orientations to knowledge, the norms, and the customs of the larger fields. The control of work shifts toward the internal controls of the disciplines, whatever their nature. And their nature, according to Norton Long, is clearest in the case of the more scientific fields:

> The organization of a science is interesting for a student of administration because it suggests a basis of coopera-tion in which the problem and the subject matter, rather than the caprice of individual or collective will, control the behavior of those embarked in the enterprise. Thus physics and chemistry are disciplines, but they are not organized to carry out the will of legitimate superiors. They are going concerns with problems and procedures that have taken form through generations of effort and have emerged into highly conscious goal-oriented activities.[3]

If these "going concerns" crosscut enterprises, then what becomes of the distinction between organization and environment when ap-plied to higher education? The disciplinary mode of organization tears it to shreds, since a large array of occupationally specified slices of the "environment" have basic representation and location within the "organization." Crucial parts of the so-called environment run right through the enterprises. It then helps little to speak of aspects of the environment that have internal location. It is more helpful to recognize the great extent of crosshatching in academic systems. Such systems are first-class examples, written large, of "matrix struc-tures," arrangements that provide two or more crosscutting bases of grouping—a way organizationally to "have your cake and eat it, too."[4] In international business firms, for example, managers of worldwide product lines have responsibility for operations that crisscross those of managers of geographical regions. Similarly, in the academic world, the disciplines are "product lines," and the enterprises are geographically centered. The representatives of the first crisscross the representatives of the second—professors paid to push physics come face to face with administrators responsible for developing a university or a set of universities. The large and

permanent matrix structures of academic systems are not planned
for the most part but evolve spontaneously, so compelling "in the
nature of things" that there does not seem to be an alternative. In
fact, there is none. Higher education must be centered in disciplines, but it must simultaneously be pulled together in enterprises.

The differing foci of interest of disciplines and enterprises are
reflected in a split in the scholarly literature. Most of those who write
about "higher education" write of enterprises and their students.
But other scholars focus on disciplines. Foremost among the latter
are historians and sociologists of science, searching for the conditions of scientific creativity within given fields, isolating the reward
structures of particular disciplines, and of science as a whole, and
devising such concepts as "invisible college" to point to informal and
quasi-formal linkages of researchers across institutions.[5] Secondary
have been those who have studied the academic profession as a
whole in various countries, pursuing the roles, orientations, and
careers of "the academic man."[6] And then a small effort has been
made to study the national academic associations that represent and
help organize the basic fields and the profession as a whole.[7] Those
who do research on science and scholarship focus on disciplines,
which link personnel within the limits of specialties, for the simple
reason that they are fundamentally so committed. In contrast, universities and colleges as entities reflect particularly the teaching and
service commitments of academic systems. They are preeminently
places for linking specialists and students; in countries where general education is practiced, they also introduce different specialists
to one another. Disciplines pressure institutions to be scholarly, and
sometimes to be interested in research. Institutions pressure disciplines to be student-centered, and sometimes to be cognizant of
other fields of study.

The discipline and the enterprise together determine academic
organization in a special way. To the extent that systems concentrate
on their knowledge tasks, the most important single fact about their
operation is that the discipline and the enterprise modes of linkage
converge in the basic operating units, the primary working groups
of the academic world. The department or the chair or the institute
is simultaneously a part of the discipline and a part of the enterprise,
melding the two and drawing strength from the combination. The
combination makes the operating parts unusually strong and cen-

tral. Naturally, organizational parts are important everywhere in the sense that the larger entities depend on their functioning. But organizations in different sectors of society vary greatly in how much their constituent parts are central, each in its own way and one from the other. As academic parts import the disciplinary connection, their centrality is enormously enhanced and even made qualitatively different from that found in nearly all other parts of society.

The argument can be summarized in three points:

(1) *The core membership unit in academic systems is discipline-centered.* As observed in Sweden, even after much modern reform,

> the most important membership group consists of teachers and researchers. They are organized in subsystems according to disciplines (departments, etc.), and their main competency as well as their professional identity is chiefly connected with the discipline. The discipline also determines their national and international contacts outside of their own departments.[8]

The disciplines in effect determine much of the division of labor within the enterprises, and give content to the divisions. Each has something approaching a monopoly of specialized knowledge, on the local scene, for a specific operation.[9] And increasingly so, since as disciplines become more thoroughly professionalized, they strengthen their autonomy by emphasizing credentials, qualifications, and jurisdictions in order to delineate boundaries more clearly. In a sense, they become more narcissistic. They are also capable of generating highly intense motivations and competitiveness. Burkart Holzner and John H. Marx were not far off the mark in stating flatly that "few contemporary institutions have insistently and successfully demanded such uncompromising loyalties and continuous efforts from their members as academic disciplines."[10]

(2) *Each disciplinary unit within the enterprise has self-evident and acclaimed primacy in a front-line task.* As two English observers noted: "Underlying the status of the department [in Britain] is its crucial characteristic of being authoritative in its own field of learning."[11] Individual and group authoritativeness holds across the great range of knowledge areas, each of which has a front-line role in teaching, research, and the other activities of managing knowledge. The academic members of a department of physics have such a role, and

no other cluster of people in the institution or the system at large can claim to know as much physics, and to know as much about its operation as a field, as the physicists. This is equally true in all the other fields.

(3) *The characteristics of core membership groups affect everything else of importance in the organization.* The special qualities of core groups preeminently render universities and colleges something other than unitary organizations; make collegial control not an accident; and require an unusual vocabulary of crafts and guilds, federations and conglomerations, to tease out the realities of academic organization that remain hidden when approached by the standard terminology of organizational life. The radiated effects will be dealt with throughout the analysis in this and later chapters.

THE FRAGMENTED PROFESSION

The centrality of the discipline affects the academic profession as much as the academic organization. The profession has long been a holding company of sorts, a secondary framework composed of persons who are objectively located in diverse fields, and who develop beliefs accordingly. Professors belong to one or more regional, national, and international associations in their own fields. Then, if they have enough money left for a second set of dues, they may join an encompassing association, such as the American Association of University Professors (AAUP), or a professional union, for collective representation, particularly on economic issues. The emergence of new specialties is generally marked by the formation of associations. In the United States, approximately 300 "discipline-oriented" associations existed in the late 1960s, organized around not only such major disciplines as physics, economics, and English but also the specialties indicated by such special titles as American Association of Teacher Education in Agriculture, American Folklore Society, Psychometric Society, and Society for Italian Historical Studies.[12] These associations constituted a class of organizations entirely separate from such institutional ones as the Association of American Universities, the Association of American Colleges, and the American Council on Education.

The large number of disciplinary associations found in the

United States is hardly typical of the world, since the United States has a strong tradition of voluntary association and the American higher education system is now the most advanced in academic specialization. But to a lesser degree, academics elsewhere similarly come together within specialties by forging associational bonds. No developed or semideveloped country is without organized academic disciplines, reflected nationally in such a common form as the learned society.

The situation of "the academic profession" is thus fundamentally different from that of every other profession. Medicine, law, engineering, and architecture, for example, are relatively singular. Despite their internal specialties, which continue to proliferate, they can be loosely, or even tightly, unified by a body of values, norms, and attitudes developed over time within the profession itself and considered an intrinsic part of it. Then an organization loaded with members of a profession, as a hospital is by doctors, can be integrated in part by professional norms as well as by bureaucratic rules. Larger sets of organizations, such as those of a "health system" of a state, region, or nation may be similarly integrated. There is a dominant occupational type.

In academic institutions and systems, however, this pattern does not hold. Here, under the general label of "professor," there are medical doctors on the medical faculty, lawyers on the law faculty, architects on the architecture faculty, and other quite distinct clusters within professional units that may number up to fifteen or twenty. Then, of course, the number of specialized clusters is much larger when we turn to the physical sciences, social sciences, and humanities. And, in turn, the major disciplines are extensively subdivided. For example, physics is broken down into such major subdisciplines as optics, mechanics, fluids, nuclear physics, and elementary particle physics—the latter dividing still further into cosmic ray physicists, who study natural particles, and high-energy physicists, who use accelerators. These major subfields, in turn, contain more specialties. Within high-energy physics alone, as Jerry Gaston has observed in Great Britain, there is a highly specialized division of labor, a community of researchers located in about twenty universities and several independent laboratories, which "is divided into theoretical and experimental roles that are further divided into types of experimentalists and theorists." The division of labor accounts for large differences in originality and type and degree of competition, more than does social and educational background and institutional characteristics.[13]

Hence, the distinct quality of academic institutions and systems is a high degree of fragmented professionalism. In the past it was possible for a faculty of law or philosophy to dominate a university. Such subject-centered imperialism may still obtain occasionally in the higher education system of a less-developed society. But in modern systems, no single discipline on a campus or in a system at large is in a position to dominate the others. Rather than a closely knit group of professionals who see the world from one perspective, academic systems are loose connections of many professional types.

Thus, we have another important principle: when professional influence is high within a system and there is one dominant professional group, the system may be integrated by the imposition of professional standards. But where professional influence is high and there are a number of professional groups coexisting side by side, the system will be split by professionalism. Academic systems are increasingly fractured by expertise, rather than unified by it.

In short, colleges and universities are indeed professionalized organizations, and academic systems are professionalized systems, with control and coordination highly influenced by the presence of professionals, but the professionalism is heavily fragmented. And it is this characteristic of fragmentation that sets the stage for our discussions of multiple authority and diverse means of integration in chapters 4 and 5.

The Division of Academic Enterprises

In focusing on enterprises as constituent units of national systems, a four-way analysis helps clarify the division of labor. Differentiation occurs horizontally and vertically, within institutions and among them. Within institutions, we refer to the horizontally aligned units as *sections*; the vertical arrangement as *tiers*. Among institutions, the lateral separations are called *sectors*; the vertical, *hierarchies*.[14] Sections, tiers, sectors, and hierarchies appear in various forms and combinations in different countries, affecting a host of crucial matters. We here examine the two internal axes of alignment.

SECTIONS

Horizontal differentiation within the individual university or college is the primary form of division by fields of knowledge. Such division has occurred typically at two levels of organization, although complex universities may exhibit as many as four, since each of the main levels develop substructures to help carry out their tasks. The broadest groupings, known by such terms as *faculty*, *school*, and *college*, encompass preparation for a certain type of occupation, e.g., law, business, or a set of "basic disciplines" like the humanities or the natural sciences. Each country arrives at a definition of these major clusterings of knowledge, which number from as low as three or four to more than fifteen, with a clear trend over time for the number to increase. For example, the French university system of the nineteenth and twentieth centuries (until 1968) had a standard set of major subdivisions throughout the country, consisting of the four faculties of law, medicine, letters, and science, with theology at one time and pharmacy at another also having faculty standing. German universities during the same period stayed largely with their four classical faculties of law, medicine, theology, and philosophy, with the latter eventually encompassing a wide range of academic disciplines. Italian universities of the mid-twentieth century found their logic in a dozen possible faculties, nine of them essentially professional, such as engineering and agriculture, and three in letters, science, and political science, with individual universities possessing anywhere from one to twelve of the faculties. Alongside a major faculty of arts and sciences that typically encompasses all the basic disciplines, American state universities often have fifteen or more professional schools for such fields as business, education, forestry, journalism, music, and social work.

The narrower groupings, which are the basic building blocks or operating units, known generally as *chair*, *institute*, or *department*, encompass a specialty within a profession (e.g., constitutional law, internal medicine) or an entire basic discipline (e.g., physics, history). For example, in the traditional French and Italian universities, departments as such have not existed, and the loci of control and organization within the faculties have been the professors occupying chairs in specialties, with the chair having a domain of teaching and research that sometimes spanned a discipline as large as political

science or physics. Hence, in a chair system, the different types of
chairs are at least as numerous as the disciplines covered, and they
become more numerous as they are used to organize subfields
within disciplines. A major university might have 50, 100, 200, or
more chairs. In contrast, in the United States, departments, not
chairs, have been the basic building blocks, numbering a dozen or
two in a small college and 50, 100, or more in modern multiversities,
usually in the form of subunits within professional schools and
within the arts and sciences.

What are the crucial fixed and varying characteristics of these two
levels of sectioning within universities (and colleges)? How do
national systems vary in these substructures? The sections of universities have two significant features that are common among national
systems: they have decidedly different contents with which to work,
and they have a low degree of interdependence. The sections vary
most sharply across nations in their internal organization.

Knowledge Content. The sections of universities and colleges vary
in the qualities of the bodies of ideas and skills with which they work.
Certain chairs and departments, faculties and schools, encompass
fields that have well-developed and relatively clear structures of
knowledge, as in the natural sciences, engineering, and medicine;
but counterpart units labor with poorly integrated and ambiguous
bodies of thought, as in the "softer" social sciences, the humanities,
and such semiprofessions as education and social work. The variation, in short, is by type of discipline, and hence cuts across
enterprises and systems. Everywhere physics, operating with a dependable corpus of theory and method, is a more structured and
coherent field than sociology. Everywhere chemists can depend on
elaborate sets of well-tested and interlocked propositions and
formulas, but professors of education cannot. Nothing is more basic
than these varying compositions of knowledge materials in accounting for differences within universities that appear as common
patterns among nations.

The consequences of knowledge contents are immediately observable. Consider the effects on student access. Access became
publicly defined in the late 1960s and early 1970s as the most
important problem of the many problems brought about by the
expansion of national systems into mass higher education. Research,
ideology, and policy alike have treated this problem largely in global

terms, as an issue of general entry into large systems. But access has long varied greatly and systematically within individual enterprises themselves, not to mention within the system at large, on the de facto grounds of the difficulty of fields. It is decided considerably by the relative need for students to move through closely regulated sequences of courses in order to master a complex body of knowledge.

Highly structured disciplines such as mathematics have been relatively difficult to enter and to remain in. Mathematicians arrange their courses in specific sequences and distinguish clearly between beginning, intermediate, and advanced students. They establish barriers all along the way, guarding the door to the classroom with "prerequisites." The barriers form a tapering funnel: the overwhelming majority of students cannot gain access to the higher levels, even if they desired. Since students perceive the difficulties, they "self-select" away from such fields: "It is really not right for me; it is too hard." Similarly elaborate course sequences are found throughout the physical and biological sciences and in engineering. Among the major professional fields, particularly medicine (in most countries) has learned how to limit access through claimed difficulty of knowledge content, and with such additional criteria as "effective clinical training," "number of laboratory spaces," and "high per-student costs."

In contrast, other disciplines and professional schools are characterized by lack of agreement on what knowledge content is basic and how it ought to be taught. Courses are only weakly stacked in sequences, if at all, since they do not necessarily precede and follow one another logically. Hence, in many of the humanities, the more qualitative of the social sciences, and such semiprofessions as education, social work, and business, it is not only easier for students to enter but also to negotiate their way, muddling through the ambiguities of the field as best they can, toward at least the first major degree. The advent of mass higher education has widened these internal differentials, with medicine, the natural sciences, and sometimes engineering protecting their standards through limited access, but with other units in the less well-structured fields taking all comers. In short, through both formal and informal means, access is differentiated across the many fields of knowledge and their supporting organizational sections, and this form of selection does not receive much argument. For the most part, it occurs quietly, student by student, classroom by classroom, course by course, specialty by specialty, and it appears legitimate.

Consider the effects on administration. Departments that operate with well-developed bodies of knowledge can arrive at a consensus more readily than those confused by ambiguous and conflicting perspectives. Decisions on the selection and retention of faculty are more easily made when all members of the department, or a major specialty within it, perceive quality in similar terms of theoretical grasp and methodological competence. In contrast, in departments where the knowledge base is vague, dissensus is more likely to reign, as otherwise "rational" people, with different understandings of the field, fight over courses and appointments.

Organizational analysts have picked up effectively on this point.[15] Working from Thomas Kuhn's concept of paradigm, they have treated ideas as the technology of higher education and suggested that academic disciplines can be viewed as technologies involving different degrees of task predictability. Janice B. Lodahl and Gerald Gordon write: "Since the structure of knowledge determines what is taught as well as what is investigated, the degree of paradigm development and accompanying predictability in a given field should affect both teaching and research."[16] This is a sensible notion and one tested in research on differences in behavior and attitudes in American departments. The results led to conclusions at two levels of organization. At the department level, "university professors in a given scientific field must operate at the level of predictability permitted by the structure of knowledge within the field. Social scientists operate in a much less predictable and therefore more anxious environment than physical scientists."[17] Social scientists have more difficulty agreeing on course and degree requirements; they have in general a higher degree of conflict, both within and among individuals.

For the enterprise level, Lodahl and Gordon argue strongly "against some current tendencies to view university structure and university problems in terms that are too simple to match the demands of technology and the associated realities of activities and attitudes found within scientific disciplines."[18] It is not true that a department is a department is a department, with all treated by administration and planners as a single kind. Rather, "any attempt to change the university must take into account the intimate relations between the structure of knowledge in different fields and the vastly different styles with which university departments operate."[19]

Thus, across the fields of the arts and sciences, across the professional schools, *and* across such major types of institutions as universities, teachers' colleges, and technological schools, the styles of operation will vary greatly depending on the respective structures of knowledge. Hence, "any attempt at universal standards for academia will impose a uniformity of activity and output which is inconsistent with the particular subject matter requirements of specific areas."[20] One can read for a long time in the literature of educational planning and reform in the United States, Great Britain, and elsewhere without encountering this simple idea—additional evidence, if more is needed, that analysis and policy need to take seriously the ways in which universities and colleges are internally differentiated around knowledge.

Knowledge contents do have important integrating effects, however, since there are organic uniformities in higher education that follow from the reach of disciplines. Each major subject matter promotes, even forces, some common contents within and among national systems. Whatever organized enterprises and formal systems do by way of grouping higher education differently, the disciplines have the crosshatching effect of carrying common bundles of knowledge and related styles of work.

Interdependence.   Compared to other types of organizations, universities and colleges do not have strongly interdependent parts. The sections have distinct materials in their subject matters. If necessary, and generally by choice, they can put out their own products—new knowledge, graduates, and services in law or medicine or the natural sciences or philosophy. Hence, as remarked earlier, ties among the sections are strongly centrifugal, since the discovery, storing, and transmitting of knowledge can take place within the units in relatively self-contained ways. Law does not need archeology; English literature does not need physics. There is not the need for close interdependence that obtains within business firms organized around the production and distribution of a set of products. In the language of organizational analysis, there is not a long-linked technology involving interdependence among units, but rather an intensive technology that, in the academic case, can take place in separate compartments.[21] The fragmentation is typi-

cally so great that "technology" is more usefully thought of as
"technologies."

However, *among* types of universities and colleges, and especially
among national academic systems, the degree of interdependence
varies considerably. One source of variation is degree of commitment to specialized or general education; a second is the primacy of
research or teaching.

Specialized training is highly fragmenting organizationally,
whereas any type of general or liberal education requires various
sections to take one another into account, fitting their work together
as integrated parts of a larger "product," such as the liberally educated person. Reflecting this source of variation, the basic fault line
among the more inclusive operating units in national systems is
between relatively specialized faculties and schools and comprehensive counterparts. The prototypic specialized unit concentrates on a
profession: law, medicine, architecture, pharmacy, engineering,
agriculture, teaching, commerce. All teachers and students therein
have a common occupational commitment and identity, providing
an important internal source of collegiality and cohesion but, at the
same time, distancing the unit from others within the university.
Students are there to specialize in one field of work, with little or
no possibility of transferring laterally to other units within the
institution.

Such units have loomed large and often dominated in Europe and
in Latin America. The French and Italian arrangements, identified
earlier, are examples. The European faculties have had mutually
exclusive personnel, clientele, and resources, despite their formal
locations within regional and national public systems that ostensibly
would bring them into close relationship. These faculties have been
so self-contained that there has been little need to group them
physically. Hence, they could scatter around a city, blocks and
kilometers apart, in a generalized version of the geographical dispersion found occasionally in the American university when the
medical school or school of business or school of agriculture is
located across the river, or miles away in the nearest big city. Some
faculty in the arts and sciences would maintain that that is not far
enough! Faculty autonomy tends to be very high in universities
composed mainly of professionally specialized units, a feature of
most Continental universities and those around the world modeled

after them. We will frequently note this characteristic in analyzing authority and integration. In the United States, the one-occupation specialized school or faculty can also be highly autonomous. Indeed, such units often take care of themselves: in private universities they may be told to raise their own income, each to become "a tub that stands on its own bottom"; in state universities they become major fixed and protected line items in governmental allocations; and, in both private and public universities, they may even become de facto arms of a national bureau, as in the case of the heavy dependency of medical schools at leading universities on the U.S. Public Health Service, one of the principal operational bases for the term "federal grant university."[22]

The prototypic comprehensive unit has been the American faculty of arts and sciences, embracing dozens of fields and their carrying departments, extending across the humanities, the social sciences, and the natural sciences. The arts and sciences faculty is typically the core personnel unit in the American university, predominating in importance over the faculties of the professional schools. In the American liberal arts college concentrating on undergraduate education, it is the entire faculty. So heterogeneous is this unit in the modern American university that it becomes difficult to hold it together by sheer collegiality. This core American unit typically has one or more dean's offices set above the departments, staffed with full-time administrators and linked hierarchically to such central campus administrative offices as president and provost. The comprehensive nature of this basic faculty has helped make campus bureaucracy characteristic of American universities and colleges.

The degree of interdependence in the structure of faculties heavily determines the possibilities of curricular reform. The university composed of specialized faculties is an unnatural setting for general education. Historically predicated on the completion of the student's broad education in the secondary school, with entry to higher education tantamount to a commitment to specialize, the specialized faculties of European and Latin American systems, and most other countries, became deeply institutionalized, connected on this basis to secondary education and job markets. Thus, what Joseph Ben-David has referred to as the abandonment of liberal education in such universities became fixed in their structures.[23]

Any reform in the direction of general education is exceedingly difficult, at times virtually impossible. It becomes a matter of attempting to develop, within areas of specialization, a somewhat more general "first cycle" of courses, to be taken by students before going on to the more specific courses in the specialties.[24]

In contrast, in the United States, general or liberal education, even while in decline, has had two key organizational supports. One has been the existence, in great numbers, of the private four-year college, where the total organization of the institution provides the framework and the authority for creating and coordinating a general-education curriculum. The other key has been the central faculty of arts and sciences within the university, public and private, which can work to foster some cooperation among its constituent departments and divisions and is driven in that direction by involvement in the general preparation of undergraduates. The consensus across disciplines that is required to effect general education can there be organizationally mustered, at least to a degree that gives plausibility to the institutional claims of providing a broad education. The arts and sciences faculty, or such units as the "undergraduate college" within the university, offers a large collegial body as a counterweight to atomistic inclinations among the departments. The faculty members of the departments come together in an inclusive faculty, or all-college faculty, that controls "*the* curriculum" and, as a body, monitors the many general and specific requirements set for students.

Thus, it is possible to speak of whole classes of universities and colleges in which it is possible to have, or not to have, general education. This is true because these institutions possess, or lack, the required internal organization, specifically in the form of specialized and comprehensive faculties and schools. Here is another instance of a general rule that holds strongly in academic systems: organization determines the fate of ideas and reforms.

The degree of interdependence among constituent units and the strength of centrifugal forces among them depend also on relative commitment to discovery and transmission of knowledge. Discovery requires an exceedingly high level of autonomous action on the part of individuals and groups, since it takes place at the leading edge of specialization within each discipline and involves venturing into the unknown. Discovery is difficult to plan and program, since higher authorities, if involved, are limited to setting general directions. In contrast, transmission involves some routine handling of what is already known and classified. It can be somewhat coordinated by a group of peers within the disciplinary unit, and secondarily by higher-level generalists and nonpeers. Hence, members of a department in an English or Swedish or Danish university, if they are to have an adequate curriculum, will more readily dictate to one another what must be taught and how it should be organized than what is to be researched. In short, "freedom of research" is more organizationally fragmenting than "freedom of teaching." Problems of coordination and control are then set accordingly, with centrifugal forces stronger in research settings than in teaching settings.

Finally, the sections of universities are rendered interdependent in varying degrees by the forms of authority, analyzed in chapter 4, that predominate in and around them. The high autonomy and low interdependence of faculties in European and Latin American universities reflect the weakness of institutional bureaucracy; the much stronger administration of the U.S. campus aids the integration of its departments and faculties.

In this regard, a notable case of extremely high faculty independence is found in contemporary Yugoslavia. There the faculties, not the universities as wholes, are very much the main units of local organization. Their strength has been increased by the deliberate decentralization of power in virtually all societal sectors, which has made Yugoslavia so unlike other Communist countries. For what does "worker self-management" mean when applied to higher education? As Geoffrey Giles has shown, it means that power flows to disciplinary clusters.[25] Individual units can set themselves up and govern themselves in whatever form they wish, with the higher levels of government even constitutionally barred, after 1974, from powers of supervision. The units of Yugoslavia in the best position to seize the opportunity of self-management were the faculties, which, numbering twenty at the University of Belgrade in 1970, have more of the disciplinary focus of U.S. departments than the wider clustering nature of the faculties in Western Europe. Thus, we have the ironic situation in which the extreme case of minimal interdependence of units within a university comes not from age-old doctrines and practices of the medieval collegium carried into the modern period, but from one of the latest and most noted socialist experiments. To the specialization of work and commitment that has caused European faculties to have quite low interdependence, there has now been added new doctrines and practices of authority that encourage the disciplines to go their own way. In the Yugoslav model, the university as a whole lies somewhere between a voluntary association and a confederation.

Thus, academic enterprises do vary within and across national systems in the interdependence of their parts. But they have in common, compared with other types of organization, a relatively low degree of interconnectedness. The metaphors of "holding company" and "conglomerate" are to be taken seriously.

Group Organization.   Now we come to the most important difference in the way that enterprises in different national systems organize their lowest operating units: chair versus department organization.[26] The chair concentrates the responsibilities of the primary unit in one person, the chair holder. He or she is in charge of academic activities in a work domain, with other staff serving in subordinate capacities. If research in the domain is organized by means of an institute, the chair holder also becomes the director of the institute or shares authority with several other chair holders. In chair systems, research institutes tend to be fused to the chairs, since the latter are the primary positions in the university structure below the faculty level of organization. In contrast, the department spreads responsibilities and powers among a number of professors of similar senior rank and more readily allows for some participation by associates and assistants. It thereby becomes a basis for collegial as well as bureaucratic order at the operating level.

Chair organization is very old. It has been the traditional form of operational control in most European and Latin American universities, with its roots in the original organization of medieval universities as guilds and guild federations of master professors who took unto themselves a few journeyman assistants and a small batch of student apprentices.[27] The internal hierarchy came from the guild model:

> At the bottom were the ordinary students, equivalent to the guild apprentices who were learning the elements of the trade and were under the full authority of the master craftsmen. Next came the bachelors, who were advanced

students and were allowed to lecture and dispute under supervision. They correspond to and derived their names from the journeymen or bachelors, who worked for a daily wage and had not sufficient maturity to establish themselves in the trade. (Hence they were still unmarried.) At the top of the profession was the master, a rank common to both universities and guilds. He was a man who had demonstrated both his skill and maturity to the satisfaction of his fellow masters. Entrance to this stage was gained after elaborate examinations, exercises in the techniques of teaching, and ceremonial investiture. . . . The three titles, master, doctor, professor, were in the Middle Ages absolutely synonymous.[28]

It is fairly certain, despite large gaps in the written record, that this key aspect of academic guilds was effectively carried forward in Europe down through the centuries.[29] When the title of "chair" emerged is unclear, but the position was there all along. What is abundantly clear is that the chair form of organization was reinvigorated and given modern trappings in the German research university, which became the most important worldwide academic institutional model of the nineteenth and early twentieth century. Centered on "the research imperative," this modern prototype "integrated research and teaching in the full professor, reinforcing his dominance as director of his research institute and as part-time policy maker at other levels of university administration."[30]

Chair organization has had some influence in Great Britain, where, more than on the Continent, it has been blended with department and all-college bodies. Where chairs and departments coexist, the chair holder is likely to be the department head, probably a permanent one, but the department will still be the basic unit for organizing work. The chair has also been tempered in the British system by the college tradition of Oxford and Cambridge, within which work is organized primarily by multidisciplinary faculty clusters in colleges rather than departments of the university. Most important, chair organization has spread throughout the world wherever German, French, Italian, Spanish, Portuguese, and English modes of academic organization have been implanted by colonial regimes or voluntarily adopted, and it has persisted as the normal way of structuring and manning the university. Thus, it has been much more important than departmental organization—a point generally overlooked by Americans—throughout Asia, Africa, and Latin America. In Japan, where public and private sectors are organized somewhat differently, the dominant sector of national universities is a striking case. There, by set formulas that vary by field, each chair is apportioned several positions for assistants, with, as the joke goes, the chair thereby becoming a sofa.[31]

Departmentalism is relatively new, a deviant form that has developed most strongly in the United States, where it arose in the context of trustee and administrative control over growing individual colleges and emerging universities in the nineteenth century.[32] Within such frameworks, bureaucratic models of subdivision could and did predominate over guild models. When the all-inclusive faculty had to subdivide in order to organize growing and disparate specialties, especially after the common classical curriculum gave way to the elective system—with free choice for students *and* more room for faculty experts to pursue their specialties—there was not already in place at the operating levels the guildlike presumptions and forms that had come down from the medieval universities in Europe.

The existence of chair organization as opposed to department organization has had major effects in national systems, and those outcomes will be pursued in greater detail in later chapters. In brief, chair organization is a persistent source of personal dominance, as against collegial as well as bureaucratic control. In contrast, the department is a less personal form. Thus, the chair scores high in concentrating authority and in creating local monopolies. Chair organization is also the more potent source of faculty control over higher levels of organization, strengthening the thrust of senatorial politics. And, as academic enterprises and systems have grown, the chair, compared to the department, has been an increasingly inappropriate unit for swollen disciplines. Systems that have both kept the chair as primary unit and have grown much larger have exhibited overload and extreme fragmentation. Most important, the chair system has a weak capacity to correct errors, particularly in the crucial area of faculty appointments. When a mistake is made in selecting a mediocre person to fill a chair, the effect is long-lasting, through the rest of the academic life of the incumbent and beyond. Hence, an important step in serious reform, a topic we return to in chapter 6, has been to replace chairs with departments or to absorb them somehow in departmentlike units. Considered a hopelessly old-fashioned unit by American reformers, the department is one of the primary means of reform elsewhere. It is capable of supporting and integrating modern disciplines to an extent not normally possible under the hegemony of chairs.

TIERS

Vertical differentiation in organizations is normally viewed as a matter of ascending administrative levels, a topic taken up in a later discussion of authority. But in the organization of academic *work*, there is the prior and more basic consideration of organizing on the basis of what Thomas F. Green has called "the principle of sequence," the notion that activities will be arranged above and below one another according to defined difficulty.[33] From the elementary school years onward, some aspects of teaching and learning are more advanced than others. Within higher education, even in the softer fields, there is beginning work, intermediate work and advanced work for students; hence, there are such curricular levels as lower division and upper division, first cycle and second cycle. The question becomes: How are the levels of training and related certification organizationally handled? Then, too, where is research placed in relation to the levels of training? Every system must develop some vertical placement of its work activities.

The differences among countries in tier construction are fascinating. Historically, most have had only one major tier; a few have had two or more. A single tier has predominated in the European and Latin American mode of organization, in which the professional school within the university is entered directly after completion of secondary education. With general education completed at the secondary level, higher education has been defined primarily as a place to prepare for the learned professions and the high civil service. Hence, the student enrolls immediately in medicine or law or another professional faculty, with law serving as the main road to the civil service. If the student enters a faculty based on one or more of the fields of the natural sciences, social sciences, or humanities, it is understood that he or she is also there to specialize.

The first major degrees, taken after some three to six years of

course work, then certifies professional or disciplinary competence—the *licence* in France, the *laurea* in Italy, the *diplom* in Germany, the *licenciado* in Latin America. This degree has been and
remains the first step in, and often the sole basis of, the extremely
rigorous state certification requirements in Continental systems for
employment in the professions and the civil service, the latter including school teaching and the academic profession itself. In some
single-tier university systems, such as Italy, there has been virtually
only the one degree; in some others, such as Germany and France,
there have been higher degrees, historically available to only a few,
but in any event not handled by a separate higher unit. Distinct units
of organization for work above the first degree have been nonexistent or only weakly developed. The higher degrees have been handled by the same faculty units that concentrate their energies in the
first tier.

Two distinct tiers have predominated in the American mode of
university organization. The first tier, the undergraduate realm of
four years, is devoted primarily to general education, with limited
specialization available as students choose a major subject on which
to concentrate in the last two years. The first major degree, the
bachelor's, does not in most cases certify any particular professional
competence, giving most of its holders a general and ambiguous
connection to the job market. Specialization has found its home in a
second major tier composed of the two distinct forms known as the
graduate school and the professional school, units that can be entered only after completion (or at least several years) of first-tier
course work. Hence, one gains entry to the top professions only
after taking a second degree offered solely by units located at this
higher level. And one enters employment in one of the disciplines
with maximum scholastic qualifications only after taking a second
and a third degree monopolized by this level.

The American vertical differentiation was created only a century
ago, at a time when "the university" was added to a domain that had
been occupied for over 200 years by "the college." The university
model of the last quarter of the nineteenth century, German-
inspired, meant a place for research and advanced training. And if
the German model had been borrowed wholesale, there would have
been no need at the time for a distinct graduate school. But the
college form was deeply institutionalized, in power and in public

understanding, and was not to be blown away, particularly since there was not enough state control to enforce a sweeping reform.[34] Most colleges existing at the time remained pure colleges (e.g., Amherst and Oberlin), a first tier committed to broad education; some colleges became both college and university (e.g., Yale and Harvard); and newly created universities found viability in being colleges as well as universities (e.g., Johns Hopkins, Chicago, and Stanford). The emergent solution was a distinct graduate and professional level with its own organization, placed in the educational sequence on top of the now "undergraduate" level, which was so well rooted in a college of its own.

The differences in tier structure are enormously consequential. For one, they markedly affect access. The problems of access in modern higher education are most severe in the systems whose primary enterprises have only one tier. Broadened entry, then, means the right of much larger numbers of students who complete the secondary level to enter into the one meaningful level, specialize in it, and graduate with a certified job-related competence. In Europe, selectivity for any of the fields, including the professional ones, became a major political issue in the 1960s and 1970s—the question of *numerus clausus*—since to introduce selection appeared to deny greater access, *and* at a time when more middle-class and lower-class students were graduating from the secondary level. In the dual or multitier arrangement, in contrast, the lower levels can even offer open-door access, and the upper levels operate selectively. No one finds it strange in the United States that graduate schools, law schools, and architecture schools can be highly selective. The lower levels screen for the upper levels, just as the secondary levels traditionally have screened for higher education. The internal vertical differentiation of levels *within* given programs of instruction, as well as within the system as a whole, allows the work of screening to move up the educational ladder another level or two. It combines open and limited access.

A second set of effects rests in job placement and the connections of higher education to the job market. The one-tier system historically had the advantage of linking higher education specifically and closely to job placement. The graduates of the first tier had a high probability of placement in the top administrative stratum of the national civil service, of entry directly into practice in one of the leading professions, or of entry into secondary-school teaching, which was under the civil service, prestigious, and so closely linked to higher education as to operate as a waiting room for openings in the universities. (Professors in the selective classical or scientific secondary school could hope to become university professors.) As long as higher education was elite in number—under five percent of the age group—this arrangement had a clarity of connection that was not possible in the multitier structure, where the terminating graduates of the first level have a more generalized connection to the job market (as in the case of B.A.-level graduates in the humanities and most of the social sciences in the United States). Here, confusion has reigned, contributing to the anxiety of that troubled age group in modern society, the fifteen-to-twenty-five-year olds.[35]

But the development of more accessible higher education in nations with single-tier systems has overloaded that type of structure, and nowhere more so than in connection to jobs. The historic promise of precise, elite placement can no longer be honored: there are simply too many persons. Often five or ten times too many enter the pipeline of training, expecting the high rewards of old, only to exit to saturated traditional markets. No more secondary-school teachers are needed after expansion has swelled those ranks with a generation or two of new teachers fixed in the permanent civil service; the administrative civil service cannot be indefinitely expanded to accommodate the flood tide of new graduates, even though countries like Italy or Mexico can push this form of conflict abatement a long way, soaking up discontent by expansion of the government's payrolls; and certain of the professions are also threatened with unemployment of the qualified and dilution of rewards as the supply of professionals expands enormously. Such systems experience a great gap between student expectations, shaped by a long history of elite placement, and the realities of limited placement at the higher levels for the much larger supply of recruits. Hence, again, as in the case of access, the problem of job placement pushes such systems toward greater vertical differentiation, *within* institutions, to sieve and to funnel and to provide a number of exit points at varying levels of preparation.

A third class of effects are to be found in the support of such elite functions as research. Research is plainly in trouble where increasingly swollen, comprehensive universities still place it in the hands of faculties loaded with the burdens of mass teaching and advising. Those whose primary commitment is to research then find their energies wrongly used and seek to escape to external research settings, encouraging governments to separate research from teaching in the form of a separate structure of research institutes. The dual- or multiple-tier structures are able to protect research in something like the graduate school, legitimating it with involvement in the training of the most advanced specialists and separating it from the needs of the undergraduate college, but still keeping it within the institution.

Joseph Ben-David has suggested that a fruitful coupling of two tiers, with different functions, is the key to the possible maintenance of general or liberal education in universities.[36] If there is not a dependable home for research and highly specialized training at second and third levels, then those operations have to be serviced at the first and only level, thereby compromising and most likely subordinating general education. When the one and only tier is deeply rooted in specialization, the revitalization or reintroduction of general education is made all the more difficult.

THE DIVISION OF ACADEMIC SYSTEMS

Academic systems, in varying degrees, have their activities separated into different types of institutions. Those institutions, deliberately or otherwise, are arranged in hierarchies. As systems become loaded with more activities, these larger forms of differentiation become increasingly important, perhaps obtaining an even greater role than the internal divisions in determining the nature and capabilities of academic systems. If there is a single structural key in the negotiating of effective modern systems, it appears to lie in sectoral differentiation.

SECTORS

Horizontal differentiation among institutions takes four general forms in the national systems of higher education of the twentieth century. From simple to complex, they are: a single sector of institutions within a single public system; several sectors within one governmental system; several sectors in more than one formal public subsystem; and several sectors under private support as well as public-system allocation.

Single Public System: Single Sector. This pattern expresses a double monopoly, one of system and one of institutional type. The whole of higher education falls almost completely under a unified national system, topped by a national ministry of education, and the system contains essentially only one form, the state university, with eighty percent or more of enrollment in that one type of institution. During the nineteenth century, virtually all of Latin America conformed to this pattern. The clearest example of this form in Western Europe in the twentieth century has been Italy, with its nationalized system of public universities, complemented by a few "free" institutions that have had to attach themselves to the national system, and with as many as ninety-eight percent of all higher-education students attending places called universities.[37] The university, then, includes not only preparation for public administration and the professions, as elsewhere, but also teacher training, engineering, and some technological fields, which in many countries are located in separate sectors. Other Mediterranean countries, such as Spain, Portugal, and Greece, have traditionally adopted this form. Sweden also had this type of institutional pattern traditionally, with a handful of universities within a unified national system absorbing eighty to ninety percent of the students.[38]

Single Public System: Multiple Sectors. In this pattern, higher education remains under the hegemony of one level of government, but the system is substantially differentiated into two or more types of institutions. This is the most common pattern around the world, the dominant arrangement in Communist societies, Western democracies, and Third World nations alike. Typically, the main sector is a set of universities, with one or more "nonuniversity" sectors organized around technological-technical-vocational instruction or teacher training, or both, but occasionally organized around esoteric functions prized by one or more departments of the central government. All sectors are financed primarily by the national government, sometimes through a single ministry but often along several ministerial avenues.

France has been and still is a striking example of this pattern, with its historical differentiation of universities and *grandes écoles*, specialized schools that for the most part rank above the universities in prestige.[39] The university sector, containing the largest share of students, has successively fallen under the Ministry of Education, the Office of the Secretary of State for Universities (1974), the Ministry of Universities (1978), and, again, the Education Ministry (1981). Some institutions in the *grandes écoles* sector also report to the Education Ministry but have "special status"; others in this elite group answer to other ministries, e.g., the *école polytechnique* to the Ministry of Defense. Then there are additional small sectors of University Institutes of Technology (IUTs) and other enterprises devoted to technical education and teacher training.

Countries as different as Thailand, Iran, and Poland have fallen within this pattern of nationalized diversity. In Thailand, nearly all institutions are governmental, with only about five percent of the students in nominally "private" institutions, which are mainly in business training, and even these colleges are "under the supervision" of a national government department.[40] The governmental institutions divide into two major types—universities, with about fifty-five percent of the enrollment, and more specialized colleges, with approximately thirty-five percent—with a third miscellaneous category making up the rest. As in France, different types of institutions come under different central bureaus: the universities under the Office of University Affairs; teacher training and vocational colleges under the Ministry of Education; and seven nursing colleges under the Ministry of Public Health. This nationalized system is an excellent example of one spawned in the twentieth century by different governmental ministries: "Originally, none of the higher institutions possessed autonomy; they were only service units in various ministries."[41] Various institutions are considered to be not only under government departments but within them: "In actual fact these colleges [agricultural, commercial, vocational, and technical] are suborgans of a larger department which is considered the juristic person."[42]

In prerevolutionary Iran, as in Thailand, educational institutions were basically governmental: as of 1975, all were supported by government funds.[43] Approximately twenty universities and fifty colleges, all founded in the twentieth century, varied widely in type, from the relatively huge University of Tehran, which had thirty percent of all the students in the mid-1970s, to specialized colleges,

schools, and institutes in accounting, hospital management, forestry, sports, and telecommunications. In this patchwork of enterprises, most fell under the Ministry of Science and Higher Education, but they did so in various ways. This was a system full of
"special statuses," such as being "directly under the trust" of some
members of the royal family, and thereby "less subject to the control
of the governmental bureaucracy."[44] And such ministries as Labor
and Agriculture had direct control over some institutions.

In postwar Poland, the private sector has consisted of only one
institution, the imposing Roman Catholic University in Lublin,
which since 1945 has been the only Catholic university in all of
Eastern Europe. All others are governmental, run by the national
government alone.[45] But the governmental realm is heterogeneous
in institutional type and bureau sponsorship. A polytechnic or technological sector of eighteen institutions (1977) had about a third of
the enrollment, as did a university sector consisting of nine institutions, leaving another third of the students in teachers' colleges,
agricultural academies, economic academies, medical academies,
and on down an extensive list to arts colleges and sports colleges.
While most of the institutions are subordinate to one national office,
the Ministry of Science, Higher Education, and Technology, others
come under such diverse bureaus as the Ministry of Health and
Social Welfare, the Ministry of Arts and Culture, and the State
Committee for Sports and Tourism.

Finally, the most important system of all among Communist countries, that of the USSR, is extensively divided between a small university sector of some 50 institutions that has only about ten percent
of the enrollment and a huge, variegated nonuniversity sector of
some 750 institutes with all the rest of the enrollment.[46] All the
enterprises are public, controlled directly by a national bureau or a
ministry at the republic level, which is in turn heavily influenced by
national policy and administration. The universities are relatively
comprehensive, covering the physical sciences, social sciences, and
humanities. But the numerous institutes are highly specialized,
focusing on such distinct areas as agriculture, engineering, medicine, "physical culture," and teacher training. Notably, only about
half of all the enterprises come under the jurisdiction of a higher
education ministry. The others come under, for example, ministries
of culture, health, agriculture, and transportation, linking them to

the tasks of many government departments that attend, in the main, to practical needs of an economy run by the national state. A manpower approach is thereby thoroughly institutionalized.

Since this type of sectoral differentiation commonly entails supervision by a number of central bureaus, it brings with it the problem of how these agencies relate to one another. "Coordination," as seen in chapter 5, is then something quite different from what is normally depicted as integrated governmental control.

Multiple Public Systems: Multiple Sectors.   This pattern occurs primarily in nations that have a federal structure of government, with higher education falling within a number of state or provincial systems, influenced in varying degrees by national government. Theoretically, multiple public systems could have only one type of institution within them, but in reality they seem always to coexist with multiple sectors, apparently for the simple reason that two or more authorities will generate more variety than a simple all-embracing one. When the formal organization of higher education takes place primarily at the subgovernment level, it will more likely reflect provincial differences in the need and preference for types of universities and colleges. In these systems, we can note a dual trend in the postwar period, especially after 1960: on the one hand, greater influence by national government; on the other, a reduction of the private sector, if it existed at all, to a small part—ten to fifteen percent or less—of student enrollment.

With considerable variation, Australia, Canada, Great Britain, West Germany, and Mexico all fall into this pattern. Australia has three distinguishable sectors: universities, colleges of advanced education, and colleges of technical and further education, with the sectors organized in the six systems of the Australian states.[47] These systems vary somewhat in character. For example, the one in Victoria, which includes the University of Melbourne, is considerably older, larger, and more advanced than the one in Western Australia.

Canada has multiple types of universities and colleges, including an important sector of two-year units similar in general form to U.S. community colleges.[48] The sectors are organized within provincial systems, eleven all together, with those systems varying considerably in type and mixture of institutions (for example, the Atlantic provinces versus those of western Canada, and especially Quebec, with its French-Canadian traditions, versus all the other provinces). Within this set of public systems, Quebec is loaded with unique features (e.g., a de facto division of postsecondary education into French-language and English-language subsystems, a heavy clerical tradition, a particular style of strict state supervision, and a sector of about thirty-seven public colleges of general and vocational education [*Collège d'enseignement général et professionel*], which contain a two-year track for transferring to universities and a three-year terminal vocational track). Canada clearly has a higher education system where differences among institutional sectors are extended by differences among provincial subsystems.

Great Britain has developed a variety of institutional types. First, there are several kinds of universities: Oxford and Cambridge as a class in themselves; the University of London as a class in itself; the nineteenth-century-spawned civic universities; and the set of new universities built essentially in the 1960s. Second, there is a host of technical and technological enterprises, some bracketed under university status and others constituting a polytechnic sector. These are the nonuniversity institutions that most aggressively challenge the privileges of the universities. Third, there are teacher-training colleges and a diffuse set of institutions of "further education."[49] Furthermore, even though the nation is not generally considered to have a federal structure of government, there are the distinctive regions of England, Wales, Northern Ireland, and Scotland, which operate in nonuniversity higher education as public authorities. The Scottish subsystem overall has long been so rooted in its own distinctive set of characteristics that "the Scottish universities" are considered to be a different type from "the English universities," even to the point of having played a separate role as a model for higher education in the United States and other countries.[50] Then, too, many of the technical colleges, teacher training colleges, and other "nonuniversity" enterprises have been sponsored by local educational authorities (LEAs), encouraging them to take on local identity and unique character.

As a fourth case, West Germany's system of the mid-1970s had about two-thirds of its students in a university sector, which subdivided into classical-type universities and technical universities; another twenty percent of the students in a vocational sector (*Fachhochschulen*) composed largely of merged units of engineering and commerce upgraded from the secondary level; another eight percent in a third sector of teachers' colleges; and six percent in a sector of new comprehensive institutions that are combinations of the other types.[51] The 200 institutions of these four sectors are grouped in eleven subsystems, following the traditional allocation of responsibility for education in Germany to the *Land* level of government, a pattern interrupted by the Nazi regime but restored after World War II. Hence, there is a fundamental structural similarity in the way public control is divided among provinces and states in Australia, Canada, and the United States—so-called federal systems— with West Germany an imposing exception to the general rule on the European continent that public control is national.

Lastly Mexico is an important instance of this federal pattern among the Latin American systems.[52] A federal republic since the mid-nineteenth century, the country has spawned institutions of higher education under national, state, and private auspices. In the 1970s, there were over 200 enterprises distributed among thirty states, including a central federal district around Mexico City, the capital. The university has been the dominant institutional type, with the technological or technical institution the most prevalent nonuniversity form. The private universities and colleges, comprising some ten to fifteen percent of enrollment, have various antecedents in early church sponsorship and post-1960 private initiatives. But amid the scatter there has also been considerable concentration. Two-thirds of the enrollment is located in the federal district and the two states of Jalisco (containing Guadalajára) and Nuevo León (around Monterrey). Over forty of the institutions and forty percent of the enrollment are in the federal district alone, with that enrollment heavily concentrated in the huge Autonomous National University of Mexico in the capital city. The system simultaneously is much divided into national and state components and tilted toward the predominance and influence of a central institution in the magnetlike area of the country, drawing and concentrating resources and thereby contributing to a gross imbalance between the center and the periphery.

Private and Public Systems: Multiple Sectors. The fourth national arrangement exhibits multiple institutional types under private as well as public sponsorship, at least to the point where fifteen to twenty percent of the students are in institutions that receive most of their financing from nongovernmental sources and have boards of control selected through private channels. The existence of one or more private sectors increases considerably the division of forms, first by providing a private-public cleavage and second by multiplying subtypes and unique institutions as the search for competitive advantage among the private universities and colleges leads some to different postures.

Japanese higher education is an impressive case, since that populous country of over 100 million people moved rapidly into mass higher education in the 1950s and 1960s by allowing the burdens of expansion to be picked up by private institutions, to the point where some seventy-five to eighty percent of the students came to be located in the private sector, a share much greater than in the United States, where the proportions of private and public enrollment are the reverse. This huge system of over 1,000 institutions and 2 million students (as of 1975) has numerous major sectors: a small set of national, formerly "imperial," universities; other national universities; universities supported by the municipal level of government; private universities and colleges, numbering in excess of 300 and varying widely in type and quality; and over 500 junior colleges, public and private, but mainly private.[53] As in the United States, each private institution is under its own board of control and governs itself. The great heterogeneity of institutions entails vast differences in selection, from exceedingly tight, as at the universities of Tokyo and Kyoto, to exceedingly loose, as in some private colleges that became virtual degree mills. Enormous differences in job placement are also the rule, from guaranteed placement to top administrative ranks in government to unspecified entry into a broad band of the total job market, including some blue-collar work, clerical positions, and sales occupations.[54]

The United States is the second great example of this pattern, with 3,000 institutions divided into about 1,500 private colleges and universities and a similar number of public ones, the latter divided into the 50 subsystems of the states.[55] Hence, in international comparison, both the public sector and the private sector are extensively fragmented. Each of the state systems has its own mixture of the three basic institutional types: the state university, the state college, and the community college. The latter in many states are supported considerably by local funds and are under the control of local educational authorities. The private universities vary from the well-known "research universities" to lesser-known "service universities" that have little endowment and have learned to survive on tuition and fees, much like the majority of Japanese private universities and colleges. The hundreds of private colleges, representatives of the type most deeply rooted in American history, run the whole gamut of selectivity and quality and, indeed, the full range of secular and religious differences in American life. The worst are a soft under-belly, indeed.

The differentiation of this system of over 11 million students (as of 1980) has been so extensive that the best efforts in the 1970s to classify institutions developed at least ten categories of types of institutions, and about twenty when the public-private distinction is made.[56] The division of labor that is thereby revealed has been largely overlooked by American as well as foreign observers. For example, on simple parameters, about one-half of all students enter-ing higher education enter the community colleges, which number more than a thousand; about a third of all enrollment at a given time is in the community colleges, another third is in four- and five-year colleges, and the remaining third is in doctoral-granting institutions. The traditionally heterogeneous university category has become ever more so as various state colleges have developed advanced programs and some research capacities and have acquired the formal title of university. Adding such places to the many private universities that have long had the character of service rather than research universities means that the images of "the American uni-versity" long formed by the Ivy League and such leading state universities as California, Michigan, and Wisconsin are poor guides to reality. The expansion of enrollment has been greatest in the enterprises that have heavy teaching loads of nine, twelve, and fifteen classroom hours a week, with large class enrollments, essen-tially precluding research and tilting the reward system away from research productivity and toward teaching performance and service to the institution.[57] Less than a fifth of American students *and* faculty are in the research universities that couple teaching and research to a major degree, following the traditional model of the university idealized in the three major systems of Germany, Britain, and the United States since the last quarter of the nineteenth century.

The higher education systems of Latin America have been mov-ing toward this pattern since 1960 and are now well rooted in it, despite a heritage of public monopoly and a widespread impression that these systems are entirely public. Private-sector enrollments doubled in the fifteen-year period between 1960 and 1975, from seventeen to thirty-five percent. Chile and Peru had become about thirty percent private, Columbia fifty percent, and the large system of Brazil sixty to seventy percent.[58] The private institutions provide various kinds of alternatives to the public realm. In some cases, they are more vocationally oriented and directly responsive to job markets; in others, they are more selective and "elitist"; in still others, they offer more open access. In each case, the buildup of the private alongside the public has meant greater institutional heterogeneity.

The division of higher education systems into institutional sectors thus has many forms, which range along a continuum from simple to complex. The divisions also vary in whether they were imposed by the central government or emerged as the products of local and regional action. Then, too, sectors vary between isolated and articulated. In most systems, isolated sectors have predominated, with a particularly sharp line between "university" and "nonuniversity." Articulation is indexed by the ability of students to move from one to another, receiving credit for courses already completed. Sector boundaries are permeable when students can cross them with transferable course credits. U.S. sectors overall are highly permeable, since there are course credits and certificates common across them, and the division of labor among sectors within the state systems is premised on a common medium of exchange. Sometimes the coin of one institution is partially discounted in the next, giving students only partial credit; but a high degree of articulation in the U.S. system generally helps weld together what would otherwise be a large number of discrete tunnels. Such linkage is partly a matter of state administration and partly a product of market-type interaction among discrete enterprises, a distinction in national integration pursued in chapter 5. But such permeability is unusual: the more common arrangement internationally has been the reverse, that is, few, if any, common units across sectors, and little or no sector transferring. Typically, a national "system" consists of national or regional authorities sponsoring a division of labor among segments that do not interact on the basis of a course-and-credit medium of exchange.[59]

HIERARCHIES

Vertical arrangements of institutions and sectors are of two sorts: high and low placement based on level of task, a hierarchy of sequence; and ranking based on prestige, a hierarchy of status, which is often but not always closely related to the first. The first form of hierarchy comes from sectors having tasks that cover rungs in the educational ladder, with the sectors themselves then taking up location at lower and higher rungs, lower ones feeding higher ones. For example, in the United States, the typical tripartite differentiation of state systems has a basic vertical component: the community college is coterminous with the first two years in the basic structure of grades; the state college overlaps those years and extends upward to take in another two or four years, through the bachelor's and master's degrees; and the state university overlaps both of the first two institutions and extends upward another several years to the doctoral degree and postdoctoral training. For transferring students, the feeder sequences run strongly from the first to the second and third, and from the second to the third, as students move upward through levels of training that are assigned differentially to sectors. This is a quite objective matter. Even if the three sectors had a parity of esteem, there would still be a noticeable vertical differentiation based on place in the ladder of education. With each place there are predictable associated activities: research is likely to locate at the uppermost levels; general education is likely to appear in the lower steps; specialized education in the higher steps.

But parity of esteem among types of institutions rarely if ever obtains. The search for such parity has been as illusory as the search for a classless society: sectors do not remain innocent of status differences. Occupational and social positions are ranked by the public as well as by incumbents; and institutions that place their graduates differentially are assigned different levels of prestige. What in comparative higher education is referred to as "institutional hierarchy" is a prestige ranking of institutions and sectors based primarily on perceived social value of graduation. Where are graduates placed in the labor force, and otherwise in social circles, that might shape life chances? The U.S. structure and others like it involve graduates stepping out into the labor force at different levels of occupational prestige, with a virtually automatic parallel assignment of prestige by the public back to the training institutions (e.g., the prestige of doctors, teachers, and secretaries assigned, respectively, to universities, four-year colleges, and two-year colleges). And sectors are even more likely to be ranked sharply by prestige when lower ones are unable to feed higher ones, but exist instead as airtight compartments that clearly place graduates at different occupational levels. When sectors designed for technical training and teacher training do not have the potential for transferring their students into the university sector, status rankings become more clear-cut and severe.

National systems vary extensively in the extent of status hierarchy, from sharply peaked to relatively flat structures, and we may note three types that range along a continuum. In the first type, several institutions have a monopoly, or near-monopoly, of elite placement that helps to give them much higher prestige than all others. Japan is an outstanding example. A small set of imperial universities were fathered and given superior resources by the central government as instruments of rapid modernization in the late nineteenth and early twentieth centuries. Within the cluster of seven institutions, the universities of Tokyo and Kyoto were given, and seized, an even more special place. They became a class unto themselves, to the point where certain high positions in government could be entered only by graduation from certain faculties, particularly the faculty of law at Tokyo.[60] As precise connections were institutionalized, a small elite sector became fixed as highly superior to all other institutions, a sharply tapered hierarchy that has persisted and conditioned the rest of the system even as the system swelled greatly in size and as diverse sectors emerged.

A high degree of institutional hierarchy has been found also in France and Great Britain. The French case is particularly clear-cut: a few institutions in the *grandes écoles* sector have had a lock on top governmental positions, and increasingly on placement in top executive ranks in industry, selecting vigorously to recruit the crème de la crème for those positions and acquiring a superior standing that has kept them well apart from the problems of university expansion. This institutional elite has been so untouchable that it never even became an issue in the great 1968 French educational crisis or in the host of attempted and effected reforms of the following decade.[61] In a less explicit but still highly effective fashion, Oxford and Cambridge have constituted an institutional elite in Great Britain, still showing in the 1970s the historic capacity to stock the top political and bureaucratic offices of the government,[62] even if, at the same time, they failed to provide industrial leaders and thereby contributed to "the British disease" of lagging economic progress.[63]

The middle ground of status hierarchy is occupied by such systems as the Canadian and the American, in which pronounced differences exist in the social standing of institutions and sectors, without a few institutions monopolizing elite placement. Institutions and sectors are definitely ranked—Canadian universities above Canadian community colleges,[64] U.S. Ivy League universities above state colleges—but placement to high office in public as well as private spheres is institutionally diversified and overlaps sectors. No one or two institutions have a lock on sponsorship of top offices, political or administrative. American presidents are about as likely to be graduates of small unheard-of colleges as graduates of leading universities. For example, Lyndon Johnson graduated from Southwest Texas State Teachers College, Richard Nixon from Whittier College, and the recruits to the central administrative agencies come from a variety of public and private colleges throughout the fifty states.

A third type is characterized by little status ranking. In Italy, there is virtually no nonuniversity sector that could be second best, and all the universities can send graduates to elite positions in government and the professions. A *laurea* in law serves as a general passport to the top administrative stratum in the national civil service, and it can be obtained at any one of several dozen law faculties scattered throughout the country.[65] The system of the Federal Republic of Germany is somewhat more hierarchical than the Italian, since its nonuniversity components devoted to technical and teacher training have a lesser standing than the universities.[66] But there are few status differences among the universities, with no one or two places serving in the manner of Tokyo-Kyoto or Oxford-Cambridge, nor, as in the United States, are there universities competing for the status advantages of attacting the best students. As the best study of the German system has put it: "In general, universities are considered to be of equal standing. There are no major differences in status among the universities of the Federal Republic as there are in

Anglo-Saxon countries." And, going on: "This is the reason why there is no competition among the universities to get the best students by way of entrance examinations, a fact that often amazes foreign observers."[67]

These important national cases make it clear that institutional sectors tend not to remain merely that, but instead become segments of hierarchies that vary in steepness and rigidity. Hierarchy is seemingly most strongly restrained by minimizing sectors and subtypes within them. If a national system works for decades to equate its institutions in resources and personnel, *and* establishes a single national degree in each field of study instead of institutional degrees, *and* elaborates a public doctrine that the state-awarded degree has the same value for employment no matter where one studies, then the hierarchical tendency is considerably restrained. If a system has multiple sectors that handle different forms and levels of training, those sectors will vary in esteem, and a steeper hierarchy is thereby produced. Beyond task differentials, higher-ranked institutions or sectors, through governmental policy or self-aggrandizement, acquire and institutionalize greater financial resources with which to attract well-regarded faculty and students, and this perpetuates and enhances their privileged position. There is a snowballing effect that is basic to the inertia of institutional hierarchies in higher education.

The pros and cons of the division of sectors and the development of hierarchies are fundamental issues in public policy in higher education and will reappear in later discussions of change and values (chapters 6 and 7). To anticipate, the issues involve trade-offs among such values as equity, competence, and liberty. Minimizing sectors, and hence hierarchies, allows for more uniformity in practices and rewards. The single formal system composed of one type of institution gives greater strength to "coercive comparisons," in which "have-nots" exercise strong leverage for equity against the "haves," the less-noble against the noble.[68] But the limited-sector system, with little hierarchy, also seems particularly vulnerable to overload in activities and to conflict among tasks. It is susceptible to structural insufficiency in completing work, as activities multiply and more people seek to be served. New functions crowd in upon old functions, as when the burdens of mass teaching and counseling in comprehensive universities absorb time and resources formerly allotted to research and advanced training. Also, what should and should not be done becomes institutionalized in the expectations and powers of the established interests in the single type of institution, with certain activities then unserved. Hence, the limited-sector systems have difficulty in accommodating an increasingly wide and diverse range of activities.

Multisector systems seem more capable of handling heavy loads of activity and reducing conflict among contradictory operations. New clusters of activities are given to a separate type of institution, as in the creation of community colleges in the United States, University Institutes of Technology (IUTs) in France, The Open University in Great Britain, and regional technological institutes in Mexico. The norms of the old sectors are then not as coercive upon the new as they would be if the new cluster of activities were placed within the old. Hence, choice is increased and adaptability of the system enhanced. But as the extensive-sector system develops institutional hierarchy, it will thereby create certain inequalities in rewards. Competitive advantages and disadvantages become institutionalized. Hence, equity tends not to be well served, at least in the short run, and those who are primarily interested in the promotion of equality are offended.

The bearing of status hierarchies upon the competence of national systems is complicated indeed. As we will note again later, extreme hierarchy has had the great advantage of guaranteeing talent to the top public and private offices. It is hardly a bad thing to have competent civil servants, but such hierarchy usually leads to some "hardening of the arteries," with major unanticipated difficulties. Japanese researchers have shown that a monopoly of top status at the universities of Tokyo and Kyoto has led to serious problems of nepotism. While producing a small output of top-quality people for government and industry, the system developed closed circles within itself that restricted a larger production of both trained people and quality research. Academic inbreeding became characteristic, as high as 100 percent at times in key faculties at the University of Tokyo. The small, closed subsystems virtually froze the life chances of university graduates and future academics at about the age of eighteen, the time of entry to the universities, with achievement criteria that had replaced ascriptive criteria in Japanese society ironically replaced at that point by precise ascription: "Achievement came to transform itself into ascription after the eighteen-plus [examinations]. After that time one's evaluation depends on the name of institutions to which he belongs or from which he graduates rather than achievement or merit,"[69] a phenomena referred to as "achieved ascription."[70]

These aspects of the top of the Japanese hierarchy contribute heavily to two basic features of student life in that country: for aspiring young people, it is critical to get into the top subsystems, and hence the preuniversity years have become a long period of intense study capped by an "examination hell"; at the same time, the university years are relatively relaxed academically, since entry is what counts, and student energies are thereby freed to flow into political and other extracurricular activities.

Hidden Sectors.   In a fourfold scheme of differentiation, we have located two forms within institutions and two within the system at large. But such analytical lines should not obscure the ways in which one form shades into another, nor the simple fact that national systems may appear in different categories and as different types, with minor changes in definition. For example, private sectors take several forms, with some completely under private finance and control; others are supported mainly by governments but maintain private boards of trustees and the appearance of being private.

A national system such as Mexico's, with only about ten percent of its enrollment in private institutions, appears in the classification above as an instance of the third type; Brazil, counting a much larger proportion in the private sector, is clearly in the fourth category. But the Mexican private sector is much more completely private, on its own; the mammoth Brazilian private sector actually is quasi governmental. Hence, the two systems could be oppositely classified. Then, too, one major form of differentiation may serve as a substitute for another, particularly in the case of divisions within enterprises acting like sectors of the overall system. Sections of universities, as in the highly autonomous faculties in continental European universities, may function much like institutional sectors. For example, faculties of pedagogy operate with much autonomy inside Italian universities. When more teachers were needed in the 1960s, these faculties could swell considerably in size autonomously, much as if they constituted a separate teacher-training sector. In a sense, there are as many sectors as there are autonomous faculties operating with virtually direct budget allocations from central offices. When the university is but a holding company for faculties, considerable sector differentiation is hidden within its nominal unity.

This point comes up later in analyzing academic change, since one tendency in recent reform has been to compose "comprehensive universities" in which virtually all fields of study are brought under the umbrella of the university designation, but, at the same time, major parts have different subgroupings of subjects and different sublabels. The German *Gesamthochschulen* of the 1970s have constituted one such effort.[71] A second and more thoroughgoing one has been the changes enacted in Sweden in the late 1970s to incorporate its small nonuniversity sector with universities—"comprehensivization" all the way, in line with the basic principle that all postsecondary education in the same location should form a single integrated institution.[72] Even in American universities, which as a general class are relatively integrated, the college of agriculture or the school of medicine may be organizationally distant from the core arts and sciences faculty, with distinct financial arrangements. When countries lump much of higher education together in omnibus organizations, "sectors" will be hidden as sections.

THE LOOSE WEB OF ACADEMIC ORGANIZATION

The work of higher education is carried out in every country in a structure that decomposes tasks within and among institutions. Some elemental features of differentiation, preeminently those centered in disciplines, have wide currency. They flow across national boundaries and thereby become similar, to a considerable degree, across national systems. Systems "break out" the natural sciences, and within that large aggregate of tasks, they break out physics and chemistry and biology and major specialties thereof. But other features of differentiation, those centered on institutions, vary widely among nations, subject to particulars of origin and context. National systems thereby make the disciplines operational in such different forms as the chair and the department, the one-tier and the two-tier university, the single-sector and the multisector national system. Whatever the combination of sections and tiers within institutions, and sectors and hierarchies among them, the prevailing structure sets many of the problems of control and conditions all important issues of continuity and reform. Hence, an understanding of the basic structure becomes the necessary footing for better comprehension of a wide range of problems and issues. To study academic differentiation is not only to determine the academic division of labor in its specific operational settings but also to pursue the expression of academic values and the foundations of academic power.

As major social units, academic systems fall between "organization" and "society." They have a complexity of tasks that is more than we expect of organizations. Their institutional parts have an uncommon primacy, always allowed in some serious measure to wander organizationally in different directions, driven by the dynamics of individual fields. The parts have limited mutual influence. Hence, even at the institutional level, academic complexes are not well understood by means of models of integrated organizations that have been fixed in the public mind by long acquaintance with business firms and public bureaus. When those models depict a division of labor, they tell of a differentiation of tasks within an hierarchical complex under a single authority. The center holds; the top manages to dominate. But universities and colleges have become entities too diverse and fragmented to be thus comprehended; and the state, regional, and national entities that are the larger organized composites, quite loosely coupled when judged by any traditional idea of organization, vary even more from standard models. Such systems, formally organized or not, are loosely webbed sectors of the larger society, to be likened as much to the way societies are organized as they are to the means of integration in unitary organizations. In societal organization, the division of labor has long been viewed by leading thinkers as a specialization of autonomous social units.[73] Further differentiation grows out of the dynamics of the individual segments and interaction among them as much as from top-down command or from simple bargaining among a few groups. Linking mechanisms operate that are overlooked or underutilized in explanations of how organizations perform as social actors: unplanned change looms large.

Because of the growing complexity of bodies of knowledge and related tasks, the division of academic labor is increasingly characterized by fragmentation within and among universities, colleges, and institutes. But this is not to say that national systems are falling apart, for there is much else that fragments and integrates. For one, as we shall now see, the beliefs of academic groups must be brought into the equations that determine an academic system, providing, as they do, a second primary dimension of organization.

THREE

BELIEF

All major social entities have a symbolic side, a culture as well as a social structure, some shared accounts and common beliefs that help define for participants who they are, what they are doing, why they are doing it, and whether they have been blessed or cursed. Outsiders generally know a formal organization more through its symbols than its technical structure, since they principally encounter official image and public reputation. They are aware of a whole class of organizations, universities, for example, by means of a diffused understanding of what that type of enterprise does and therefore what it is. Thus, the cultural side of human affairs involves the construction of meaning, something we are incapable of doing without no matter how narrowly rational our purpose or how technical our organization. It is always present, in micro form for smaller groups as well as in such macro concentrations as "the scientific culture" and "the humanistic culture."[1] As Everett Hughes puts it: "Whenever some group of people have a bit of common life with a modicum of isolation from other people, a common corner in society, common problems and perhaps a couple of common enemies, there culture grows."[2] Organizations and their components are natural producers of subcultures, since they throw members into the same boat, confront them with the same inescapable problems, make them cope with the same forces and the same kinds of people. They bring individuals together—coal miner, logger, sailor; accountant, doctor, social worker; historian, econometrician, space physicist—to share a distinct social fate. "All of us, if we have a sense of solidarity with some occupation, are in some measure members of a community of fate. We are also by the same token participants in a subculture, although it may not include song."[3]

The symbolic side of modern organizations has been vastly understated in research. Those who study purportedly rational organizations have in the main ignored intangible and seemingly unformed culture in order to be hardheaded about such problems of management as budgeting and productivity, and to track those features of structure that could most readily be quantified or concretely depicted. But, with increasing momentum, organization watchers have turned to the study of ideologies and other sets of symbols. In an early classic study, Philip Selznick highlighted the "administrative doctrines" of the Tennessee Valley Authority and the part they played in defining the character of the organization and in rationalizing its actions.[4] In a comparative analysis of managerial beliefs in the course of industrialization in nineteenth-century England, tsarist Russia, contemporary America, and the new Communist state of the German Democratic Republic, Reinhard Bendix sought out "the ideologies that the managers of the new productive techniques and their supporters have woven out of their own roles."[5]

In a later systematic distinction, Amitai Etzioni set forth three principal forms of compliance in organized systems—the coercive, the instrumental, and the normative—and grouped organizations according to the dominant form used: prisons under coercive, business firms under instrumental, and churches, colleges, and nonprofit organizations under normative. The normative grouping encompasses sectors in which common attachment to perspectives and ideas, symbols in general, seemingly predominate over forced compliance and monetary rewards.[6] Herbert Kaufman went further by proposing that organizations are held together by five types of bonds—the physical, the habitual, the expedient, the moral, and the emotional—and by suggesting that the emotional bonds are often the strongest, forged by attachment to a common symbol and a common idea, as well as by love of a common leader or love of all by each.[7] John Meyer has gone all the way in claiming that even the most technical system will be held together and made effective by the shared commitments of its members as much as by specific technical rules and procedures.[8] Generally, the late 1970s saw organizational theory develop a subfield that pursues organizational beliefs, ideologies, stories, legends, and sagas, the different terms grappling with the same general phenomenon and versions thereof.[9]

Analysts of academic systems have noted that academic sites often reek with lofty doctrines that elicit emotion, in a secular version of religion. Small liberal arts colleges in the United States, and even some good-sized universities, have constructed definitions of themselves that elicit deep personal and collective commitment,[10] signified in most dramatic form by tears of joy and sadness at college ceremonies and captured historically in the deeply emotional appeal made by Daniel Webster on behalf of Dartmouth College before the United States Supreme Court in a famous case of 1818: "It is, sir, as I have said, a small college, and yet there are those who love it." This was a peroration of such intensity as to reputedly bring the chief justice, John Marshall, to tears.[11]

One U.S. management analyst who has attempted to compare "the cultures of management" has gone so far as to maintain that universities are naturally disintegrative organizations held together by "love," pointing to a more emotional attachment than that typically found in business firms, public agencies, trade unions, and most other organizations.[12] Those who staff academic systems of all sizes and shapes are not only "men of ideas," handling materials that are intrinsically ideational, but they are also known for a certain piety in self-definition. There is much comfort in believing that one has committed a lifetime to serving knowledge, youth, and the general welfare, avoiding the crass materialism of the marketplace. The purported altruism of one of the world's oldest professions is frequently brought into play. Thus, as a general type, academic systems are symbolically rich, with participants devoted to bodies of specific symbols, frequently attached to broader robust ideologies, and often uncommonly bounded by affect despite elaborate pretensions to the contrary.

To explore why this is true, it is appropriate first to disaggregate academic culture, in order to seek primarily those self-defining ideas and beliefs that are generated within the academic system or that are so thoroughly incorporated that they become systematically positioned within it. As the ideas that steer academic people are identified, they should be connected to their social foundations. Since little has been written about academic beliefs in any serious detail, especially in comparison across nations, national patterns can only be suggested by examples and illustrations. We then turn analytically to the way that beliefs interpret outside trends and demands, and hence mediate between other parts of society and the higher education system itself. This point needs special attention in order to escape from the simple cause-and-effect stories told by those observers who refuse to take seriously what goes on within the black box of academic organization and hence merely project automatic, passive response to immutable external forces. Finally, we consider the possible symbolic disintegration of academic systems under the steady pounding of larger scale, greater specialization, and multiplying complexity. The centrifugal tendency is strong. Yet that tendency generates countermovements at all levels of the systems, producing new symbolic linkages that provide some reintegration. The interesting question is whether the quality of symbolic integration necessarily shifts over time in modern systems from the unspoken to the spoken, the soft to the hard, the informal to the formal. Do the cultures of law, constitutional framework, and administrative rule figure importantly in the symbolic construction and integration of academic systems?

THE BASIC TYPES OF ACADEMIC BELIEF

Academic systems are ideologically rich in part because they provide a plurality of nested groupings that manufacture culture as part of their work and self-interest. A German professor of physics at the University of Heidelberg partakes of the culture of physics, the culture of the University of Heidelberg, the culture of the academic profession at large (in Germany and internationally), and the culture of the German national academic system. There are additional external sources of ideology and belief that vary from one society to another, such as political and religious orientations imported from the broader society, but a systematic approach to the ideologies of academic life needs to emphasize those sources naturally generated or most firmly positioned within the system, and therefore to distinguish the cultures of discipline, enterprise, profession-at-large, and national system. Discipline and enterprise, the primary forms of organization, are also powerful sources of belief, working locally in the department and the subfaculty, as well as in the university or college as a whole, and producing the more specific sets of beliefs that academics live by. The academic profession and the national system, more inclusive groupings, bring to bear more general traditions, ideas, and categories of thought. They are also the environments of first importance for the more specialized units, exercising their own constraints and filtering the influences of the more remote parts of society and its general culture.

THE CULTURE OF THE DISCIPLINE

In chapter 2 we identified the disciplines as the primary "going concerns" of academic systems, with their own procedures that had taken form through generations of effort. Around distinctive intellectual tasks, each discipline has a knowledge tradition—categories of thought—and related codes of conduct. Most strongly the case in advanced systems, there is in each field a way of life into which new members are gradually inducted. Physicists, economists, and historians of art are socialized into their particular fields as students and later through on-the-job interaction with disciplinary peers. As recruits to different academic specialties, they enter different cultural houses, there to share beliefs about theory, methodology, techniques, and problems. "A paradigm is what the members of a scientific community share, and conversely, a scientific community consists of men who share a paradigm."[13]

The culture of a discipline even includes idols: the office of the physicist often has pictures on the walls of such greats as Albert Einstein and Robert Oppenheimer; the sociologist, with all due respect to Einstein and Oppenheimer, prefers to pay homage to Max Weber and Emile Durkheim. The photographic images convey sternness and seriousness, hooking followers to those who have led in setting perspectives and standards. The idols of disciplines, particularly in the humanities, may go even further to include those embedded in the subject: those who study Dante or Shakespeare as a lifelong specialty are normally elevated in self-esteem, since prolonged association with such greatness is bound to make one feel superior to all those who have not been so lucky. Such elevations in identity may even be noted when the subject is an eminent general culture, as in the case of specialists in French history and literature.

Disciplinary cultures are hard to pin down, since they are only vaguely sensed by their own members, difficult to perceive by outsiders, and easily dismissed as romantic, self-serving portraits when articulated in speech or prose. The clearest cases appear in the fields most structured by a body of systematic knowledge and arcane categories of thought that set them apart. Consider mathematics, as seen from the top by Stanislaw Ulam:

> The aesthetic side of mathematics has been of over-whelming importance throughout its growth. It is not so much whether a theorem is useful that matters, but how elegant it is. Few non-mathematicians, even among other scientists, can fully appreciate the aesthetic value of mathematics, but for the practitioners it is undeniable. One can, however, look conversely at what might be called the homely side of mathematics. This homeliness has to do with having to be punctilious, of having to make sure of every step. In mathematics one cannot stop at drawing with a big, wide brush; all the details have to be filled in at some time.[14]

The culture of mathematics stresses the internal logic and consistency of a set of numerically specific ideas. The basic style combines elegance and precision, a combination found also in classical music. The math-music syndrome has been widely noted—he who likes mathematics likes Bach and Mozart. The materials with which they work push mathematicians toward a style of thought and communication radically different from that found in most other disciplines, especially the qualitative ones in social science and the humanities. Written communications are short, perhaps several pages of highly condensed knowledge expressed in mathematical symbols. In contrast, a historian can hardly get started in three pages. Others may need a desk, a room, a library full of books, but the creative mathematician needs to stare at a wall or fiddle with coffee cups by the hour, or work with chalk and eraser at a blackboard. From early in his career he is likely to have a deep sense of being different from others, including scholars in such bordering fields as physics and chemistry.

In contrast, physicists, closely related to mathematicians in the broad spectrum of fields, see themselves as more concerned with reality. Even theoretical physicists have a firm sense of reality, leading physicists generally "to hold their subject superior to one which

involves 'making chicken scratches on paper.' " They too value
highly the property of elegance, but with an empirical bent: "It
seems almost an article of faith, related to the physicist's belief in the
unity and simplicity of nature, . . . that the right answer is always the
neatest among two or more apparently valid interpretations of the
same phenomena. Complicated solutions are suspect; the ideal
explanation 'can be put in one sentence.' " And no other field has a
greater sense of its own universality. While the process of building
up the subject may be parochial, discernibly different in France, the
Soviet Union, Britain, and the United States, the corpus of knowledge is seen as universal: "what counts as a valid finding is not
dependent on geographical or cultural considerations, and the process of establishing or refuting a claim knows no frontiers."[15] At the
root of it all is a peculiar bundle of knowledge possessed only by a
few. The we/they distinction that underlies subculturing could
hardly be sharper.

Even the most general subjects contain perspectives and technical
doctrines that are shared by most insiders and that set them apart
from those outside the field. Philosophy is a "soft" field, but it is also
one that has become enormously specialized in subject matter as well
as fragmented internally in the last half of the twentieth century. In
the United States this field underwent professionalization in the
decades around the turn of the century, primarily at the hands of a
dominant department at Harvard that contained, among others,
William James, Josiah Royce, George Santayana, Alfred North
Whitehead, and Ralph Perry. In a perceptive analysis of the role of
this group in the rise of American philosophy, Bruce Kuklick points
to a unified set of basic beliefs:

> To some extent this set of beliefs reflected complexities
> that would justify the need for disciplinary expertise, but
> it was also a rich and nuanced perspective that defined
> concerns and fixed the terms of philosophic debate.
> Harvard Pragmatism was a form of neo-Kantianism
> whose adherents drew from a set of connected technical
> doctrines: a constructionalist epistemology stressing the
> changing character of our conceptual schemes; a com-
> mitment to a kind of voluntarism; a concern with the
> nature of possible experience; a distrust of the tradition

of phenomenalistic empiricism; a recognition of the importance of logic for philosophy; discomfort with the dichotomy between the conceptual and the empirical; and a refusal to distinguish between questions of knowledge and of value.[16]

A "set of beliefs," a "rich and nuanced perspective," a "set of connected technical doctrines,"—and much jargon, in the eyes of the nonphilosopher—went into the making of a specialized pattern of speculation. Produced by outstanding people grouped in a department of the most influential U.S. university, the pattern, for a time, virtually became the content of all of American philosophy:

> From the mid-1890s to James' death in 1910 Harvard Pragmatism controlled American philosophy. The philosophic world looked to Harvard for stimulation, and when the Harvard speculators themselves wanted stimulation from contemporaries, they looked to their departmental colleagues. Within the department itself, Royce and James developed a common vocabulary that set the limits of philosophical discussion in the United States.[17]

Indeed, everywhere at the core of a disciplinary subculture we find a "common vocabulary," one increasingly so arcane that outsiders find it mystifying and call it jargon. One way to investigate changes in the beliefs of a discipline is to track changes in vocabulary. The internal splitting of a field will be reflected in a differentiation of terms.

Professional areas of research, teaching, and service also develop subcultures of their own that reflect the different technologies and work patterns of their respective occupations and partake of the values and norms of those extended fields. As we have seen, the professional schools in most countries reside in the first and only significant tier, side by side with the natural sciences, social sciences, and humanities, with exclusive membership and usually no lateral transferring of students. Hence, they encapsulate faculty and students even more than does the American professional school. In either case, a distinctive medical-school culture, law-school culture, engineering-school culture, etc., arises.[18] The more professionalized the occupation, the greater the cultural separation. Hence, medical and law schools seem to have the most distinctive subcultures, with a great buildup over time of norms decidedly peculiar to the occupation (e.g., the importance in medicine of having not "crocks" but really sick people upon whom to apply one's knowledge and technique, or the adversarial relationship in law in which even the most obviously guilty person must have representation and a day in court). The schools of the semiprofessions, for the most part, especially those based on the social sciences (e.g., education and social work), show less firmness and clarity in the integration of their own ways. This tendency is rooted in their "knowledge uncertainty." As a medley of thought drawn from such unsure disciplines as psychology and sociology, their symbolic constructions are more diffuse.

The associations, learned societies, and academies that disciplines and professional areas develop generate a steady flow of symbolic materials about themselves. The materials include: admission and membership requirements that help distinguish between insiders and outsiders; reaffirmations of the special virtues of the field; reports on how the field as a whole is doing, particularly if it is engaged in delicate relations, or even border warfare, with other fields; prizes and tributes for outstanding performers and "tribal elders"; sometimes a code of ethics; and always an obituary column, the repetitive honor paid to surviving colleagues as well as the deceased. From such materials, and associated activities and rewards, come self-identities that may be more powerful than those of mate, lover, and family protector, or those that come from community, political party, church, and fraternal order. As the professor comes to care about the welfare of his discipline or profession as well as the advancement of his own work, there is less reason to go home at five o'clock.

But in all such cultural matters, disciplines and professions vary greatly. We have already reviewed the way in which fields vary from unified to fragmented in consensus on one or two paradigms, with social scientists and humanists operating in less predictable symbolic settings than natural scientists. Disunited within their own fields on grounds of basic approach, theory, and methods, social scientists and humanists are thereby rendered more vulnerable to specific political views or world views brought into one's work from outside sources. Sociology, political science, and history are relatively open in this sense, with, in comparison, mathematics, physics, and chemistry operating more like closed cultural systems. The autonomy brought by systematic knowledge proceeds along symbolic as well as material lines.

The comparative strength of disciplinary cultures among national systems is principally dependent on how advanced is the system's state of knowledge. Such advanced systems as the German, French, British, and American, containing the highest degree of disciplinary specialization, experience a relatively intense distinguishing of related subcultures. But subculturing is also subject to the effects of age and international transfer. Old systems such as the Italian have had centuries in which to accumulate traditions in a host of professional fields and disciplines. Culture begets culture: "cultural inheritance" is high in fields that have a sense of a long history—a "community of fate" stretched over decades and even centuries. And the transfer of academic forms from one country to another, analyzed in chapter 6, brings with it related cultures that may be taken more seriously in the insecurities of the new setting than in the relative security of the old. It never has been functionally necessary to drink port wine in order to understand the classics, but this particular happy ritual has been of more than passing interest in the universities of many former British colonies.

THE CULTURE OF THE ENTERPRISE

The second source and type of academic culture is that which is generated by and attaches to individual universities and colleges. Such enterprise cultures vary widely in strength and in content, within national systems as well as among them. The bonding power of institutional symbols is affected by: organizational scale, with smaller units better able to forge unifying ideologies than larger ones; organizational integration, with interdependent parts more inclined than autonomous ones to share a self-definition; organizational age, with historical depth producing a larger storehouse of lore; organizational struggle, with dramatic events of birth or transformation producing more heroic symbols than an uneventful institutional life; and, especially, the competitiveness of the larger organizational setting, with competition for survival and status generating claims of uniqueness and a sense of common struggle. Competitive distinctiveness is the sharp edge of enterprise culture.

Extreme examples of institutional culture have been studied intensively in the liberal arts college sector of the American system.[19] Crucial in the movement of several colleges—Antioch, Reed, Swarthmore—to a top ranking among some 800 colleges was the working up of an intensive and integrated self-belief. Notably, no particular program or bit of structure was necessary: all the specific items that are endlessly debated in the U.S. system—sequences of courses, freshmen seminars, senior requirements, departmental versus divisional organization, and so on—were not in themselves of any great importance and could vary almost randomly, with one college doing it one way and another college another way. What counted was the meaning assigned to the bits and pieces, the way in which the participants saw their practices as the expression of a unified and unique approach devised by hard work and struggle. A good share of the faculty, students, administration, and alumni came to hold a credible story of uncommon achievement. The story was not always accurate, since it was highly selective and exaggerated. But it had important ingredients of truth and was based on a historical reality. The colleges possessed, and were possessed by, a saga—a collective understanding of current institutional character that refers to a historical struggle and is embellished emotionally and loaded with meaning to the point where the organization becomes very much an end-in-itself.

These three colleges, and many others in the same sector, have been moved toward vibrant institutional cultures by the conditions specified above. They have been small in scale, with people and parts thereby made more visible to one another. Their components have been relatively interdependent, since the colleges were not involved in graduate work or big science but concentrated instead on undergraduate education. They have had to pull together in order to implement, or at least make plausible, the college's particular approach to liberal education. Each college has been around long enough, from the mid-nineteenth or the early twentieth century, to be covered with the ivy of historical events—great presidents, fires, debts, exploits of misbehavior, birthdays. Most saliently, each went through an easily dramatized struggle to win their unusual standing in an arena in which competition through the decades has led many other colleges to unexciting mediocrity, lingering sickness, and even death.

As a matter of degree, the concept of organizational saga is applicable to other colleges and universities as well as to other types of organizations. Even a predominantly pragmatic and instrumental organization will develop some stories, even legends, about itself, if personnel turnover does not destroy all continuity of group connection. Those who have worked together for a decade will develop some shared feelings about "their" organization, a set of beliefs that helps to define their place in life and gives meaning to the fact that they have contributed so much time and effort to a particular institution. The meaning provided by shared symbols offers rewards beyond the material ones for having contributed so much of oneself. But it is the broad classes of organizations loosely known as normative that are most inclined to stress symbolic bonding, and thus to range along the middle-to-high parts of a continuum of saga building. And competitive situations push colleges toward the extreme. There is good reason why the first pages of the catalog of a U.S. liberal arts college tell a story that begins with the college sitting on a high hill overlooking a lovely valley, a location that allows it to combine rural charm and urban convenience, and then proceeds to detail the many features of the college that compose a general and attractive uniqueness.

No matter how they are produced, enterprise cultures generate loyalty. Symbolically bonded faculty do not leave when they have a better material offer, but avoid the "exit" choice and take the option of exercising "voice" to maintain and improve things where they are.[20] A saga-enriched culture also helps to turn the organization into a community, emotionally warming the institution and giving individuals a sense of place. Enterprise community, like occupational community, has a valuable role in modern societies in partially compensating for the erosion of geographic community and the rapidity of social change. The inducing of such community remains an important reason why colleges and universities appear so often not to be "organizations." Then, too, full-bodied ideologies constitute moral capital, an additional resource for institutional health.

Institutions move into troubled times with quite different characterological abilities to survive and remain strong. Financial capital helps, but, in addition, people's depth of belief in the value of the institution makes a difference in response in the days of illness and decline. For example, the troubled days of student protest in the late 1960s affected individual American colleges quite differently according to their characters. Some that were weak in self-belief and quite fragmented were severely ripped apart (e.g., San Francisco State College). Others that had strong self-belief, and that were relatively united around it, went through extremely troublesome days but were able to snap back fairly rapidly and to feel that they had been made stronger by the common experience of working their way out of the troubled waters (e.g., Wesleyan University).[21] A potent institutional myth is a resource deposited in the bank of institutional morality, an account on which one can draw without going under when difficulties arise.

Sturdy institutional beliefs also serve as bridges to the outside world across which resources flow. Especially in competitive arenas, the institution that believes deeply in itself, and has at least a small social base of believers on the outside, has some advantage in raising funds and attracting clientele and personnel. The belief is an institutional reputation as well as a self-image. Reputation is important in nearly all sectors of organizational life but especially in those realms where resources must be privately assembled.

Such intense ideologies have their dangers. As seen in the academic world, they involve narrow commitment and possible loss of adaptability. The first is the hazard of the specialized niche in the ecology of similar organizations. Organizations normally diversify as a way of hedging their bets, protecting themselves against sudden changes in the environment that might make any one operation obsolete. Those that choose the path of a narrowly specified, unique role must live with the hazard of putting all their eggs in one basket. They are unable flexibly to orchestrate a set of roles, emphasizing first one and then another as environmental change suggests a shift in commitments. Thus, a saga may freeze commitments. But the contents of sagas make a difference in the degree of rigidity. For example, the traditional self-belief of Antioch College developed in the 1920s and 1930s was more open to experimentation and structural change than that of Reed, since it encouraged such nontraditional perspectives and programs as a work-study program and intense student participation in campus government.

The second danger is that self-love can rigidify responses. A specialized enterprise is particularly surrounded by its own trained incapacities when it is full of pride about its distinctive accomplishment and is publicly perceived as especially good at a particular thing. Competence is then narrowly staked, with interest and ideology together helping to ensure that any shift to new duties and points of view will be wrenching and sometimes impossible. An intense sense of craft may be a great thing, until an organization wants to shift from one craft to another or transform craft workers into assembly-line workers. That is generally so hard to do that it is preferably done by turnover of personnel rather than by exhortation and retraining of existing staff.[22] But then personnel turnover is not possible where academic tenure, civil service position, or union rights provide job protection. A tenured senior faculty member highly competent in a collegiate specialized task and carrying a unified belief about a distinctive role can be unshakable. For example, it is not easy to induce those who have developed an intense commitment to a particular interpretation of the liberal arts over several decades of hard work to change their minds in the course of five or ten years to a quite different definition.

Thus, there is good reason that in public sectors of higher education in the U.S. system, and even more so elsewhere, zealous pursuit of special organizational culture is often deliberately avoided. The public enterprises need the internal diversity that allows them to relate to many publics. The state may mandate similarity across a set of institutions, or institutions may voluntarily converge on prestigious models, or make common cause with similar institutions to avoid risking their revenge on a prideful deviant. Yet, even in state-supported sectors, this "safe" game has its own set of dangers. When a general turndown occurs, the nondistinctive institution has no special claim on resources other than a fixed place in the budget. As a duplicate part, interchangeable with other parts, it may be the redundant unit selected by budget cutters for major surgery or a bankruptcy sale. Various public authorities may be inclined even to attempt to reward those campuses that reach for distinctiveness rather than remain in a comfortable uniformity. There are ample reasons why even timid public enterprises try not to go symbolically flat, but rather claim some distinction in mixing particular qualities and services and in relating to external support groups.

The *structural* feature that most determines the nature and strength of enterprise cultures in higher education is tightness of organization. American universities are more loosely integrated than American colleges on the symbolic dimension, since they incorporate more of the fragmented professionalism of the disciplines. In turn, European and Latin American universities are even more loosely integrated symbolically than their American counterparts, since the individual faculties are traditionally highly autonomous and require little or no lateral linkage. As we have seen, their confederational nature is often reflected in a geographic scattering of faculties throughout a city. From structural fragmentation, in this case, comes cultural fragmentation.

But there is always some symbolic unity of the whole. In this respect, the conditions of the U.S. system have led to the exploiting of extracurricular activities, with athletic valor the raw material of institutional legends. Year after year, extending back through a long tradition, football teams, for example, represent the whole institution, offering integrating symbols that give wholeness and magnetism to enterprises that need to compete for attention, affection, and support from external sources as well as to overcome internal fragmentation.[23] In Europe and Latin America, in contrast, the extracurricular realm has been weak, undeveloped and unused as a contributor to integration. The need for competitive distinctiveness is much less: as we have noted, in all the many nationalized systems in the world, university buildings, personnel, and programs are sunk costs in national budgets. In most countries, we may conclude, sheer age is the main source of hallowed symbols and of the sense of continuity of ideals and activities that comes from the stone and mortar of bygone centuries—a sense of institutional roots that is hard to come by on the new campus, whether it is constructed of plate glass, cement block, or old stone. Elders in the institutional tribe quite simply have more culture than the young because they have extracted symbols from experience over a longer time, including ideologies that legitimate position and power.

Subcultures of the Enterprise.   In the conglomeration that we call a university, subcultures are bound to develop on grounds other than disciplinary location. There are more general roles, those of student, faculty, and administrator, around which subcultures form. As the enterprise grows, subculturing around such major roles grows apace, setting student, faculty, and administrative worlds further apart and developing further differences within each. For example, in a study of students at the University of Melbourne, Graham Little noted a great gulf between Australian student and faculty cultures.[24] Faculty remained oriented around the ideals of a "community of scholars" and assumed that the university was made up of people whose sustained interests were intellectual, hence focused on "problems" and "issues." Their myth assumed that students, too, are scholars, searching and highly motivated. But the student culture was more uncertain and more fitfully intellectual. Students were much less certain of where they were going and what the university was all about, causing them to turn to a host of different definitions for symbolic support.

Student culture has been studied intensively in a large body of research on students' attitudes and values, principally in the United States.[25] The most widely used typology has pointed to four general types of U.S. student culture: the academic, the vocational, the collegiate—Joe College himself—and the nonconformist.[26] But four types are not enough in such a heterogeneous system, since among 10 million students there are widely varying ways of being academic, from premature Don to passive grade-grubber; or of being nonconformist, from radical political activist to member of a religious sect. The structural diversity of the system has a counterpart in a plethora of subcultures, making it difficult to comprehend the ways in which students orient their behavior by shared beliefs.

Simplified approaches have suggested central tendencies, orientations common across large bodies of students. From a study of undergraduates at the University of Kansas, several sociologists pointed to the overwhelming importance of a "grade point average perspective," with students ever mindful of the importance of individual course grades in the U.S. system and how they add up to an average grade for purposes of graduation and certification.[27] But how many and what types of subcultures we identify in student life depends on how discriminating we want to be. A perspective on "making it" by means of satisfactory academic performance is surely widespread in and across national systems. But then there is much more that makes a difference: the intellectual intensity of student life, the amount of emphasis on vocational preparation, the encouragement to live now while young, the support given to political or artistic nonconformity. Highly accessible universities and colleges will contain all such orientations, and still more, in a grand diffusion, whereas highly selective enterprises narrow and focus student subcultures.

In the extremes of "elitism," student subcultures can be powerful in shaping lifelong attitudes and in binding individuals to one another. An outstanding study of university preparatory academies flourishing in Japan from the late nineteenth century through World War II showed how these schools operated like castles under siege, insulating the inmates from the "evil ways and sordid customs" of the world outside.[28] All students were boarded and encountered physical training, ritualized hazing, and patriotism of a most intense sort. They dressed in common in huge capes and high wooden clogs. A small set of these schools produced a highly self-conscious elite, welded together by a "schoolboy tradition" that went on to play a large role in the development of Japanese business, politics, and literature.

Elsewhere, numerous literary accounts have revealed something of the intensity of student cultures in British selective secondary schools and at Oxford and Cambridge. In its most precious form, as exhibited in the 1920s and 1930s, the subculture could entail a sense of uncommon esthetic background and interest, attracting and shaping young men from cultivated families and traditions who already knew they were different from others in having absorbed much good literature and having been introduced to the art and architecture of England and the Continent at an early age. Selection to a particular Oxford or Cambridge college heightened the sense of specialness. Small, esthetically centered groups could and did form that had some connection to the life-styles of some of their teachers but for the most part had a life and continuity of their own, expressing rebellion and deviance as well as the values of the establishment. Those who might still believe that such small student subcultures do not matter very much need to review the effects of one tiny cluster at Oxford and Cambridge between the two world wars, in which a dominating estheticism mixed with adolescent rebellion and political reaction to fascism. Out of a mere handful of kindred spirits came the most important moles of Soviet espionage within the British government: Guy Burgess, Donald Maclean, Kim Philby, and Anthony Blunt—the latter also to become an ornament of esthetic scholarship and the personal curator of the Queen's art.[29]

Faculty culture has been less studied, but it clearly becomes more segmented as universities and colleges grow in size and complexity, splitting the whole into the disciplinary subcultures noted earlier and into larger orientations centered around such primary activities as research and teaching. For example, in the U.S. state university one can note faculty oriented primarily by one of four different commitments: research, scholarly teaching, professional training, and outside professional work.[30] In pure form, there is the fanatical scientist who locks himself in his laboratory; the Mr. Chips who disdains specialization and devotes his life to chatting up undergraduates; the academic dentist who checks the drillings of students in training; and the professor of business, education, or engineering who spends so much time consulting outside the university that new rules must be enacted to ensure his or her presence some of the time. These four types cross the normal distinction between pure and applied with the older analytical one between locals and cosmopolitans to yield two kinds of locals—the "disinterested" teacher-scholar and the practical professional—and two types of cosmopolitans— the researcher and the consultant.[31] Notably, in a good share of the systems of the world, the many faculty who are not full time are a type of reverse cosmopolitan for whom the academic enterprise need not be the primary source of occupational identity.

Least noticed in the subcultures of academic enterprises and systems but of growing importance is the separation of administrative cultures from those of faculty and students. As cadres of professional experts replace the professor-amateur, in campus, provincial, and national administration, a separate set of roles and interests emerge around which separate definitions of the situation form. This phenomenon has been best identified in studies of the University of California, where there has existed a large statewide administration over and above the nine campuses of a multicampus system. Grouped in a separate building off the Berkeley campus, the senior experts in this cluster, who together with supporting staff numbered over 1,200 persons in the mid-1970s, interact largely with one another, have daily role mandates radically different from teaching and research, increasingly do not come from faculty ranks, and have ample reason to see professors and students as, at best, lacking in understanding and, at worst, troublemakers and enemies.[32] A separate culture is generated. As Terry F. Lunsford puts it:

>University executives and faculty members are increas-
>ingly isolated from each other in their daily lives, while
>each is encouraged toward contacts mainly with their
>own "kind." . . . On many large campuses, a dozen or so
>high-level administrators meet regularly in an "adminis-
>trative council," sharing perspectives on specific prob-
>lems of university management. . . . Increasingly, also,
>university officials meet their opposite numbers in other
>institutions away from their campuses, at meetings of the
>many regional and national boards, commissions, advi-
>sory councils, interuniversity groups, and "professional"
>associations of administrative specialties. Literally scores
>of voluntary groups are peopled principally by campus
>administrators. Their meetings are at once Rotary con-
>ventions and "scholarly" conferences for the partici-
>pants. Some of the administrative specialty groups work
>deliberately in these sessions to develop "professional"
>identities, and foster self-conscious sharing of "exper-
>tise" or "viewpoints" on problems typically met by their
>members.[33]

As other groups in the university see "the Administration" as a
distinct and even alien segment, symbolic separateness grows. In
response, administrators develop a special self-interest in creating
and spreading certain official ideologies. "They themselves have
special needs for those 'socially integrating myths' that help to hold
the loosely coordinated organization together and give its members
'a sense of mission.' "[34]

In most countries of the world, administrative culture has developed primarily at the national level, since overhead services have
been located in the ministry of education or some other national
service. Such offices can be small and amateurish and well integrated
with the understructure, rotating a few professors in and out of
dusty, sleepy quarters, but they can and do grow rapidly and become
staffed with full-time administrators as education becomes big business. Thus, even small and homogeneous Sweden made such a
change between the 1940s and the mid-1970s;[35] and even Britain, *the*
model of amateur professorial control, moved strongly in the same
direction.[36] In systems that have long had major national ministries

or departments of education, whether in France or Mexico or Thailand, central staffs are known for their encapsulation as well as their large size, with attention possessed by the day-to-day demands of office and with attitudes heavily conditioned by the administrative culture that accumulates as a legacy of efforts over decades to grapple with those demands. Thus, one important distinction among academic administrative cultures is between those that help administrators define their situation at the university level and those that provide definitions at system levels. The first typically takes the point of view of the enterprise, which generally includes autonomy within the system; the second is necessarily imbued with the requirements of regional and national linkage, the canons of fairness across institutions, and the need to operate in arenas where national public administration meets national politics.

THE CULTURE OF THE PROFESSION

While the discipline and the enterprise provide the immediate cultures, the academic profession at large offers one that is more remote and ambiguous. Sweeping across all the fields and institutions, assumed by professors of biology, sociology, and classics alike, is the identity of "academic man." All such men and women, in the doctrines of the profession, are part of a single "community of scholars," sharing an interest that sets them apart from others. Community members are entitled to special privileges, particularly "freedom of research" and "freedom of teaching." Downgrading all external controls, the culture of the profession everywhere emphasizes personal autonomy and collegial self-government. It portrays altruistic commitment, suggesting that it is a high form of service to society to create knowledge, transmit the cultural heritage, and train the young to fulfill their highest potential. And if academics have such an exalted role, then the more senior among them should rank with ambassadors and admirals in the civil service. The culture of the profession is not reticent in asserting professorial rights to power and status.

Within the profession, major segments have symbolic unities of their own. The respective identities of natural scientist, social scientist, and humanist stretch across groups of disciplines, mediating between the part and the whole. Here again the myths of "community" are strong. For example, "the scientific community" is such a powerful symbolic construction that we can virtually feel its presence, if not touch it—and no wonder, since the norms of science permeate the daily activities of the scientist. Across literature, history, languages, and classics, academics are bounded by the mutual sense that they are humanists, members of a larger flock that also has some common needs and interests, including protection against domination by scientists.

The culture of the profession overlaps and fuses with the cultures of individual disciplines to the extent that often we can hardly separate the one from the other. We are helped by a distinction drawn by Walter Metzger between the ideologies of "academic freedom" and "scientific freedom." These are different species of freedom:

> The key differentia is this: academic freedom is the ideology of a profession-across-the-disciplines, the profession created out of the common circumstances of an academic appointment in a college or university and of the common duties and anxieties that this entails; scientific freedom is the ideology of the diverse professions-in-the-discipline, the professions based on the regularized advance of knowledge in distinctive fields.[37]

The problems of academic freedom center on restraints within academic institutions, and organized systems thereof, that could apply to all professors regardless of specialty. In the United States the specific formulations cultivated by the American Association of University Professors (AAUP) attempt mainly to ward off control by trustees and administrators. Affirmation and defense take no account of the freedom of similar specialists and researchers who are located outside of academic walls.

In contrast, the problems of scientific freedom center on restraints on work in the discipline, whether inside or outside academic systems—for example, the freedom of chemists to proceed according to the canons of chemical science whether they work within governmental bureaus, business firms, nonprofit organizations, independent laboratories, or universities and colleges. In the United States, emerging formulations and incidents of perceived abuse of this form of freedom have centered on control by government bureaus and business firms rather than control by campus trustees and administrators. Hence, "academic freedom" is an ideological response to certain problems of the broad academic profession that follow from its location in specific educational institutions. "Scientific freedom" is a proclamation that reflects problems of the specialized scientific fields as they are quartered in both educational and noneducational institutions. The axes are different, with disciplinary beliefs running along the reach of the sciences to locales outside the profession.

But in other respects science and academia increasingly converge. Basic norms of the profession are the norms of science. As conceptualized by Robert K. Merton, they are "universalism," the idea that the same standards should apply everywhere, without regard, for example, to politics or religion; "disinterestedness," a commitment to the advancement of knowledge; "organized skepticism," the norm that everyone should suspend judgment about a contribution until it has been critically reviewed; and "communality" or "communism," the belief that the results of inquiry should be fully disclosed and made readily available.[38] These four sets of imperatives comprise not only the ethos of modern science, following Merton, but also much of the ethos of the academic profession.

How strong, how intense, how unified is the culture of the academic profession in one national system compared to another? The matter has hardly been explored.[39] But the structural features applied earlier to explore the strength of enterprise cultures are also relevant here. The size of the profession affects the strength of its cultural bonds. One of the reasons why older professors in numerous systems can reminisce happily about their lives in the old days of "elite" higher education is that the overall profession was much smaller. It is easier to encounter and to identify with one's colleagues across disciplinary lines, nationally as well as locally, when they number 100 and not 1,000, or 1,000 and not 10,000, let alone 100,000. Functional interdependence is critical. Colleagues forced to associate with one another to effect general or liberal education are more likely to develop a sense of common profession than those who operate in airtight compartments. Hence, the coming together of faculty in the colleges of Oxford and Cambridge enhances the culture, whereas the autonomy of faculties in Continental universities undermines it. Autonomous chairs at the operating levels turn local clusters inward and fragment the profession. In U.S. universities, faculties of the more autonomous professional schools, off in their own worlds, are less identified with the profession than those in the college of letters and science who feel closer to the heart of the profession as well as to the center of their own university.

The age of the system makes a difference. Whatever the difficulties of the Italian system, its eight centuries of university life since the founding of Bologna have added great meaning to the process of becoming and being an academic person, whatever one's discipline. Struggle and drama, too, make a difference: perhaps one's predecessors had to beat back king and pope time and again to protect the entire guild from external dominance—as in Italy, France, Britain, and Germany; or perhaps academic intellectuals helped create the soul of the nation and carried it symbolically through decades when outsiders ruled and even abolished the nation as a political entity— as in Poland. Despite its inherently fragmented nature, there are combinations of conditions that have and can still virtually turn the academic profession into a secular church, infusing it with a richness of meaning second to none among the professions.

At the core of the doctrines of the profession everywhere is the idea of freedom. Professors have an "elective affinity" for this idea.[40] It fits their tasks well, and even, as we later argue, becomes necessary for efficiency and effectiveness. Hence, leaving aside personal and group aggrandizement, the valuation of freedom can be intense. Academics are notorious for suffering fools in their own ranks: it is the price of freedom, they say. Students, administrators, and politicians are less likely to do so, since they are less committed to the many specific doctrines of academic freedom and perceive the functional necessities differently. Hence, "freedom of research" and "freedom of teaching," "academic freedom" and "scientific freedom," are the banners under which the profession marches, the intensively felt myths that pull academic people together and turn them often into a united fighting force. Cases of resistance to abuses of freedom become the legends shared by otherwise disparate and often factious groups.

With the fixation on individual and group freedom from domination, there comes increasingly a normative assertion of individual rights. Scholars everywhere expect to have the right to criticize one another and to serve as critic of the actions of others outside the academy, including state officials. They virtually have property rights in ideas and formulations, supported by prohibitions as well as such rewards as recognition for creativity. Across the profession, plagiarism is a serious offense, a high crime and misdemeanor. Even to skim off the cream of someone else's work without attribution is morally offensive, whereas in journalism, for example, it is part of a good day's work. While rooted in material conditions and interests, the culture of the profession becomes a force in its own right. Even in the largest, most diffuse contemporary system, the total body of academics possesses some guild mentality.

THE CULTURE OF THE SYSTEM

Certain academic beliefs have their principal source and attachment in the national system as a whole. We may speak of national traditions in higher education. The German system has been relatively scientific, the Italian system relatively humanistic; the U.S. system relatively oriented to general education for its entering students, the French system to specialized training. We also find beliefs about the right character of postsecondary education amid the broadly formulated goals of systems reviewed in chapter 1. Communist systems believe more strongly in a manpower-planning approach than do democratic ones. Certain primary values that we later examine (chapter 7) are differently emphasized. Loyalty to the state has much greater weight in decisions of the system in the German Democratic Republic than in Great Britain.

Four system beliefs are noteworthy and variable, reflecting and affecting the character of a system: how accessible it should be; how specialized its training; to what occupations it should connect; and whether it should center on research.

The Access Belief.   National systems vary greatly in assumptions about breadth of access. Should people be "qualified" to enter the system? If so, at what level of qualification? And how many should be expected to pass that threshold? The expression "open door" can mean "universal admission" (everyone is free to enter), as in the U.S. system. The same expression can also mean "open to all those who qualify," as that is defined by certain grades in prior schooling and by scores in examinations, with "experience" seemingly dictating that no more than twenty percent of the age group, for example, belongs in the defined category. More restrictive beliefs as well as constraining structures helped stop the recent expansion of Continental systems in the range of ten to thirty percent. In those systems, conceptions of access had indeed changed to the point where everyone assumed that two to five percent was no longer appropriate. But it was quite another matter to slide into the belief, found in the national systems of greatest accessibility, that virtually all are welcome. The ideas that stuck in the craw of expansion centered on the notion of "qualified": certain requirements have to be met; most students will not measure up; and therefore, higher education is surely not for everyone—no matter what the Americans do!

The Specialization Belief. As noted earlier, national systems possess different traditions in regard to general education. The Anglo-American tradition glorifies a liberal education, within which British and American approaches point the curriculum in somewhat different directions, with the English system emphasizing a concentration in one or several related fields, such as classics or "reading in PPE"—philosophy, political science, and economics—and the U.S. approach pressing the undergraduate to spread his attention across a wider range of fields. The Continental tradition, assuming the completion of general training, points the student immediately into a specialty. Students enter specialized faculties, or parts thereof, and do not roam across subjects. Hence, a commitment to general education is not found in thought or in structure. In both types of systems, belief constrains structural change and structure constrains change in belief.

The Employment Belief. There are fundamental differences among national systems in what they believe is proper employment for graduates. *The* basic difference is whether the system has been oriented traditionally to governmental employment and the professions alone, largely to the exclusion of the business sector, or whether it sends graduates to business as well. The university systems of France, the Mediterranean countries, and Latin America have been strongly oriented in the first direction. From higher education, one naturally entered one of the leading professions or governmental service, the latter including school teaching. The university did not need the support of business; in turn, industry did not need higher education. Bridges were not built: graduates understood that a job in business would be a placement of last resort, a status-lowering, largely improper fate.

In England, the Oxford-Cambridge tradition made it perfectly clear that the "best people" did not go into industry and commerce, unless it was already in the family line, but rather did their classical studies and then went on to run the government and, in days past, the Empire. That was proper; industry was not. As earlier noted, the effect has been enormous: British government has been more effectively manned than British industry; the leading politicians and civil servants have not understood industry, nor the necessity for systematic training of professional scientists and engineers; and the country's leadership has thereby come up short in their respect for the entrepreneurs and technologists who promote economic progress.[41]

From such Continental and British roots, the orientation to government and the professions has become widespread in systems throughout the world, reflected in the systems of such former colonies as Tunisia and India. The avoidance of placement in industry and commerce has been a dominating, deeply ingrained set of beliefs, one that has been difficult to alter as systems have expanded, produced more graduates, and then found there was not enough employment for all of them in government and the professions. Graduate unemployment is accentuated as a problem when large sectors of employment are avoided because "that is not where a university graduate goes."

The contrasting orientation of legitimate employment in the business sector has been strong in the U.S. and the Japanese systems. In the United States, employment in the private sector has long been legitimate, even preferred. Leading private universities, supported by private wealth, sent graduates to Wall Street as well as to Washington, preparing captains—and lieutenants—of industry as well as embassy personnel and chiefs of public bureaus. State universities began with a strong service orientation that focused on agriculture and industry of all sorts as well as state and local government. Likewise in Japan, where leading faculties as well as lesser universities developed specific and strong ties to business. Proper employment did not mean avoidance of the world of industry and commerce. As in the United States, less desirable placement into lower

white-collar and even blue-collar jobs has also been a steadily growing, systematic aspect of the system. One might hope to go to a
high-status position, but one is not surprised when the first job
proves to be automobile salesman, mechanic, or office secretary.

The Research Belief. National systems vary considerably in how
much they believe research can and should be integrated with teaching. The German, British and American ideals have emphasized
such integration, with, as a matter of course, a heavy assignment of
research to universities and a blending of research and teaching in
the professorial role. In contrast, the French system has long incorporated the belief that the university tests and teaches (for a long
time in the nineteenth century, it was primarily a testing enterprise),
and while it is all right and even necessary for the professor to do
research, the latter activity needs the support of a separate structure
of academies, institutes, and centers.

Joseph Ben-David has noted that France was the Western European country least influenced by the German model. Lacking a
nineteenth-century tradition of integrating teaching and research,
the French effort to develop research in the twentieth century led, in
1939, to "a distinct organization that has facilities of its own and that
has no concern with teaching": the *Centre national de la recherche
scientifique.*[42] In the French scheme, research appointments are full
time and tenurable—a graduate school without teaching! University
students may be hired as research assistants. Some senior staff may
be full time; some may be university professors on part-time appointment to do their research. Thus, professors and students from
the university may be involved, in some cases simply walking across
the street to an academy building. But as a separately financed and
administered system, research is pulled away from the interaction of
teacher and student. The French system also offers the great
anomaly that its most prestigious sector, the leading *grandes écoles*,
consists principally of places devoted to strict professional training
that leave the research function out almost entirely.

The separation of research and teaching is most ingrained in the
Soviet model of a "national academy of science." As put by Loren R.
Graham:

> Of all the scientific institutions in various countries in the
> world, the one which is by far the most important, relative

to the scientific life of its nation, is the Academy of
Science of the USSR. No other academy, society, university, or research foundation dominates the field of science in its country to the degree the Academy of Sciences
in the Soviet Union does Russian science. . . . Founded
early in the 18th century, its predecessor, the Imperial
Academy of Sciences, was already a venerable institution
by the time of the Russian Revolution. Only since the
political overturn, however, has the Academy come fully
to occupy its unique position among scientific institutions.[43]

Thus, in the broad underpinning of science, the Communist regime
followed and intensified the tradition well-established in tsarist
Russia. A separate home for research was the right way: "The
universities would be primarily centers of teaching, while the institutes of the new Academy would be the centers of advanced
research."[44]

Such beliefs, then, are not characteristic of any discipline alone,
nor are they separately attached to individual universities or colleges. They are normative definitions characteristic of the whole
and held, often unconsciously, by many factions in the many parts.
Establishing commonalities rather than differences, such generalized understandings thereby promote the integration of the system.
There is a discernible French way or British style in higher education: each is composed of particular beliefs as well as specific
structures.

BELIEFS AS MEDIATING BUFFERS

In the famous metaphor of Max Weber, beliefs act like switchmen,
helping to determine the tracks along which action will be propelled
by interests.[45] A fascinating part of that determination is the way
that beliefs held within a societal sector mediate external pressures.
Steered by their own ideas, those within the system interpret the
meaning of societal trends and decide what responses are appropriate. Beliefs about access, specialization, employment, and research produce different national responses to common trends and

forces. To grasp the relation of external events to internal operations involves comprehending the way that beliefs intervene to give
the external a particular form and relevance.

The clearest examples for elucidating this principle and establishing it in our conventional wisdom are found in the impact of
beliefs about expansion and contraction in the face of broader
trends that seemingly dictate one or the other. As Thomas F. Green
has persuasively argued:

> What could be clearer than the claim that what *caused* or
> *produced* educational expansion in the United States
> during the sixties was an enormous increase in the size of
> the school-age population . . . together with an increase
> in the participation rate? . . . There were more people to
> be educated and more people stayed longer in the system
> [emphasis in original].

Ostensibly, these increases produced expansion in a simple cause-
and-effect manner. But beliefs intervened, particularly the unspoken one that "all children should have some education within the
system, however defective, than that some have none at all."[46] The
facts about demography and aspirations, *plus* the belief, produced
the expansion. If we substitute another belief, there is no expansion.
If we believe, for whatever reason, that only a certain number of
students can be educated decently, then we find ways to select as
numbers increase.

This is precisely what has happened in various higher education
systems at both enterprise and system levels. Many individual universities and colleges in the U.S. system have had their intake of
students determined more by their own beliefs than by demographic trends and levels of aspiration. While the system as a whole
became considerably more accessible in the decades after World
War II, Harvard, Yale, Princeton, and a host of other private colleges became more selective. They raised entrance qualifications;
they increased in size only modestly; they became a smaller part of
the whole. It was thought preferable to be better than to be larger.
These colleges seized the opportunity to be more selective and
relatively small, rather than open and much larger, as demography
and aspiration would dictate. U.S. state universities have shown
modified forms of this response, increasing their selectivity so that a

smaller proportion of those who enter the system will enter their particular doors, thereby expanding at a slower rate than the other segments of the state systems.

At the national-system level, belief about qualification can narrow entrance into certain fields at the same time that access beliefs about the system make it more accessible. Under rapid expansion, the automatic right of entry of qualified secondary-school graduates in many Continental countries soon ran into the belief that certain subjects and faculties should not have to reflect the great increase in size—in effect, they should not be driven by demographics and aspirations. It might be thought permissible to expand many times over certain of the humanities and social sciences, but it was not appropriate to let enter all who aspired to do so in medicine, science, and engineering. These fields had a stronger claim that they should not be "swamped": around their different tasks and technologies, beliefs in limited access are well rooted.

Beliefs about contraction are even more compelling. When demographic trends and changing aspirations subtract possible applicants, enterprises and systems almost never make an automatic parallel decrease in their size. For many interests in the system, any turndown in size is a threat. We do not find systems passively adjusting their scale downward; to the contrary, they fight it all the way. It is thought undesirable to educate less. Broad ideologies are mobilized: injustices will be done to deserving young people; now is the time to improve quality with better staffing ratios, etc. Using such ideas, educators are able to elicit some support from specific outside groups and from the general public. And in the name of maintaining at least the current scale of education, enthusiasm can be mounted for old ideas treated nominally in the past.

For example, the idea of adult education has been around for a long time, with some gradual implementation in some national systems. But there has been much natural resistance from the ingrained belief that in education the young come first, pushing the education of adults to the margin.[47] But when the young are in short supply, enterprises and systems become more interested in adults. The natural interest in protection of job and function then pushes the belief in size to the forefront and reinterprets the value of adult education. We then say that "the time has come for the idea": in various guises—"lifelong education," "recurrent education," "continuing education"—enterprises strengthen their belief in the value of instructing older students.

In general, beliefs about the damage that will be done by contraction help make the higher education system anywhere sticky on the downslope—always failing to follow the predictions of those who merely extrapolate from broad trends. In higher education, enterprises and systems are more than stubborn about decline. Smaller scale, not to mention institutional death, is seen as immoral, and there are many who will fight hard to see that it does not occur.

Symbolic Integration

The symbolic side of academic organization clearly exhibits disintegration. Academic people divide ideationally as well as structurally: it cannot be otherwise. Specialization proceeds, and each field, new or old, delimits its tenets of thought around certain facets of reality and adopts its own way of viewing the world. If it does not have a different perspective, it is not a basic field. On the basis of disciplinary subculture alone, those in academia will go on having an ever harder time understanding and identifying with one another.

Then, too, the segmenting of systems in sectors divides them culturally. Universities and colleges committed to different roles in a system possess different overviews and varied assortments of student, faculty, and administrative subcultures. Such major sectors as research universities and community colleges in the United States, *grandes écoles* and universities in France, and Oxbridge and teacher-training colleges in Great Britain develop different faculty orientations. Expectations are adjusted to the mix of institutional tasks. In the United States, for example, the community college presses for a total commitment to teaching and student counseling, setting its face against the cosmopolitan orientations of research and professional consulting. This type of college seeks both the pure undergraduate teacher and the practical person who can give apprentices how-to training. The American short-cycle unit is illustrative of the newer sectors in mass higher education in many countries, in which the institutional culture is vastly different from that idealized in the traditional research university.

But cultural disintegration is only half the story, since there is much symbolic development that proceeds in the opposite direction. At the disciplinary level, roles emerge that link the specialists within a field. From a study of the specialties found within high-energy physics in Britain, Jerry Gaston offers the principle that "when roles become segmented one role will emerge whose function is to bind the separate components into a cohesive group." In high-energy physics, this role fell to persons known as phenomenologists: "Phenomenologists are specialists but they are specialists at being generalists. Their status is derived from the role of being the 'middle man,' and from the usefulness of their role for the scientific community."[48] Gaston concluded that a similar process must happen in other sciences, and in all professions, as they become more specialized. Indeed, in a host of fields "methodologists" and "theorists" are specialists at being generalists, working with procedural approaches or substantive ideas that reach across specialties. When fields reward for such roles, and they generally do, the roles will be robust. In a field confused by a plethora of perspectives, such as sociology, the vocabularies of the methodologists offer some commonality. And without regard to whether they are right or wrong, those who work on general theorizing may be seen as offering some integrating categories of thought. What Talcott Parsons wrought for major parts of American sociology in the 1950s and 1960s no person could put asunder.

At the multidiscipline level, approaches focused on problems not special to a particular discipline are often symbolically as well as structurally integrative. The identity of the study group is formed around a broad social problem, such as environmental pollution, or a geographic area, such as Latin American studies, or an occupational sector, such as health. Such groups may provide the primary and even exclusive membership for faculty and students, especially as they become firmly fixed and able to recruit and reward on their own. More typically, they become a second center of association for staff and students who are still rooted in the traditional disciplines, providing within the enterprise, as we noted earlier, a matrix form of organization that pulls specialists out of their specialties some of the time and mixes them with other specialists on more general problems or projects. The dual assignments provide crisscrossing lines that partially overcome the divisiveness of ever greater concentration on ever narrower specialties. Academics who thereby belong to two cultures partake of a matrix form of symbolic integration.

At the enterprise level, as earlier stressed, the need to elicit some common commitment from all the many specialists and the need to appear to outsiders as a single entity leads toward integrating doctrines and symbols. That need deepens when enterprises have to struggle for survival, viability, and standing. It also deepens as the centrifugal force of disciplinary fragmentation threatens to break all pretensions of unity. Growing central administration then creates roles in which an integrating frame of reference is natural. The rector, the vice-chancellor, the president are joined by a host of others who take an all-campus or all-university point of view. Such specialists as the registrar, the vice-president of finance, and the dean of student affairs work across the many divisions of professorial specialization. Their specialties slice on a different plane, making connections among autonomy-straining units. Hence, they present and work with a different imagery, primarily that of the whole rather than the part, no matter how narrow their own specialty may be.

At the multi-enterprise level, the reputations of leading institutions can be significantly integrative. The sharper the prestige hierarchy of institutions, typically, the greater is the symbolic dominance of the styles and traditions of one or two or a handful of places. Academic drift is then integrative, with divergent institutions moving toward a common viewpoint as the less prestigious consciously and unconsciously imitate their betters. Voluntary convergence, as well as mandated similarity, proceeds along the symbolic side as well as the technical side of organization. Drift does not always have this outcome and, in fact, may have the opposite effect, as sets of institutions, constrained by different conditions, become fixed in niches that vary in distance from the top. But the reintegrative pull is there, and often strongly operative.

At the national level, various groups work at cultivating common pride and loyalty to the whole. An important counterforce to the natural symbolic disintegration of the operating levels is the standardization of academic culture that comes about, largely unconsciously, as state and national administrative systems, omnibus academic associations, and nationwide unions generate hundreds of categories of common definition. All promote common symbol systems that diverge from and cover the vast individuation at the operating level. Of course, national systems vary greatly in the form and degree of such standardization. The form may be largely that of the administrative category, as strongly exhibited in the French and Italian systems, where professors are united in a common civil service. Or it may be that of common professional identity and linkage, developed to a high degree in England, where common understandings of the professor and his work, and the student role, emerged mainly from within the profession itself. Still another form is the transferable course unit that serves as a common medium of exchange, a standardized category of tremendous integrating importance that developed in the United States largely from the interaction of institutions with one another.

There remains the possibility that other general beliefs integrate national academic systems, and indeed academics internationally, but are so much in the shadows of observable activity that we can barely sense their presence. It takes only a slight pinch of Durkheimian perspective to suggest that academics may be powerfully bonded to one another by their strong valuation of individualism. As Durkheim put it, this societal ideal "has as its primary dogma the autonomy of reason and as its primary rite the doctrine of free inquiry."[49] Of all people, academics enshrine reason and free inquiry. Their favorite doctrines—freedom of research, teaching, and learning—are heavily individualistic. At first glance, these ideas are completely atomistic, since each person is to judge and choose for himself. But individualism remains very much a shared value, one that academics sense they share and one that inculcates respect for the choices and actions of others. Values do not have to produce similar behaviors to be integrative. While acting differently, according to individual judgment and dictate, we may also be aware of moral bases for such actions, share attachment to the premises, exchange respect, and grant authority accordingly. Individualism is a flexible normative pattern, one that has an elective affinity for the evermore variegated nature of academic work. It stretches considerably to legitimate and rationalize so much variety, and, at the same time, to operate as a shared perspective.

It is not difficult for academics to understand that individual divergence can be good for collectivities. As Becher and Kogan note:

> Where most other social institutions require their members to adopt convergent values and practices, universities—and, to a growing extent, polytechnics and colleges—put a premium on creative divergence. Individual distinction, competitively assessed, in research or consultancy or scholarship, is held to strengthen the reputation of the basic unit which has housed and sponsored the work, and more remotely that of the institution which has provided resources for it.[50]

Thus, academic systems may be integrated in many different ways. Individuals diverge and yet have a sense of serving one another. They go down different disciplinary paths yet belong to the academic profession. They become identified with one enterprise yet are made common members of a national system. Symbolically, modern academic systems are vast congeries of crosscutting lines of integration and overarching unities. There is so much to counteract, to overcome, since in the contents of knowledge and all the meanings associated with academic subjects, fragmentation is the dominant force. It is in the nature of academic systems to be increasingly pluralistic in the production of patterns of thought and in the precise definitions of proper behavior. But the specifics are lodged in generalities, and system making proceeds along cultural lines and according to administrative procedure.

FOUR

AUTHORITY

Now we come to the third basic element: authority. Who rules? How do the many academic groups articulate their interests? Are the fragmenting forces of work and belief counterbalanced by integrating forms of authority? Such questions follow closely upon our prior analyses. It is not possible to discuss work and belief without implying related aspects of authority: a professorial chair in a Continental system is a form of authority as well as a way of structuring tasks. But structures of work and authority are not the same thing; nor are they mere overlays of one another. France and the Soviet Union may appear together in a typology of sector differentiation, but the two systems vary greatly in how the state exercises control. Over and around chairs and departments, faculties and schools, universities and colleges, there are differing arrangements of deans, rectors, vice-chancellors, presidents, trustees, and ministers of education, about whom we have thus far said little. It is time to take "authorities" seriously, both those designated as such and those who exercise influence without benefit of administrative title.

To seek the realities of academic power is not in the first instance to pursue hidden hands and power plays, the rough and tumble of academic infighting in an Italian *Facoltà* or a college at Oxford or a department in an American university. The fundamental task is to discern broad patterns of legitimate power, authority rooted in the dominant locations of certain groups. As we have seen, the various groups come equipped with certain interests and beliefs, even their own myths and rules of the game. System structure is then a mobilization of bias, following the acute observation of E. E. Schattschneider, steadily presenting certain points of view, furthering the cause of certain groups and subordinating others.[1] Structure grants and withholds voice, not only in determining who sets agendas and tells others what to do—decision making—but also in restricting the scope of what will be decided—non-decision making.[2] Such "faces of power" become all the more complicated in academic systems where legitimate power has many forms, including the subtleties of influence that attach to expertise. Professional or scholarly expertise confers a crucial and distinctive kind of authority, entitling certain persons to act in certain ways that entail some dominance over others.[3]

How an academic system distributes and legitimizes power may well be its most important aspect. Lord Eric Ashby has put it most clearly: "The health of a university depends upon whose hands are on it *inside* its own walls [emphasis in original]."[4] The point may be applied to the higher education system as a whole: what difference does it make whose hands are on it from among those in its immediate environment, and especially from among those inside its own ranks?

To move effectively across national systems it is helpful first to identify major levels at which authority can be explored and compared. A sense of levels restrains the tendency to run up and down the scales at will, sounding such notes as "academic community" about the whole when we mean a small part, or to compare the authority structure of "the French system" with "the California system" without appreciating the key dissimilarity. Second, it is possible to construct an almost exhaustive battery of forms of academic authority, sorted out by level and observed in one or more major systems. Such dichotomies as bureaucratic/collegial no longer serve, since these forms have components and locations that need to be distinguished, and there is much else to highlight if analysis is to stay reasonably close to reality. With levels and forms in hand, we are then able to turn to entire national systems, offering profiles of networks of authority that vary significantly, and with marked results, among nations.

LEVELS OF AUTHORITY

Six levels, not all found in every system, keep matters reasonably clear and simple.[5] From bottom to top, the first level is the lowest major operating unit: the department, as developed most strongly in the United States; or the chair-institute combination typical in the widely imitated European model. The second level aggregates the operating units and functions as part of the university or college. As described in chapter 2, its main name is "faculty," as in the traditional four faculties of law, medicine, theology, and arts or philosophy in many European universities, and the faculty of arts and sciences in the U.S. university, where, in addition, this second, more-inclusive unit may be known as a school or even a college, as in the school of medicine or the college of engineering. Trust Americans not to keep their terms straight! These two lowest levels will sometimes be referred to later as the understructure of a national system, whenever the complexity of comparison requires that six levels be reduced to two or three. Besides, as we shall see, the two levels are closely interlocked in the way that authority in one determines authority in the other.

The third and most readily distinguishable level is the individual university or college in its entirety, in the traditional sense of an institution limited largely to a single locality and aggregating under one name the operating units and faculties. Referred to earlier as the enterprise, we will have occasion later to portray it as the basic part of the "middle structure," fixing attention on its middle and mediating position between the two lower levels and the higher levels of national systems. National variation here is great, with faithful consequences.

The fourth, fifth, and sixth levels of authority organization are administrative entities of increasing inclusiveness. The fourth level, the least sharply defined because of its recent emergence, is multicampus academic administration, all of the superbodies that try to pull the enterprises into systems but at a formal level of authority below government itself. These bodies are many types: multilocation or federative universities, as in the case of the University of California system, with its nine universities, or the University of Wales, with its five units; state or regional subsystems that encompass a sector of institutions, as in a state community college system; regional boards, as established in Sweden in the late 1970s; or councils of rectors, as found in many Latin American nations. The fifth level is state, provincial, or municipal government itself, where "the authority" is concretely a ministry or department or bureau, and where influence normally also flows from a chief executive and a legislature. The sixth and highest level is the national government, with its own relevant parts in bureaus and legislative bodies. In later simplification, these levels will be referred to as the superstructure.

The levels vary greatly in importance in different national systems. For example, centralized systems have little or no autonomous power lodged at the provincial level. If administrators exist at that level, as in prefectorial structures, they are arms of the central offices. The levels may be seen as places where problems come in or are lodged, what in organizational theory is called "problem-access structure."[6] Consciously or not, problems are sorted by level, never to reach certain positions in the layers and steered to others. The levels may be seen also as places where decisions are made, what in theory is called "decision structure." Problems may slip and slide up and down the levels in search of those who can decide, certain groups holding certain authority because of tradition or formal delegation. The levels are also places where certain forms of authority are lodged, ones that can clearly be identified and compared across nations. With the forms attached to groups, used by different interests and helping to define them, we then have critical cues on who has power.

Forms of Academic Authority

Starting from the bottom of national systems and working our way up, what different types of legitimate rule can we observe? A half-dozen basic forms make up a battery of possibilities that individually, and then in characteristic compounds, occur strongly, moderately, or lightly in various systems.[7] The forms are rooted, in turn, primarily in disciplines, enterprises, and whole systems. Although based at one level or another, they are naturally imperialistic, inclined to spread into and over other levels. We shall have cause to note one or two derivative forms that have migrated to levels from which they did not originate.

DISCIPLINE-ROOTED AUTHORITY

Personal Rulership (professorial). All modern organizations, usually characterized as impersonal and bureaucratic, nevertheless contain much personalized and arbitrary rule by superiors over subordinates.[8] Systems of higher education are saturated with this form of rule. Individual professors exercise extensive supervision over the work of students and often over that of junior faculty as well. Their judgments typically are not closely circumscribed by bureaucratic rules, or by collegial norms that would foreclose individual discretion. The personal rule of professors has many sources. As noted in our discussion of chair organization, it has historical roots in the dominance of the master in the early academic guilds. It is ideologically supported by doctrines of freedom in teaching and research, which in practice have been interpreted to mean that senior professors in particular should be free to do largely as they please. It is functionally based in expertise and the need for conditions that would promote criticism, creativity, and scientific advance. Moreover, as professors in some systems acquired fixed slots in national bureaucracies (for example, in Italy and France), they accumulated protected rights and privileges that strengthened personal rule—an outcome opposite to the intention of bureaucratic order.[9]

A national bureaucratic structure can not only protect and administer the particularism of personal rule but may even help cause it. If the formal system places a chaired professor in charge of a domain of work and then does not enforce its many laws and codes through checking-up procedures that would detect deviation—typically not done in higher education—it invites avoidance of rules. Unless collegial controls intrude, the rewards of particularism may surpass the rewards of universalism. The advantages of being a crony outweigh those of being a neutral instrument of larger governmental policy. A unitary administrative framework can help turn professors into barons.[10]

Thus, personal rule has been extremely high in chair-based systems, particularly where collegial supervision is nominal and state supervision too remote from operations to be effective. Such authority exists to a lesser degree in department-based systems, such as the American, where power is formally held by an impersonal unit and spread within it among a number of permanent professors. But even there personal rule exists, most noticeably in advanced research and teaching (for example, in the supervision of the graduate student in dissertation research). Although personalized authority is always potentially subject to abuse, systems of higher education apparently cannot function effectively without it, since it is involved in the conditions of freedom for individual initiative in research, individual freedom in teaching, and personal attention to students as a basic method of advanced training. It would have to be invented if it did not already exist.

Collegial Rulership (professorial).   Collective control by a body of peers is a classic form of traditional authority, within the fundamental Weberian typology of traditional, bureaucratic, and charismatic authority.[11] Like personal rulership, it has been widespread in the academic world from the twelfth century to the present; it has had exceedingly strong ideological support in the doctrines of freedom of teaching and research. It is also congenial to the expression of expert judgment; the growth of specialization in recent decades has increased the influence of collegial control in the form of peer review and decision in an ever-increasing number of occupational fields.

In chair-based systems, collegial rule has often been virtually the sole mechanism for coordination at faculty and university levels of organization. Central to its strength is the election of a head from within a body of peers—"appointment" from below instead of appointment from above by a superior official or chief. With election by peers, amateur administration results, but so too does a close connection between "administration" and "faculty." The dean or rector is a temporary chief representing the group, aware that his or her elevation is at their pleasure. Besides, his electors assemble to vote on all important matters. Such one-person-one-vote authority naturally encourages some politics, open or concealed, since majorities must form from among individuals and factions. Senatorial courtesies and tacit agreements also then serve to keep order and get the work done.

In department systems also, collegial rule at the operating level is likely to be quite strong. It is difficult to imagine a university, or a college of any size and renown, in Great Britain or the United States today, in which we could not find department meetings of all instructors, and/or meetings of full or tenured professors alone, in which issues were discussed and then voted on by all those present. Collegial authority is so natural at the operating level as to be virtually an assumption of the higher education system—a far cry from traditional business management. Collegial authority is the governance side of what academics mean when they speak of "the academic community" or its twin, "the community of scholars."

Thus, collegial rule is the professors' strongly preferred way to run a department as a whole and other such larger accessible units as the faculty, college, school, and university. In normal form, it is expressed in several-hour meetings when, typically, after teaching "chores" are finished, there is time for prolonged discussion and negotiation. While preferred as a means of self-rule, such meetings are distasteful for many. Those who do not enjoy debate and conflict would rather steal away to their books or other pleasures. Those most sure of their own judgment find much of the conversation foolish at best and outrageous at worse. Since collegiality means being outvoted some of the time, colleagues, like politicians, have to learn how to lose.

In some countries, the collegial meeting stretches on and on, a virtual end in itself when many members of enlarged groups need and want to exercise the right to have their say if not their way. During the late 1960s and the 1970s, most noticeably in Japan and some Continental universities, meetings stretched to six and eight hours. No one ever said that collegial authority would be fun! In these extreme cases, "meeting time" drives out teaching as well as research time and leads cynics to remark that collegiality is ten minutes of action crammed into six hours.

Guild Authority. This type of authority is a notable and characteristic derivative compound of the first two, blending the personal and the collegial. In guildlike arrangements, the individual master has a personal domain within which he controls subordinates; the masters then come together as a body of equals to exercise control over a large territory of work.[12] The controlling stratum in a guild is thereby composed of persons who are simultaneously autocrats and colleagues. This combination never disappeared from certain sectors of society, including academic systems. Notably, such structures moved inside the bureaus created in modern nation states. The capacity of guildlike authority to survive inside governmental agencies now seems surprising mainly because of two prevalent misconceptions: that guilds are voluntary associations independent of government, and that governmental agencies are entirely bureaucratic in form. But even in the days of old, the connection of guilds to state authorities included their having virtual inside location as they served as arms of government.[13] And modern agencies reflect a host of organizational tendencies, other than the bureaucratic, that are currently captured in conceptions of guild, profession, community, and bureaucratic politics.[14]

Academic systems have continued to be guildlike at their lower levels: personal rulership and collegial authority together commonly dominate the substructure of even fully nationalized universities. In the blending of autocracy and collegiality, one element or the other can predominate. In Italian academic life, personal rule has been dominant, primarily because of the way that the system encouraged chair holders to elaborate their roles. In Great Britain, collective control has been stronger, largely because of the way in which the college substructure of Oxford and Cambridge modeled collegiality and because of the combining of departments and chairs in the other universities. The dominance of personal rule means virtually full personal control over a private fiefdom; collective rule dampens that tendency by locating decision making in a body of the whole that attempts to monopolize control over a larger domain of work, even if that work territory is increasingly a formal part of the apparatus of government and thereby subject in theory to the control of general public policy.[15]

Hence, guild authority must remain a key concept in analyzing academic power and modern power generally, even though it is difficult to rid the concept of negative connotations and to stress its appropriateness in the face of the addiction to broad ideas of bureaucracy and profession. Then, too, the belief lingers that guild forms disappeared when the state and the factory took over. Karl Marx claimed that "all in all, the entire guild system—both master and journeyman—dies out, when the capitalist and the labourer emerge," since "the monetary relation between worker and capitalist" replaces "the patriarchal relationship between journeyman and master."[16] But not so, either in academic work or in the other key occupations of the twentieth century that have acquired the status of profession. Especially in academia, authority relations were not preempted by the likes of profit-seeking entrepreneurs building factories, hiring wage laborers, and producing for extended markets, even if universities sometimes took on some of these characteristics. Rather, guildlike features of authority persisted inside academic and other professions and, around experts, crawled deeper into government. If we want to understand why real professions and governmental agencies deviate extensively from professional and bureaucratic principles, the concept of guild authority is a useful tool. It helps us characterize the operational authority inside professional hegemony, or what Leon D. Epstein has referred to inside academia as "professorialism" or "departmental colleagueship."[17]

Professional Authority.   Professional authority, like pure bureaucracy, is supposedly rooted in universalistic and impersonal criteria, but with standards drawn from the profession rather than the formal organization. It is thereby viewed as based on "technical competence" rather than on "official competence" rooted in formal position.[18] But the classic literature on professional authority has been unduly idealistic in assuming that altruism is the dominant characteristic of professional life, with behavior shaped generally by doctrines of service to society and specifically by objective expert judgment. In practice, however, professionals exercise authority in a host of ways: through personal rule, collegial control—and hence guild authority—and bureaucratic position and political struggle. Overall control is typically weak within a large profession, with discretion radically decentralized to operating levels, where it tends to take autocratic and collegial forms. The actual expression of professional authority is thus problematic: taking different specific forms, professional authority may be particularistic as well as universalistic, oriented to personal profit as well as to service in society, and used to subordinate clients and allied personnel as well as to serve ideals.[19]

Thus, the concept of professional authority may be broadly relevant in understanding academic power, as later used in juxtaposition to bureaucracy and market. But with such general use should go the realization that professionalism breaks down into more specific forms. There are vast differences in the "professional rule" of academic experts, with, for example, that rule considerably more universalistic in the United States than in Italy, more universalistic in Great Britain than in Japan. These variations are not primarily a function of the degree of professionalization. Rather, they are related to differences in institutional structures: as we noted in the case of strong personal authority in the Italian structure, the structure of the system can virtually demand autocratic behavior, rewarding for particularistic sponsorship and intense political actions on behalf of one's own interests and the interests of friends, dependent staff, and students. Overall, academic professionalism is ambiguous, diverse, and complex. It tilts toward specific forms of authority according to the pressures of context.

In sum, among the forms of authority rooted in disciplinary understructures, the personal and collegial are primary. Guild authority is a blend of these two forms, with subtypes according to proportions of each primary type. "Professional" is a broad characterization of authority rooted in expertise, one that in the more global comparisons leaves open the strength of the more specific forms.

ENTERPRISE-BASED AUTHORITY

Trustee Authority (institutional).   As we search for legitimate power above the operating levels, trusteeship is immediately prominent as a common form in Anglo-Saxon higher education, an educational form that has been transferred internationally to numerous nations that are former British colonies and to countries, such as Japan and Mexico, that have been influenced by British and American models. Trusteeship means supervision of an enterprise by outsiders—"laymen"—who are part time, generally unpaid, and have their primary commitments elsewhere. The outsiders have been variously designated, in Britain and America, as "trustees," "overseers," "regents," or simply lay members of governing bodies.

Six years after its founding, in 1642, Harvard University acquired a board of overseers, who were given, by the Massachusetts legislature, "full power and authority to make and establish all such orders, statutes, and constitutions as they shall see necessary."[20] In Britain, in the civic universities that emerged in the nineteenth century, "the governing bodies were a large (and largely inert) court and a smaller (and executive) council, each with a heavy lay majority."[21] In the case of the American state university, also emergent in the nineteenth century, "a governing board of externally chosen nonacademic citizens" became the conventional method by which the university conceived its authority "as legitimately public and yet largely autonomous."[22]

In the doctrine of trusteeship, then, the outsiders represent a larger interest, that of the general public in a public institution or a specific constituency and supporting group in a private institution, or some combination of the two. They are the long-run caretakers, finally responsible for the fate of the enterprise, and, as a body, are commonly the legal owners or legally established managers. In its many variations of public and private boards, trusteeship can therefore be seen as a form of dispersed public control, with specific publics, as narrow as a few families or as wide as the population of a state, "represented" in different institutions. "The board [in the American state university] exercises authority in the name of the people of the state, but it is not as directly responsive to the will of the people as are governors and legislators. And it is not, in principle, as directly responsive to governors and legislators as are most state agencies."[23]

In systems that do not have trustees, the interests of various publics are legitimately pursued through mainline governmental channels. Publics then participate more diffusely and indirectly but more globally in the control of a whole set of institutions, by means of elected representatives in the legislature and elected and appointed officials in the executive branch of government. These are different ways of connecting institutions to the public, with trusteeship putting certain outsiders in an immediate position of authority.

Although originating in English higher education, trustee authority has found its strongest expression in the United States, pervading all important subsystems, public or private, those sponsored by local as well as state authorities.[24] Throughout, it has served as an instrument of institutional aggrandizement, linking the interests of specific constituencies and the participation of influential citizens, generally from business, to the welfare of the individual college or university. Administrators and professors expect trustees to help the institution, particularly in garnering and giving money: college presidents joke that the basic rule for trustees is "get, give, or 'git' off."

The influence of trustees, however, has varied widely across U.S. enterprises, and has shifted over time as first administrative authority and then faculty control was strengthened. Its influence has also become problematic as trustees have moved from the campus to a more encompassing level in multicampus subsystems, and as state and national governments have increased their supervision. In contrast, the period since 1960 has seen trusteeship grow in Latin

American systems, particularly in private universities, such as Columbia's University of the Andes, but also in public universities under state as well as national control, as in Mexico.[25] Private academic enterprises, it seems, virtually require trusteeship if they are to be more than proprietary. Public institutions find the form useful. Notably, some of the nontrustee systems of the European continent began in the 1970s to search for quasi-trustee ways of associating outsiders with institutions, in order to break old patterns of guild and bureaucratic control and to relate higher education to other sectors of society. Thus, the Swedish corporatist pattern discussed in the following chapter entails the systematic insertion of outsiders in the equations of control.

Bureaucratic Authority (institutional). As the best-known idea in twentieth-century analysis of organization, the concept of bureaucracy needs little explanation. It refers to formal hierarchy, with explicit delegation of authority to offices and positions, codified coordination of those units, and impersonality in recruiting personnel, judging individual worth, and deciding what will be done. Bureaucratic authority is the antithesis of personal rule and collegial control as well as lay control and charismatic authority. In pure bureaucracy, the expert manager draws power solely from an explicitly defined position. Of course, in practice there are degrees of bureaucracy. Thus, it is useful to speak of a bureaucratic tendency and to ascertain its strength in various settings rather than to assume that organizational personnel follow bureaucratic dictates.

It is centrally important to distinguish who are "the bureaucrats," which comes down largely to determining where administration is located in the system. Administrators subject to the bureaucratic tendency may be found largely in central ministries, in which case bureaucratic authority at the university or campus level may be very weak or virtually nonexistent; or they may be lodged primarily at the institutional level and very little at ministerial levels of coordination; or they may be more than noticeable at both institutional and system levels. Such different concentrations are of great importance in determining what bureaucratic authority does. When it has local position, as in the buildup of campus administration in the U.S. system since the late nineteenth century, officials become boosters of their "own" institutions, since even more than professors, job rewards and career successes depend directly on the apparent success of the enterprise. Their perspectives and interests can then be fundamentally different from those of officials in central offices as much as they are from those of faculty and students. And, as noted earlier, when large numbers of campus administrators interact largely with one another, a quasi-autonomous culture of their own making will form alongside the faculty and student cultures of the campus.

In short, it is not true that a bureaucracy is a bureaucracy is a bureaucracy. Bureaucratic authority can be coupled to different chariots; it functions in different ways in systems depending in part on the organizational level at which it operates.

SYSTEM-BASED AUTHORITY

Bureaucratic Authority (governmental).   As we rise above the enterprise level to multicampus, state, and national linkage, the bureaucratic form is omnipresent. Whenever government assumes some responsibility for the provision of higher education, certain public agencies must become the loci of administrative implementation. Much legitimacy then rests on official hierarchy, precisely in those positions that are recognized as part of the administration of government rather than part of its politics. But the influence of agency staffs varies widely according to the historical relation of the state to higher education.

High administrative involvement has been presupposed and exercised in the European and Latin American systems that used ministries of education as embracing frameworks; whereas, for example, low involvement occurred in Great Britain throughout the first four decades of the existence of the University Grants Committee (UGC) (1920–1960).[26] Even though the national treasury became increasingly the main means of financial support, the UGC, which was not under the jurisdiction of the education department, had only a small borrowed staff and was controlled largely by persons from the universities. But the older British pattern was atypical; the Continental pattern has been widespread and continues to be. Recent governmental policies in any number of countries have induced a buildup of central administrative staffs, as public officials have responded to problems of growth, equity, accountability, and duplication by enacting laws that require larger central offices to disburse funds, set uniform requirements, check compliance, and otherwise implement public policy.

But like the concept of professional authority, bureaucratic authority at the governmental level, once distinguished, needs analysis in terms that go beyond those of the classic concept. For one, the staffs of governmental bureaus are conditioned by national cultures, especially as those cultures are expressed in the styles of politics and public administration. For example, there may be a particular French style of bureaucratic behavior, one that leads unduly to rigidity and stagnation, a thesis proposed by Michel Crozier that has stimulated a debate in comparative politics and public administration about the character of French bureaucracy and national differences generally.[27] The central staffs also develop a separate administrative subculture of their own, as we have seen, which conditions the uses of their authority. Then, too, central administrative staffs are not neutral tools of higher policy, but rather become interest groups themselves, ones with privileged access, vested rights, and self-sustaining points of view.[28]

Each agency staff battles for its own interests. A staff in a central educational agency, in need of allies and supportive exchanges, will develop tacit agreements with key legislators and staffs of legislative committees, political appointees in executive agencies, staff peers in bordering agencies, trustees and administrators at lower levels, and professors. The nature of the authority of such staffs needs to be seen as problematic, a mixture of bureaucratic, guild, and political elements that vary from one society to another. And for whom the authority speaks is also problematic. The bureaucratic authority of neutral administrative staffs would speak for higher political councils of government, but the "bureaucratic" authority of staffs turned into specific interest groups speaks for those interests.

Political Authority. From the beginnings in Bologna and Paris some eight centuries ago, organized higher education has faced the problem of relating to the controls of state and church. As the nation state increased its strength in the last several centuries, it became the dominant framework; throughout most of the world today, higher education is primarily an organizational part of national government, there conditioned by the nature of the branches of central government and affected by the exercise of general political authority.

For example, coalition governments as exist in Italy are hard put to enact major reform legislation, but rather must move by studied indirection and incremental adjustment in order to safeguard a precarious ruling consensus; a more dominant state authority, as existed in France under De Gaulle in 1968, can push through a big bill promising extensive reform of higher education, even if implementation is later slowed and attenuated by countervailing resistance from central policy makers as well as professors and students. But in either case, authority acts as agent of the state. A generalized right is given to government, particularly when it is the main sponsor, even as various interests quarrel over the specific uses of that right. At bottom, legitimacy rests here on positions in the official structure that are recognized as political rather than administrative and that are generally seen as above administrative concerns in the hierarchy, grappling with the broadest issues and representing government in its most general form.

The widespread acceptance of political authority is also rooted in a belief in the rightful power of the purse, a version of the golden rule in which he who has the gold has the rule. If higher education is a private matter, then government may possibly be denied influence. But if it is a public good, so defined by public financing, then "government" cannot be denied some voice. There is no national system today in which this form of authority is absent. But its strength varies widely according to the extent to which governmental rule is centralized and monopolizes the provision of higher education. Its weight also varies greatly according to the large differences among regimes that affect all of society, from democratic polities that permit multiple political parties and autonomous private associations, to authoritarian governments based on single-party rule with some autonomy for churches, trade unions, and other forms of association, to the state that strives to eliminate all autonomous association and achieve total control for a one-party regime. The dual control of party and government, each with its own centralized apparatus, which is characteristic of the Communist model, is an extreme example of providing strong political authority. Of all the forms, political authority is the most open to extended variation. Its subtypes will be identified in the examination of national coordination in chapter 5.

Systemwide Academic Oligarchy.   The imperialistic thrust of modes of authority is particularly striking in the way that personal and collegial forms, rooted in the disciplinary bottom of a system, work their way upward to have an important effect on enterprise and then finally system levels. We have observed in passing that national systems can legitimately be ruled by professors. By election and appointment and informal transaction they may transfer local oligarchical power to the national level. Operating as the major professional group within the sector, they have had, in many systems of the world, privileged access to central councils and offices, and they have been the most important constituency to please for top bureaucratic and political officials.

In Britain, for example, a few senior and influential members of the academic profession have served on the important central bodies that have allocated resources, dominating decision making, until recently, to the virtual exclusion of bureaucratic staff. Even in the United States, where systemwide academic oligarchy has been relatively weak, academics sometimes have imposing, if fragmented, influence: the leaders of national academies and associations of scientists advise government; science advisory committees operate within the White House; committees of professors and scientists exercise peer review as standard operating procedure in major governmental agencies that disburse funds for different segments of research and education.

The systemwide roles of small numbers of professors vary greatly according to such factors as the traditional prestige of academics, the guild strength of senior professors, and the countervailing power of other interested groups. There seems not to be any clear unilinear trend toward diminished influence of professors in control at the highest levels. Everywhere the need increases for those in top positions to seek and use the judgment of experts. Among those who gather to whisper words of advice into the ears of the modern-day prince—the chief executive, committee chairman, or bureau chief—are notables based in academe. At bottom, legitimacy here rests on expertise, specifically the belief that its expression is necessary, and therefore acceptable, at the highest levels, as well as "down" in the classrooms and laboratories, departments and institutes. Oligarchical coordination will loom large when we turn, in chapter 5, to the major alternative ways of integrating national systems.

THE WILD CARD OF AUTHORITY: CHARISMA

The concept of charismatic authority refers to the willingness of a group of people to follow a person and accept his or her dictates because of unusual personal characteristics—in the extreme, "a gift of grace."[29] The authority of the leader thus derives not from position in an administrative structure or from established right in a traditional line of descent, but from personal qualities. Hence, it is the wild card, the least systematic and most unpredictable form. In a higher education system, it may pop up anywhere, from within the ranks of students, professors, administrators, trustees, politicians, or interest-group representatives. It carries its own legitimacy in the perception of uncommon personal qualities, which means, however, that charisma is directly situational: the personal qualities of the leader or would-be leader must be perceived and valued by actual or would-be followers. The authority disappears when followers are disillusioned and turn away. Hence, instability is a central characteristic and problem.

That instability is reduced when charisma is attached to specific social positions, and hence to persons who occupy them, instead of to specific individuals alone. The position of priest in the Catholic church is an excellent example—and so has been the office of chaired professor in many traditional systems of higher education. Strong personal rulership within the guild form encourages the assignment of charisma at the operating level of chair and institute. The professor becomes a Large Person as the situation dictates that he or she accumulate and elaborate a set of commanding roles— head lecturer, institute director, fund raiser, consultant, sponsor— and thereby maintain a large gap in status between him or her and subordinates.[30] The position evokes a steady stream of deference, encouraging the assumption of personal superiority and leading toward the adoption of a commanding presence. Such statements as "he thinks he's God" have not been without point.

Situations open to personal authority are situations open to cha-risma. Thus, the influence of charisma may appear fairly often when the operating level tilts toward a high degree of personal influence; or it may occur at higher administrative levels when systematic controls of guild, bureaucracy, and other regular forms are weak, as took place in the U.S. system during the late nineteenth and early twentieth century when faculty forms were not yet strong, rule by amateur trustees was giving way to more professional admin-istration, and a bevy of presidents were given or seized the responsi-bility for building and sharply reshaping entire institutions. The opening narrowed considerably by the mid-twentieth century as the more regular forms grew stronger. The boundaries of routine authority normally control the intrusion of charisma, keeping out or clamping down upon the person who would say "follow me!" But crises as well as situations of new organization occasionally beckon the person with special gifts of leadership. And even stable organi-zations will sometimes deliberately open themselves up to such per-sonal intervention, as when a college or a professional school or a department becomes ambitious to do better or become different and invites in a builder, an agent of change.[31]

More frequent than the dramatic cases of charisma are the occur-rences of modest personal elements of leadership that are more readily compounded with bureaucratic position or such traditional locations as those of chaired professor or trustee. A leader then draws authority from both personal and structural sources, making it all the more evident that his authority is agent for the collectivity.[32] In modest doses, charismatic authority still occurs repeatedly in higher education systems. Its role is particularly to help clarify directions of effort and to impel change. It seems most likely to occur outside the realms of professor and official, where and when systems reward for initiative and hence for leadership.

*   *   *   *

Thus, legitimate power takes many forms in academic systems. No wonder participants are often confused, laymen bemused or irritated, analysts reduced to "organized anarchy." As soon as we move away from the grand and often misleading sweep of the more global concepts, i.e., bureaucracy and profession, in order to get closer to reality, analysis plunges into a swirling mixture of a half-dozen or more major ways in any given system that some people quite legitimately possess influence over others. Then there are also forms not here presented: e.g., the unusual regularized power of students in many Latin American countries. And if we were to take a further step into reality, we would confront the many informal patterns of friendship, exchange, and group protection that are reflected in stories of hidden hands and power plays. But the forms here identified provide an appropriate middle ground, bringing analysis down out of the clouds of the broadest concepts but maintaining it at a level where we can concentrate on basic structure and systematically state major similarities and differences among academic systems.

NATIONAL MODES OF AUTHORITY DISTRIBUTION

Three national combinations of authority, here called the Continental, the British, and the American, cover much empirical ground. We see them best and grasp their rudiments when they are presented starkly, without nuance, without the details that make each country a case unto itself. But to indicate how these basic combinations may be combined in other countries, we will also describe a "Japanese mode."

THE CONTINENTAL MODE

Authority has been distributed traditionally in most of the academic systems of the European continent in a combination of faculty guild and state bureaucracy.[33] Guildlike authority has predominated within the universities, with much personal authority at the operating level and with groups of professors exercising strong collegial rule over the higher levels of faculty and university. Trustees have not existed, and bureaucratic authority has been located on high, generally at the level of national government, as in Italy, France, and Sweden, following upon the placement of all or nearly all universities and colleges under one or more ministries of central government. In a federal variant of this pattern, the embrace of governmental officials occurs at a subnational level, as in the *Land* structure of the Federal Republic of Germany.

The national-federal distinction is an important one, since the national system is a single-system monopoly and the federal structure normally promotes more competition. But it remains useful here to lump together the systems of the Continent in order to emphasize a similarity in authority structure that expresses primarily the interests of two groups: senior professors and officials located in a state ministry, two relatively small groups in the vast conglomeration of interests found in modern nations. Thus, the main contest for power traditionally has been between these two groups. Professors generally controlled the lower levels, but not everywhere and not continuously; for example, the minister of education, using formal powers inherent in the office, may sometimes intrude in the appointment system to make his own choices of chair holders.[34] State officials have tended to control the higher levels, but again not everywhere and not continuously. The senior professors, as the most powerful constituency, typically acquire important rights of advice and consultation in central decision making. As emphasized under the concept of national academic oligarchy, the professors, as in Italy, may devise and elaborate procedures that ensure their primacy in the exercise of centralized control.[35]

Notably, in comparison with the British and especially the American mode, the Continental mode has exhibited weak autonomous authority at the levels of the university and its constituent faculties. The professors have not wanted a separate administrative class and have simply elected deans and rectors as amateur administrators on short appointments and easy recall. The distant ministry has preempted overhead services and has seen institutional personnel on the business side of organization as its own arms reaching into the field to apply uniform standards. In this classic pattern, bureaucracy working down meets oligarchy working up, and neither powerful group has been interested in creating an autonomous third force in the middle.

Excellent evidence on this point was uncovered by Lyman A. Glenny in a comparative study of the funding of higher education. He notes:

> Collectively, the chairs control the internal governing and budgetmaking patterns of institutions and spend the

resources after appropriation. The university administration is delegated very little separate power by the state,
except for maintenance of buildings, and hence cannot
control the allocation or reallocation of funds without the
consent of the chairs.[36]

The result, in effect, is a vertical bypass:

> Much of the money going to disciplines, chairs, or de-
> partments within institutions in the European countries
> bypasses the institution as an administrative unit. Rather,
> funds from the central state agencies go directly to pro-
> fessors or to internal units, without considering any insti-
> tutional position on the subject.[37]

The largest funding item of all, the salaries of teaching faculty and
support personnel, is not even in the budgets of institutions. As civil
servants, the personnel are paid out of the general salary budget of a
ministry or the government at large.

Thus, in vertical profile, the traditional Continental distribution
of authority has placed authority at the bottom, in guild forms;
secondarily at the top, in ministerial bureaucracy that accommodates to the faculty guilds; and has only weakly provided for authority at middle levels of the system, in the form of institutional administration or trusteeship. As systems have grown in complexity and
size, the latter feature has been viewed increasingly as a serious
weakness, stimulating efforts, taken up in chapter 6, to provide
stronger rectorial and presidential offices at the enterprise level and
stronger deanships at the faculty level, and, at the same time, to
weaken the powers of the professors. In Eastern Europe, the newer
Communist model introduced after World War II strengthened the
administrative capacity of the universities, as well as the hands of top
officialdom, with campus heads appointed by government and
thereby made more dependent on those at the top and less so on the
professors.

THE BRITISH MODE

The traditional British style of authority distribution has combined faculty guilds with a modest amount of influence from
institutional trustees and administrators.[38] Individual colleges and

universities have been chartered corporations responsible for self-management, each to admit its own students, arrange its own courses, and hire its own faculty. In this context, guild authority has flourished, especially in the colleges of Oxford and Cambridge, which have provided the system's most influential models. But trustee authority and some administrative authority in the form of the vice-chancellorship have also been present, interfused with the guild forms at the local levels.

Since the British did not early develop the Continental devices of placing institutions under a governmental bureau and teachers within a civil service, there has not been a formally organized system either nationally or at provincial levels. Even as the national treasury became the main means of financial support, the device of the University Grants Committee, a central allocating body composed of professors, kept primary influence in the hands of senior professors and university administrators.

Thus, in vertical profile, the British mode has placed strong authority at the bottom, in guild forms, but has emphasized the collegial over the personal approach more so than the Continental systems. It has given some strength to middle levels of coordination, providing a modest degree of administrative leadership and allowing for the participation of lay trustees as well as collective faculty rule. Governmental bureaus traditionally had little power, with national coordination instead chiefly provided by a body of academic oligarchs.

Until recently, the main contests for power were located within the university itself and were largely contained by an elaborate web of tacit agreements among faculty clusters, each of which had primacy in its own domain, and between those clusters and all-university administrative staff, trustees, and faculty bodies. Hence, the contest was not, as on the Continent, faculty versus state officials. But the subordination of ministerial control has been viewed increasingly by government as a weakness—a system that is not a system—and reform in the 1960s and 1970s moved in the direction of strengthening central forms of authority—the political, the bureaucratic, and the national oligarchical.

Beginning in the mid-1960s, British higher education moved firmly into a de facto national system: (1) the Department of Education and Science (DES) took on some of the attributes of the Continental ministry, able and inclined, for example, to tell some colleges of education that they must consolidate with other units, or even that they must cease to exist; (2) the University Grants Committee developed a larger staff and was relocated within the government, from working directly with the Treasury to answering directly to the DES; and (3) the legislature and the top political councils of the executive branch became more determined to have explicit national policies in higher education and to use the DES and the UGC as central instruments to carry out those policies.[39] With this thrust, the power contest moves toward the European mode of professors versus the state apparatus.

THE AMERICAN MODE

The American mode, like the British, has combined beloved faculty forms with institutional trusteeship and administration. But in comparison with the British, faculty rule has been weaker and the influence of trustees and administrators stronger.[40] The mechanism of the chartered corporation, used historically by many hundreds of independently established units, meant separate boards of trustees, each fully in charge of its own institution and, sooner or later, creating its own administrative staff, from president to assistant dean, to "run" the place. With faculty authority developing late, largely in the twentieth century, and thus within the context of the established powers of trustees and administrators, the faculty forms of personal and collegial authority did not achieve the influence they had in the European and British modes. As emphasized in chapter 2, the chair did not become the building block. The emergent departmental form both dampened personal authority and had to blend the internal collegiality of the department with its place in a larger structure that was decidedly more bureaucratic than that found within the European and British modes.

Thus, the American mode localized bureaucracy. No national bureau had an important role. Even the departments of education of the separate states, where public responsibility for education became lodged, often had little influence. The private institutions, in the nineteenth century, became entirely independent of state officials; the leading public institutions had their own boards of control and chartered autonomy. Thus, in vertical profile, the

American academic structure developed a strong middle, in the form of institutional administration and trustees. Second, authority grew at the lower levels of the department and multidepartment college or school, in a blend of guild and bureaucratic forms. Weakest, in comparative perspective, have been the governmental levels. But around this mode this enormously diversified system exhibits much variation in the top-middle-bottom relationship. State colleges, developing later and less rooted in traditions of research and scholarship, have been closer to state bureaucratic control than the state universities, especially the older "flagship" campuses. Community college faculties, under local boards and local administration often conditioned in thought and practice by secondary-school antecedents, have developed less personal and collegial control than the university faculties.

Reform has had one main thrust: to bring more administered order into what is the most disorderly of all major advanced systems of higher education. The drift of authority for a quarter-century has been steadily upward, toward a growing web of multicampus administrations, coordinating boards of higher education, state legislative committees and executive offices, regional associations, and a large number of agencies of the national government.

THE JAPANESE MODE

A summary look at Japan illustrates how these several primary modes can be combined in other national systems, especially where efforts in national development cause them to look to central international models and then, under the restraints of local traditions and conditions, to evolve a unique mixture—a matter explored in greater depth in the chapter on change. The Japanese authority structure has elements similar to both the Continental and American modes.[41] The greatest likeness is to the European, since the system as a whole has been dominated for a century by the handful of leading national universities, particularly the University of Tokyo, which exhibit the classic pattern of faculty guilds formally located within a national state bureaucracy. In the old "imperial" sector, as chapter 2 made clear, the chair holder has had a high degree of personal control over subordinates. In turn, as in the German model, the chair holders have exercised strong collegial control within faculties and universities; and the superstructure, as in France, has centered in the bureaucratic staff of a national ministry. Institutional trustees are absent and institutional administration has been relatively weak.

But other sectors have organized differently. The huge private sector, unlike anything in Europe, has important similarities to the American private sector: e.g., trustees, relatively strong campus administrators, and departmental organization. Since the private institutions must struggle individually to stay alive, like poorly endowed private institutions in the United States, trustees and institutional administrators become much involved in the welfare of the enterprise. At the same time, since there exists a powerful central ministry and a prestigious set of national universities that come under the government, the Japanese private sector has not been able, as much as its American counterpart, to avoid governmental pressures and influences. They had to come to an accommodation with the government. T. J. Pempel states that, beginning in 1918, "with the promulgation of the University Ordinance, the private universities were subsumed into the system they had originally been established to counter, and with few exceptions they mollified their high levels of independence from the government."[42] There was no Dartmouth College case here legally to run up the banner of private-college independence; the private sector was to be closer to government.

Thus, the Japanese mode is a fascinating mixture of contrary forms of organization and authority. The mixture is a structural source of conflicts and cross-purposes that appears dysfunctional to many, especially to central state officials held responsible, much more so than in the United States, for the welfare of the whole. Thus, in the 1970s, worried about low standards in many of the private institutions, the government took responsibility for upgrading the private sectors, offering financial support on the condition that the private institutions meet certain centrally established and monitored guidelines.

THE ACADEMIC SYSTEM AS AN AUTHORITY SYSTEM

The effects of the different arrangements of authority are fundamental. They affect the way that systems operate as systems, the types of changes that occur, and the values that are implemented, as the following chapters clarify. Seemingly basic among the numerous general and specific effects is how authority structure liberates and constrains initiative. Who can act? Personal authority turns loose the individual professor, collegial control the academic group. Institutional bureaucracy widens the discretion of administrators at one level, state bureaucracy the influence of another administrative class. From discretion comes active identities: the important professor, the self-ruling college, the swashbuckling president, the minister of education in charge of every nook and cranny. Notably, institutional identities are strengthened when authority is centered in the enterprise, as in the U.S. system. Responsibility is localized, with such groups as trustees, campus administrators, and senior professors put to work on the construction and protection of a corporate identity. Such identity formation is dampened when authority becomes large at other levels, as in most systems of the world. Power is then behind an all-system point of view, on the one hand, and the identities of smaller faculty clusters, on the other. When it comes to initiatives and identities, what you see in the structure of authority is largely what you get. The distribution of authority goes a long way toward determining how much the individual university or college is an organization.

Across the many national systems, and relative to organizations in other sectors of society, the bottom-heavy division of labor previously highlighted translates, in summary form, into a bottom-dominated authority structure. Personal and collegial forms are uncommonly prevalent, giving operating personnel uncommon influence over nominally higher supervisory levels. There is much discretion at the bottom. The loose coupling noted in the division of work also has its parallel in balkanized authority. So-called decision making at higher levels then becomes considerably a mobilization of the lower "atomic" interests of chairs and institutes in chair systems, departments and related research centers in departmental systems.[43] There is much that trickles up and happens by slow accretion.

"Decision" is increasingly a weak concept for describing aptly the flux of activities that engage officials, even on the top rungs. Those normally described as decision makers or as authorities, in public office, for example, "recommend, advise, confer, draw up budgets, testify, develop plans, write guidelines, report, supervise, propose legislation, assist, meet, argue, train, consult—but *decide?*" [emphasis in original].⁴⁴ Decisions typically take shape gradually, without the formality of agenda, deliberation, and choice. With numerous problems and issues to be dealt with simultaneously and over a protracted period of time, such small steps as writing a memo or editing the draft of a regulation, each with seemingly small consequences, gradually foreclose alternative courses of action and imperceptibly produce a choice. Such accretion occurs particularly when there is a wide horizontal dispersion of responsibility combined with a vertical division of authority. The balkanized authority of the academic system provides a setting in which authority is rarely pinpointed in specific persons or found in clear-cut policy actions.

Thus, compared to organized life elsewhere, academic authority structures are characterized as both bottom-dominated and subject to much diffusion of influence and decision accretion. *But*, national systems vary extensively on these characteristics. Middle tiers and superstructures have varying counterweights against bottom domination. In the American mode, institutional bureaucracy and institutional trusteeship are often decisive in overall enterprise control and able to drive wedges into the faculties and departments, turning them into bureaucratic units as well as centers of collegiality and personal privilege. As the long-run reform of the American structure gives rise to a larger and more complicated superstructure, it too counters the weight of the bottom tiers and slices along segmental as well as general lines into the business of faculties, departments, and individual professors. No characterization of bottom-dominated—drawn across societal sectors—should be taken to mean a monopoly of influence held by American professors. This is true as well for the European mode, where, as seen, state bureaucracy and national academic oligarchy have been the historic counterweights. Within that widespread pattern of strength at the top and the bottom, individual national systems have developed their unique ways and characteristics, shared with small groups of nations. Thus, there has been the counterpoising top dominated by national academics; the national center possessed by regular civil service bureaucrats; and the peak, in some authoritarian and totalitarian societies, in which political personages, in state or party office, at least for a time have had sufficient power arbitrarily to decide something—a five-year plan, a top-to-bottom overhaul, etc.

The national systems obviously also vary within our general characterization of diffusion of authority and decision accretion. The European mode has offered a gathering-in of authority in the superstructure—*the* ministry—but ironically has contained simultaneously, with its weak middle structure, a confederative autonomy within the universities in which, in one country after another, the faculties have been the main inclusive units and the university as a whole has been largely a nominal organization, more loosely joined than its American or British counterparts. Hence, decisions indeed accrete slowly and quietly and behind the scenes, produced more by senatorial courtesy than by rectorial muscle. In contrast, the U.S. mode integrates authority more at the enterprise level, leaving it more to the winds at those levels where, in Europe, the traditional regional or national bureaucracies would have well-worn ways, or the small cliques of national academics would know what to do.

Thus, our points of comparison give us different characterizations, ones that we can extend even further in the next chapter as we range beyond formal structures to consider state and market alternatives. But the final note here is that academic authority is extreme in its complexity, diffusion, bottom-up nature, and decision making by accretion.

II
Integration and Change

FIVE

INTEGRATION

In an infinitely complex world, the higher education system has difficulties in pulling itself together that belie simple descriptions and answers. Tasks proliferate, beliefs multiply, and the many forms of authority pull in different directions. Yet in each case, some order emerges in various parts: disciplines link members from far and wide, universities symbolically tie together their many specialists, bureaucratic structures, local and national, provide uniform codes and regulations. And the bureaucratic, political, and oligarchical forms of national authority contribute to the integration of the whole. But even when grouped in national patterns, the many modes of authority leave out much of the story. A good share of the order that governs relations in higher education in Brazil, Japan, and the United States is produced not by bureaucrats, politicians, or academic oligarchs but by marketlike interaction. Other systems, in lesser degree, also exhibit the play of markets. Such undeliberate effort to effect order mingles with more deliberate initiative in baffling combinations. The rudiments of linkage require much additional disentangling, and a reassembling of forms by which academic action can be concerted.

We begin on the simplest ground by constructing three ideal types—state system, market system, and professional system— which, in combination, offer two- and three-dimensional spaces for comparing national systems. Greater complexity is then introduced by specifying some pathways along which each major type of integration moves. Since the machinery of the state becomes the central tool, even in shaping the markets of higher education, the analysis then highlights the fusion of state and market, and turns to the main interest groups that in various countries have strong hands on that machinery. Finally, there is the important matter of the limits of

136

state control. Time and again the modern state stumbles over the academic system. A concluding review of some twentieth-century efforts to fashion compelling chains of command suggests their self-defeating nature.

STATE, MARKET, AND OLIGARCHY

Let us establish a dimension that extends from tight to loose linkage in the parts of a system.[1] The tight end is a unitary context in which all units are parts of an inclusive formal structure and have common goals. Moving down the continuum we find a federative context in which the units have primarily disparate goals but possess some formal linkage for shared purposes. Still further along the line is a coalitional setting in which disparate goals are so paramount that there is only informal or quasi-formal collaboration among the parts. And at the far end there is a "social-choice" context in which there are no inclusive goals, and decisions are made independently by autonomous organizations.

The concept of social choice, as opposed to central decision, was developed by Edward Banfield:

> A *social choice* . . . is the accidental by-product of the actions of two or more actors—"interested parties," they will be called—who have no common intention and who make their selections competitively or without regard to each other. In a social choice process, each actor seeks to attain his own ends; the aggregate of all actions—the situation produced by all actions together—constitutes an outcome for the group, but it is an outcome which no one has planned as a "solution" to a "problem." It is a "resultant" rather than a "solution" [emphasis in original].[2]

Resultants, as well as planned solutions, coordinate. Rooted in the interested groups, they may result in new viable structures that become permanent solutions. For example, as noted earlier, the rise and spread of the graduate school in the United States as a solution to the problem of underpinning research and advanced training was never a centrally planned solution, nor was it apparently even a tacit agreement among a small group of leaders. It was more a social choice, a resultant rooted in the competitive interaction and voluntary imitation of autonomous institutions.

Reformulating slightly, in order to address more effectively national sets of universities and colleges, the two ends of the continuum may be seen as state administration and market in pure form. The antithesis, at the societal level, has been stated by Charles E. Lindblom:

> Historically the alternative to governmentalization of a national politico-economic system has been the market. And just as hierarchical, bureaucratic, and governmental systems arise from the authority relation, so market systems arise from the simple exchange relation. . . . Not merely a method for reshuffling the possession of things, exchange is a method of controlling behavior and of organizing cooperation among men.[3]

Higher education systems vary widely between dependence on authority and dependence on exchange: the more loosely joined the system the greater the dependence on exchange.

Thus, for example, the four divisions of institutions identified in chapter 2 ranged from one form of dependence to another. The first pattern was unitary and unified state administration; the second was unitary in general control but broken into several independent sectors; the third was a looser arrangement consisting of divided governmental authority and multiple sector-interests, shading down, as in Canada, into confederation; and the fourth contained much social-choice or market-type interaction.[4] The continuum was one of decreasing state-system inclusiveness and of increasing market-type interaction, with such in-between combinations as federation, confederation, and coalition. Thus, in this broad meaning of market, it is synonymous with nongovernmental, nonregulated.

We can illustrate how democratic national systems of higher education might locate on this dimension, without regard to precise spacing, by placing six nations on a limited continuum:

Sweden	France	Britain	Canada	Japan	United States

Unitary and unified   Market
state administration   linkage

In this set of nations, Sweden has the most inclusive and tightest system of state coordination, with highly developed planning capacity and central state machinery integrated in a small system. France also has such a state system, but with some disparity introduced by multiple bureaus and sectors and more looseness resulting from much larger size and complexity. England has moved along the continuum from right to left since 1965, from coalitional linkages with strong elements of market, to tighter federative connection, and then to important elements of inclusive state structure, but is still in the middle range. Canada remains heavily confederative and even coalitional, with the authority of the provinces straining mightily against national linkage. Japan has extensive market characteristics in the interaction of its 1,000 institutions, but state influences have been greater there than in the U.S. The United States, qua national system, remains the most heavily endowed with characteristics of autonomous choice and market exchange.

Movement along this continuum is possible in either direction. The years since World War II, especially the 1960s and 1970s, have seen a general shift from loose arrangements to tighter and more inclusive formal systems. Even the United States has not been immune to this shift, since the costs and complexities brought by expansion have strengthened the perceived need to bring order out of disorder, first at the level of the fifty states, where the formal machinery of coordination has changed qualitatively in the last two decades, and second, at the national level.[5] But systems that are already unitary often see reform as movement away from tight controls; e.g., the efforts in Sweden, France, and Italy to decentralize political authority and/or to deconcentrate administration authority. Furthermore, a country that has provinces attempting to move away from national unity, as in Canada, may remain an exception to the rule that modern countries that have been loosely structured are straining to heighten state coordination.

A third possibility picks up on what we already have learned about national academics. A national system may be coordinated primarily by such oligarchs, for good or for bad, rather than by either political-bureaucratic dictate or market-type interaction. For example, the Italian nationalized system has severely dampened market relations, reducing to a low point the initiative of individual universities and competition among them. At the same time, since the coalition government has been relatively weak and the state bureaucracy relatively mediocre, especially in the Ministry of Education, state authority has functioned largely as a mock bureaucracy, a facade of public control behind which senior professors have had primary power.[6] The power vested locally in chair-holding professors in Continental systems was used to build control in bodies responsible nationally for finance, personnel, curriculum, and research. On some issues, such control has been exercised with the unity of a small oligarchy, as superbarons have come together in a central council or maintained informal contact. On other issues, particularly in those specialized along disciplinary lines, such as the allocation of research monies, the small-group control has been more polyarchical in nature. In either case, there have been "authorities" in charge, not market mechanisms, but the authorities are professors rather than bureaucrats.

Some coordination by academic oligarchy exists in all national systems of higher education. It is most prominent in chair-based organization, since so much concentration of power locally in individuals, amounting to small monopolies in thousands of parts, establishes conditions that propel some of these persons to national power, by means that vary from sheer inflation of status to steady participation in central councils. The guild-bureaucracy combination is inherently contradictory, since chair power fragments the formal structure. The situation is then ripe for substitute mechanisms based on the power of the chairs, ones that will, in a different way, pull the parts together. Thus, the extensive powers of clusters of senior professors, even in the face of a strong and competent bureaucracy, have been a notable feature of traditional French academic life.[7] German professors have had powerful collective voices at national as well as provincial and local levels, in such bodies as the Science Council (*Wissenschaftsrat*), the West German Rectors Conference, the University Association, and the disciplinary committees of the German Research Association.[8]

National systems not strictly organized as state systems are likely to depend heavily on the many ways that academic oligarchy can link persons, groups, and institutions. When institutions are funded mainly by government, academics normally first seek the privileged autonomy of a direct and unfettered lump-sum grant from the national treasury to the individual institution—leave it on the stump, please—with past commitments and budgets guaranteeing an adequate sum. But once coordination in some formal sense becomes probable, as it has virtually everywhere, the common second preference is to have a buffer body that "understands the institutions," is "sympathetic to their needs," and will represent them to government. On grounds of expertise and representation, academics have a persuasive case that such bodies should be staffed with persons who are influential within and outside their disciplines and institutions. Here the classic case has been Britain's University Grants Committee, which, manned largely by prominent academics, has long modeled to the world an effective way of taking the government's money without taking orders from the government's officials.

Thus, although not the only means of such high academic influence, the intermediate body is a key one that has been seized upon in one system after another, for different sectors and at different levels of government. In Australia, for example, where such British traditions as the UGC have been borrowed and adapted to a more extended federal setting, intermediate bodies have developed at both national and state levels and for all three major institutional sectors. At the national level, in the 1970s, there was the Australian Universities Commission for the university sector, the Commission on Advanced Education for *that* sector, and the Further Education Commission for *that* sector, with all three commissions reconstituted in 1977 as statutory councils for their respective areas under a new umbrella Tertiary Education Commission.

Somewhat parallel bodies, especially for the second and third sectors, were spawned at the state levels, amounting to six subsets.[9] And especially at the state level, the sectors and their respective commissions have a background in which historically they were generated by, or have interacted with, different government departments. The situation, only a short time before, was that "in each state except New South Wales, a single university related directly to its state government, while teachers colleges, institutes of technology, technical colleges, agricultural colleges and similar institutions generally came under the direct control of a particular state government department."[10] The specific commissions emerged as buffers between specific sets of institutions and related government departments, with the latest reforms establishing broader commissions and attempting to regroup departmental sponsorship. For a nation of less than 15 million people and only six states, Australia is not short of intermediary bodies!

Thus, the buffer form of oligarchical influence is likely to develop most extensively in those systems historically rooted in federative, coalitional, or market environments of institutional development. The vacuum of an official top is filled, at least in some minimal part, by the professionals coming to some resolution. Systems rooted in ministerial control exhibit fewer buffers. In these nationalized systems, there are two main possibilities. One is that central civil servants will keep power in their own hands to a degree commensurate with the systemwide responsibilities that they carry. Delegation of administrative authority is then a matter of line officers placed in the field, as, for example, in the traditional French style of prefectural supervision. The other stronger possibility is that power will pass into the hands of academic notables as they penetrate and surround the ministry with forms congenial to their rule.

With academic oligarchy omnipresent or lurking in the wings, our continuum from state authority to market can be reshaped as a triangular model of state, market, and oligarchical forms of coordination. Each corner of the triangle represents, then, the extreme of one form and a minimum of the other two, and locations within the triangle represent combinations of the three elements in different degrees. For example, we place within this triangle the six countries that we previously arrayed on a continuum, after stretching the conceptual space by adding the USSR and Italy as cases nearer two of the extremes.

The Soviet Union is the purest case of the triumph of the state over oligarchical and market interaction.[11] Sweden remains relatively close to the extreme of state coordination, since that country developed strong capacity, during the last two decades, for state officials and allied interest groups to override the traditionally strong power and privileges of professors. By 1980 it had become a country in which academic barons feel particularly pushed around by the state and by outside groups. France locates somewhat further away from the state extreme and more toward oligarchy, since, despite a strong and competent ministry, the continuing situation has something of the character of a standoff between the formally superior powers of the central officials and the capacities of university personnel to ward off, reshape, and attentuate state-imposed

The Triangle of Coordination

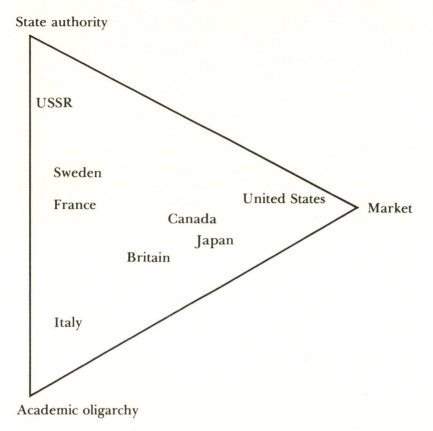

State authority

USSR

Sweden

France   United States

Canada

Japan

Britain

Market

Italy

Academic oligarchy

rules and policies. Italy is well down toward the oligarchical extreme, since its prestigious and powerful national academic oligarchs traditionally have been more than a match for a relatively impotent bureaucracy. None of these four countries impresses with market dynamics.

Britain locates fairly closely to rule by academic oligarchy, because of the extensive role of such intermediate bodies as the University Grants Committee and the Council for National Academic Awards, in which academic notables have been dominant. Even after the significant increase in state power that has occurred since the mid-1960s, deliberate coordination in Britain remains a blend of the bureaucratic and the professional. In their study of the British system, Tony Becher, Jack Embling, and Maurice Kogan note that the "central government has the determinate role in the overall shaping of the system":[12] this is left neither to the market nor to academic judgment. Yet, given the traditional respect for institutional autonomy and individual academic freedom, the government is "coy" about stating national objectives, and the intermediate bodies, although increasingly to be seen as parts of the machinery of government, retain "academic judgments" and are heavily involved in "resource decisions."[13] The indeterminacy of objectives and the freedom of these bodies mean that "coordinative planning" by the state is generally weak: compared to the strength and style of a Continental ministry, British national coordination appears implicit, covert, and indeterminate.

Canada is located close to Britain in this three-dimensional conceptual space, with a somewhat weaker tradition of oligarchical influence. If we drop, for the moment, from the national to the provincial level of government—Canada's strongest level of state supervision—then we find state officials exercising considerable bureaucratic influence upon subsystems, particularly in Quebec and Alberta.[14] Japan, given its complexity, is difficult to place in a summary fashion: on the one hand, national coordination is formally left largely to ministerial officials and not to bodies analogous to the British University Grants Commission; on the other, the chair system, mixed with certain Japanese characteristics of small-group loyalty and cohesiveness, has given senior professors a strong power base.[15] The towering status of the Universities of Tokyo and Kyoto has also given academics at those institutions national influence as well as privileged autonomy.

The United States, inordinately varied, exhibits little coordination at state or national levels by senior academics. Lacking the power base of European and Japanese counterparts, American academics are poorly represented in the higher reaches of the superstructure of control. American professors might control their departments and their multidepartment faculties, colleges, and professional schools, and even occasionally might have an important coordinating role in the campus at large (for example, as in the powerful academic senate on both the Berkeley and Los Angeles campuses of the University of California); but, outside of research councils, they are not found in significant number and strength at the higher levels of control. Indeed, it is noteworthy that even voluntary commissions established to address national issues in higher education, such as the Carnegie Commission on Higher Education, are manned by administrators representative of important sectors and institutions rather than by prestigious professors.

In this triangular conception of types of integration, most of the overt action in most national systems is located to the left of the midpoint: the open battle is between state officials and professors. The market is either not perceived as a form of coordination or is seen as one that gives undependable and undesired results. On the part of responsible academics as well as state officials, political and administrative, there is the assumption that there should be an authority, someone in charge. But the state officials are not automatic winners in this battle, easy victors in an unequal contest. They do move toward dominance in a host of ways—through ministerial control over the location and expansion of facilities, segmental budgeting, the administrative staffing of coordinating bodies, legislative program evaluation. But as chapter 4 stressed, academics have imposing counterbases rooted in the expanding need for experts to participate in the making of competent judgments. Hence, the need for peer review by experts within subareas, and for "advice" by councils of experts, grows rather than diminishes at national as well as local levels. Nations need national academics.

PROCESSES OF INTEGRATION

Each of these three broad forms of integration of national systems can vary considerably in its internal nature and will be variously shaped as it is mixed with the other types. And each has certain dynamics of its own, particularly the processes of its growth. To explore these processes is to dig deeper into the natural complexity of each, moving away from any single explanation of the integration of a higher education system. Contradictions are normal in practice, and so they become in theorizing as soon as we give up simple conceptions of "coordination" that encompass only ministries of education and formal boards and move to the broader spectrum of ways in which the actions of organizations, groups, and individuals are concerted.

By splitting state authority into bureaucratic and political components, a necessary step sooner or later, natural processes of integration will be identified under the rubrics of bureaucracy, politics, profession, and market.

BUREAUCRATIC COORDINATION

The general phenomenon of bureaucracy, located in chapter 4 at institutional and system levels, may be broken into at least five pathways of development that have been observed frequently in higher education in recent decades.

Layering. Bureaucracy expands by increasing the levels of formal coordination, governmental or quasi governmental. Decentralized systems add new higher levels; centralized systems introduce more intermediate levels. The United States and Australia have been adding higher levels of coordination in essentially new or vertically extended administrative superstructures; Sweden, already centralized, has introduced regional councils. This pathway may be denoted as "layering," a phenomenon noted in public administration as a lasting structural effect of reforms. Reforms necessitate reorganization, and "reorganization often results in layering—the piling of administrative echelon upon administrative echelon in an unremitting quest for coordination, symmetry, logic and comprehensive order."[16]

Layering makes administrative pyramids taller. It is intended to provide linkage vertically in larger and/or more complex systems, to put the top, middle, and bottom more in touch with one another. It also allows for the participation of more interests from within and without the system, e.g., national bureaucrats added to the U.S. system and lay groups introduced into the Swedish system at the regional level. Everywhere the common understanding of "coordination" pushes in this direction as it pictures the symmetrical pyramid of accountability that will finally provide comprehensive order. But layering may have major unanticipated and undesired effects. The additional layers distort communication between the top and the bottom and multiply participants and perspectives, thereby rendering administration less rather than more consistent and dependable.[17] A small number of posts at the top are made highly attractive, but a large number of now "lower" posts are made less attractive, thereby inducing a loss of talent and initiative at middle and lower levels. For example, the highest positions on public campuses in the United States became less attractive as three or four layers were laid over them in the form of multicampus administration, state governing board, state government surveillance, and a web of national government regulations. Most of all, reforms enacted today by means of layering, whatever their immediate intent and outcome, help establish massive command structures that become rigid and resist reform tomorrow. Layering is central to the paradox of reform by bureaucratic means: the more you do it, the less likely you can do it meaningfully in the future.

Jurisdictional Expansion. Another pathway of bureaucratic development is an increase in the jurisdictional scope of administrative agencies, singly and in combination. Existing ministries of education are given or seize expanded responsibilities; additional departments are established; quasi-governmental commissions become more comprehensive, replacing specialized commissions or topping them. Such expansion in the scope of central bodies is widespread, notable in one country after another as efforts are made to pull together formerly separated domains and to cope with the creeping disorder of a bewildering variety of tasks. Ideas about public accountability are a basic force behind such expansion.

The wider jurisdictional responsibility has the effects of making administrative pyramids wider and more firmly structured. In Japan, the jurisdiction of the Ministry of Education has expanded in relation to the huge private sector of universities and colleges, making that sector quasi public to a greater degree. In the United States, a host of national departments have developed an administrative reach into and over hundreds of universities and colleges as they attempt to supervise proper expenditure from various accounts. In Australia, the new 1977 supercommission encompasses the domains of the three formerly more specialized commissions. In Sweden, the jurisdiction of the central agency has successively expanded. In the United Kingdom, pressures have grown for a super-UGC.

Much reform by means of bureaucracy has the combined structural effects of layering administrative echelons and of expanding administrative jurisdictions.

Personnel Enlargement. There is an increase in the number of administrators who attend to matters of higher education. Layering and jurisdictional expansion generally result in such enlargement, but it can come about, too, in such simple ways as the expansion of personnel attending to old duties in an old bureau. This pathway of bureaucratization has been noted virtually everywhere, in part because it can readily be observed by counting administrative staff. Thus, in Sweden, the central staff who attended to higher education in the mid-1940s amounted to a few people within the Ministry of Education and only three civil servants in the Office of the Chancellor of the University. As late as 1960 there were only 17 in the chancellor's office. But by the mid-1970s, these staffs had grown to over 25 in the ministry and 170 in the chancellor's office. The growth of personnel in the chancellor's office was stimulated not only by the general expansion of the system (tenfold in students between the mid-1940s and the mid-1970s) but also by a deliberate change in the character of that office from "a representative of the universities," elected by the rectors, to "a regular state agency," appointed by the Cabinet and operating "wholly in line with the pattern of Swedish state agencies in general."[18] In Britain, the administrative staff of the University Grants Committee grew from about 6 in the early 1950s to over 140 in 1975. Many of these permanent staff members of the UGC were civil servants holding appointment in the present Department of Education and Science.[19] In France, the department responsible for universities within the Ministry of Education grew into "a ministry within a ministry," leading to a succession of structural reforms attempting to straighten things out, including an effort to have an entirely separate ministry employing several hundred professionals.[20]

Administrative Specialization. Expertise in administrative work increases. A shift from amateurs to experts occurs in the line positions, from top staff to institutional administrators, with the amateurs replaced by persons who make a career in administration, become expert in specific administrative areas, hold long terms in office, and are appointed rather than elected. The composition of coordinating bodies also shifts toward greater dependence on full-time, permanent staff and less on the part-time, temporary generalists, as in the case of the British UGC. As administrative work becomes more specialized, administrative credentials and experience become more essential for entry into formal positions of coordination. A separate administrative class then develops a separate culture.

The professionalization of administration has been uniquely strong at the institutional level, as previously remarked, in the United States.[21] But observers in Britain have also noted there a "greater emphasis on the roles of vice-chancellors, bureaucrats, and council" in university government, with a concomitant decline in the relative power of faculty and with the possibility looming that "practicing academics" will be replaced in key decision-making areas by "full-time professional bureaucrats."[22] Such professionalization will occur strongly in the layers of coordination above the institutional level, since the higher staffs need skills applicable across larger and more complex systems and a related mentality appropriate to a view from the top. Such staffs are notoriously removed from faculty and especially from students. The typical bureaucrat in the French or Italian Ministry of Education (or Higher Education) can hardly encounter faculty and students in his daily rounds, since he or she is spatially separated and, even on coffee breaks, interacts with other administrators. Hence, the dilemma of systems turning increasingly toward "nonacademic" academic administrators: it is difficult to keep the higher reaches of a system in touch with what professors and students think and do when those centers are distant and peopled with specialists who have little or no background in teaching or research.

Rule Expansion. There is an increase in the number and complexity of formal rules designed to effect consistency in the actions of people within the system. The growth of rules is a universal aspect of what is commonly meant by bureaucracy. The rules may be of various types: some attempt to guide or "preform" decisions, as in the case of budget categories; others are meant to check the compliance of personnel with policies or decisions already made, as in the case of auditing and inspecting practices.

This route of bureaucratic coordination is relatively easy to measure in gross terms, cross-nationally and over time, since it can be observed in the indices, pages, and volumes of administrative codes and commission regulations. For example, national laws and regulations that pertain to higher education in Italy already required, by the mid-1960s, a twenty-page index of 800 items to guide readers through a thousand pages of specifications.[23] But then rule enforcement becomes an additional matter: when it is weak, as in Italy, the administrative structure can be a mock bureaucracy, a paper tiger. In any event, rare is the system of higher education that has not seen, in recent decades, an evermore closely meshed network of laws and administrative regulations. The principal counterforce to this trend from within governmental administration itself is found in efforts to reduce detail and broaden scope: e.g., to pass not specific legislation but broad "framework" laws that cover more activities but in less detail. It is possible to enact broad procedural rules, regulating who participates and the channels by which they do so, without specifying directly the many substances of exchanges and behaviors.[24]

Layering stretches the administrative superstructure vertically; jurisdictional expansion thickens it horizontally; personnel enlargement fills it with more people; administrative specialization, with more experts; and rule expansion ensures that the larger, better-manned structure will have a commensurate massive body of regulations. These processes, separately and together, increase the coordinating influence of bureaucrats. As a result, administrative officials in central committees, commissions, and councils, as well as in ministries and offices of education, become more implicated in the forming and implementing of policy.

The influence of the bureaucratic tendency is affected by numerous features that vary from one nation and context to the next, especially in the administrative organization and culture of the national executive branch. In some cases, generally in less-developed countries, state bureaucracy is relatively passive and benign; in others, commonly in the most developed societies, it is assertive, multiplying regulations in excess of legislation and accumulating autonomous authority. Higher education systems move from benign to assertive bureaucracy as they are goaded to modernize, become efficient, and plan.

POLITICAL COORDINATION

If the bureaucratic avenues of coordination have seemingly gained the most in strength in recent decades, political means have not been far behind. As noted in chapter 4, political authority is a legitimate form of power in and around higher education systems, serving as a basic alternative to bureaucratic and professional forms at the broadest reaches. The pathways to integration that are essentially political in nature are those that strengthen and formalize the representation of various factions, from those long legitimated as entitled to control to new claimants for influence. Since less is known about these matters than in the case of bureaucracy, we need to pay them greater attention.

Ascending Political Priority. There is an increase in the extent to which higher education is seen as an issue worth attending to by the regular channels of politics and government: ministries, parliaments, interest organizations, the mass media, elections, and public opinion.[25] A more widespread popular interest in access, the dramatic events of student discontent and rebellion, sometimes a government interest in scientific productivity and available manpower, and always the matter of rising costs cause legislators and the highest reaches of the executive branch to become more attentive and involved. Voters want to know where legislators stand on specific issues of access. The legislators and the chief executive are pressed for policies and laws that will ease or suppress student discontent. Military leaders and others in departments dependent on science and technology call attention to the connection between the scientific capabilities of universities and national well being. Budgets for higher education more often appear as political issues as the greatly increased volume of accessible higher education helps produce leaps in the magnitude of costs. Student riots may come and go, but higher costs go on forever, making higher education a more political issue year in and year out.

A clear example of how increasing costs give higher education greater political priority, for bureaucrats and politicians alike, was what occurred in Great Britain when the University Grants Committee had its status changed in 1964 from a statutory body receiving funds directly from the British Treasury to one receiving its allocations from, and reporting to, the British Department of Education and Science (DES).[26] For Treasury, the annual allocation to the UGC was negligible, even as costs increased markedly with early expansion, since Treasury's domain was governmentwide. Compared with the amounts that went into the military and the other social services, the cost of the universities would always seem a small matter—this on top of the historic relationship of trust that had built up between the gentlemen of the Treasury and the gentlemen of the UGC, *and* the fact that Treasury was not responsible for educational theories and could willingly leave all that to those who were given the money. It did not expect to be much involved and no one—well, almost no one—expected it to.

In contrast, the higher education bill, amounting to over seventy percent of the DES budget in the mid-1970s, was bound to make it a larger issue in the new setting. No education minister could quietly ignore such a major part of his or her jurisdiction. Also, of course, education ministers and their senior civil servants are supposed to have educational preferences and policies—even theories!—as well as implement in education the political will of parties and regimes. In effect, the change in budgetary location helped change the status of British higher education as an issue. The example illustrates the importance of different administrative locations in drawing attention to higher education. The relative as well as the absolute size of costs determines issue importance, and relative cost is a matter of context as well as historical comparison.

The Deepening of Political Involvement.   As higher education matters assume greater importance as issues, they flow more readily through the regular political channels of government and the related structures of the political parties where they exist. As these instrumentalities institutionalize their handling of such matters, they in turn further contribute to the heightened status of higher education matters. More committees, and stronger committees, of the legislatures have higher education business on their regular agendas. The chief executive and his cabinet, and the appointed education minister and his staff, assume more "responsibility" and thereby become more assertive and intrusive. The courts then follow, as they have in many countries, since judicial interpretations are sought for the laws passed by the legislature and for the actions taken by executives. The greater usage of regular political channels clearly includes the emergence and strengthening of a relevant jurisprudence.

In addition, the flow of higher education matters through these regular instruments of government attracts the attention of existing political parties. The issues then become subject to the internal politics of the parties and their interaction with the legislature and the executive, involving straight political bargaining and compromising and the mixing of educational concerns with other interests of political factions. A proposal to initiate a new university in the north of Norway becomes mixed up in the broader issues of regional development, with location, in Tromsø, then decided by "politics," e.g., by the regional commitments of the dominant parties. A new university in the south of Italy is located in a particular city as a trade-off for a rival city having been made the regional capital. With such involvements, some party officials as well as legislators become acknowledged experts on higher education and develop a supporting staff who can keep them informed and help them make judgments.

In the sense of strengthened political channels as the structural corollary of greater importance as an issue, higher education in Western Europe, whether in West Germany or Sweden or Denmark or Italy, has become more politicized in recent decades. The issues have moved more fully and deeply into the party caucus, the session of the legislative subcommittee, the cabinet meeting of the executive, and the calendar of the courts. Similarly in the United States, the years since World War II have seen a great increase in legislative, executive, judicial, and party attention to a realm that has become much more costly and troublesome. The change occurred first at the state level, where in some cases it has evolved into "legislative program review," in which legislators and their staffs scan and criticize in detail the educational programs of specific universities and colleges. It has also taken place in the national capital, where a qualitative change has produced a willingness to engage in "federal supervision" of higher education, a conception that was decidedly illegitimate as late as 1970.

Meanwhile, in Eastern Europe, Communist rule since 1945 has been devoted to a great strengthening of the explicitly political forms of coordination, by means of the dual and interpenetrating dominance of the single political party and the one-party regime over all such public sectors as education.[27] Then, too, in many developing societies, regimes can hardly afford not to be deeply interested in control of the higher education system. They tend to see it as a basic sector for nation-building efforts, from the training of essential experts to the building of national culture and consensus. They tend so often to feel they must intervene to ensure the system's relevance to pressing practical problems—poverty, land use, industrialization—that the professors might otherwise ignore as they follow the academic models they know best but that come from the highly developed societies.[28] Politicization in the most primary sense is frequent and intense in developing societies in the contemporary period, producing often bitter struggle between state officials and the academics.

Hardening of Internal Interests. Much of the more obvious politicization of higher education in recent decades has involved the representation of internal interests. More groups have clamored for "participation" in decision making, across the many levels from the operating units to the top. In the expanded contest, the methods of representation have moved from the informal to the formal, from the soft to the hard.

This participation phenomenon, sometimes also referred to as democratization, occurred most sharply, in Western European systems, in the late 1960s and early 1970s.[29] Junior faculty, students, and such nonacademic personnel as custodians sought a piece of the power long monopolized by senior professors and state bureaucrats in the European mode of authority distribution described in chapter 4. They demanded, and often got, a formal allotment of seats and voting rights in various bodies. Noted changes occurred in West Germany and Denmark, where, in certain areas of decision, such as course formation, the votes of senior professors were reduced to one-third of the total, in a *Drittelparität* (1/3-1/3-1/3) distribution of votes among senior faculty, junior faculty, and students.[30] The allocations in West Germany varied from one *Land* to another, and were often different according to decision area; e.g., more votes were reserved for senior faculty in matters of research, more influence given to the new groups in arranging the curriculum. Notably, the formal recognition of the representation of a larger set of interest groups was enacted by legislation and hence written into law. It thereby became formalized by codification as well as explication, to the extent that the judiciary became involved in interpreting the appropriateness and application of the law. Thus, a 1973 court decision in West Germany that applied throughout the country "rolled back" some of the liberal distribution of votes effected in earlier legislation. The court decided that senior professors had certain inherent rights that should be reflected in predominant power—half of the votes or more—in such matters as research and appointments.[31] Thus it went in varying degrees in, for example, Austria, Belgium, Italy, the Netherlands, and Sweden. The main idea throughout was simultaneously to reduce the power of senior faculty and abate the discontent of the other internal segments.

This general form of politicization—explicit powers allocated to different major internal segments—has historically and comparatively been developed in two radically different contexts: the conditions of the original medieval universities in Italy and those of twentieth-century Latin American universities. The first universities in Italy were constituted as student and faculty guilds.[32] The students banded together to buy the services of teachers, to protect themselves against landlords and town ruffians, to maintain some order among themselves, to obtain certain jurisdictions and rights, and in general to give themselves a civic personality, in cities where they were aliens. The heyday of student power, never later surpassed, occurred in this setting between the twelfth and fifteenth centuries.[33] Such power became virtually eliminated when the universities settled into permanent locations and came under municipal finance, with the professors then freed from their dependence on the payment of students. The high point of student power in all of Western history came from market conditions under which students, as organized customers, could often dictate freely.

In Latin America, the Córdoba Movement of 1918 ushered in an age of politicization in Latin American universities, in the sense of a high degree of student power.[34] Students obtained strong formal power in ruling councils; for example, Mexican students generally comprise one-fourth to one-half of the membership of university-wide councils. They also developed additional influence through the power to disrupt. Their uncommon power has been formed in a context where universities have assumed the role of principal critics of society, within political systems which feature few other institutionalized outlets for criticism and dissent.[35] Within that role, the students have seen themselves as both necessary critics and leaders of change, before they move from the privileged sanctuary of the university campus to ruling or influential positions in government and the professions. Their power, legitimate and otherwise, has been aided by the weakness of institutional administration—the absence of trustees and the weakness of elected rectors and deans, characteristic of the European mode—*and* by the limits on professorial involvement that stem from part-time status and commitment to outside employment.

In examining how "conflict and mediation" take place in a Latin American university, a Mexican anthropologist has characterized the National University of Mexico (UNAM) as

> a battlefield for political feuds, both figuratively and actually. There are plenty of opportunities for professional and amateur politicians among the student body to participate in political activity. One might think of partisan struggles within the National University as tournaments, such as used to take place during the Middle Ages, where knights in shining armor publicly clashed. Until recently, the National University campus was the ideal setting for these jousts because of its relative isolation and autonomy.[36]

As a battlefield, the university is "useful also as a training ground for future political leaders of all persuasions," with 70 percent of top political leaders having been National University graduates "who earned their first political stripes within the university."[37] Thus, politics, in the most direct sense of the word, is a principal activity of such student-politicized universities and university systems—a worthy contender against the knowledge activities elsewhere seen as central. At UNAM, "academics" and "professionals" are simply two interest groups serving academic and professional interests that must contend with "politicians" and "fighting gangs" serving the interests of politics and adolescent rebellion. At the same time, "the immense majority of students . . . are confused and habitually passive," mobilized only "by causes and contingencies of a purely sporadic and circumstantial nature."[38]

The pathways of increased political coordination entail forms and processes that in the long run are not likely to stand up as well as the bureaucratic means of coordination. For one, issue importance is a fickle thing. It has indeed risen, for higher education, during recent decades. Yet, at any one time, governments nearly always have a number of other issues to face that are more important and that crowd the agenda. In an examination of higher education policy making in England, France, and Sweden, Rune Premfors has shown that issue importance fluctuates fairly rapidly: up with dramatic events that demand attention for awhile; down when the crisis lessens, with higher education typically ranking quite far down the governmental agenda.[39]

In an examination of the role of the U.S. presidency in educational affairs, as such matters were drawn toward Washington by federal funding, Chester E. Finn, Jr., has pointed to the low issue importance of education generally, let alone higher education, in the executive branch, where the staff is always overloaded with burning issues of the day.[40] The regular political instruments of government everywhere tend to become operationally overloaded. Paralleling the flood of issues is a flood of work, clogging those channels and reducing their effectiveness as ways of supervising higher education.

Finally, while the representation of internal interest groups widens and hardens, sustained representation on complicated issues in a complex setting becomes a matter for small elites rather than mass involvement. In the metaphor of front stage, backstage, and understage, as three arenas of academic discourse,[41] large representational committees and councils operate on the front stage in order to make ritualistic and high-minded assertions of value and purpose and to sanction decisions taken elsewhere. That "elsewhere" is in much smaller groupings, working understage and backstage, that do the hard bargaining and form alliances that can carry the day. Students tend not to get understage and backstage, but younger academic staff have been better located to do so and hence have gained more than the students in the struggle for influence.[42]

In comparison, the bureaucratic processes are more immediate, focused, and durable. Higher education does not go up and down in issue importance for a higher education ministry or department or council or committee. It is *the* business, all the time and for all time. Issues and work loads from other domains do not readily intrude. To the contrary, the bureau expands its rules and regulations around its singular commitment, struggling to enlarge the domain within which its personnel are dominant and higher education is seen as the paramount issue. A full-time, career-centered civil servant, in blunt imagery, can outsit politicians as well as students: he has more time now and for the long haul. It thus becomes no secret why, out of the joint struggle of politicians, bureaucrats, and students in the 1960s and 1970s against the dominating power of professors, in so many systems, the bureaucrats were the great winners and the students gained least. Those who are full time and expert have great advantage over those who are part time and amateur; those who are permanent are likely to prevail over those who are transient. The steadiness and continuity of administrative entities have long been primary reasons for the bureaucratization of the world.

Of course, political coordination can be made as strong as bureaucratic coordination: political groups can become authoritative and be given the durability of bureaus. Communist regimes seek such control by means of a single-party monopoly of political power and a party structure that parallels the state machinery.[43] Party regulars move into all sectors of governmental activity and at all levels of supervision and surveillance, right down to the grass roots. A party person can be as legitimately in the room as a bureaucratic person. The vast party structure, itself bureaucratized, but separately from the state bureaucracy, thereby achieves focus as well as durability, in the form of party officials and members, paid and unpaid, who concentrate on educational sectors.

In the contest of will between political and bureaucratic groups, the final irony is that the political become more powerful as they become more bureaucratic—in higher education systems, as elsewhere.

PROFESSIONAL COORDINATION

Chapter 4 depicted authority rooted in expertise as the common basis for personal, collegial, guild, and professional forms. Graeme C. Moodie, in discussing "the survival of academic rule" in British universities, writes: "Within the universities, broadly speaking, the prevalent outlook may be summarized as 'knowledge is authority.' By this is meant that the right to decide in any area ought to be shared among the knowledgeable, with those knowing most having the greatest say, and the uninformed having no say."[44] Hence, while lay members of higher boards and councils may rightly judge finances, building, and public relations, and bureaucrats certain matters of general administration, faculty members should judge in their specialties and generally in anything to do with academic work. Academics, as emphasized, have also transmuted local authority into national power in many systems, with national academics thereby becoming worthy opponents of bureaucrats and politicians in putting hands on the levers of decision. What are the pathways for expanding this form of influence and coordination?

Expansion of Subject Expertise. Authority is pulled downward in the structure of national systems, toward professional rather than bureaucratic or political bases, as the need increases for thousands of judgments at operating levels to be based on the evermore esoteric knowledge of professors. The primacy that each department is able to claim as the authoritative unit for a given discipline or professional field gives a stubborn centrality to the parts where knowledge is authority. The great strength of the understructure, in comparison to the superstructure of national systems, is a remarkable phenomenon, one rooted in the inexorable expansion of subject expertise and hence of professional authority.

If the superstructure of state control should be able to impose its will on the understructure of faculties, departments, chairs, and institutes anywhere among Western democratic nations, it should be in Sweden, where state political authority is strong, the bureaucracy is competent, and planning capacity is relatively developed—all in a small homogeneous society. Yet an insightful 1977 research report from Sweden notes an ongoing "antithesis of central importance" between the real governance mechanisms in universities and colleges and the mythology of central governance. Against the rules and formal organization of central control there is the reality that professional authority at the department level sweeps upward to have great influence at faculty and university levels. Central governance must take this fact into account and adjust accordingly. Otherwise, it becomes "out of step with real local governing mechanisms, in which case it becomes unrealistic and inefficient."[45] Thus, precisely because of the embeddedness and strength of professional authority, the understructure is not simply passive, forced to give way to superior powers of the bureaucratic and political tendencies that strengthen state authority. Rather, state coordination becomes "unrealistic" as it becomes out of step with the organic professionalized understructure. Professional authority is the bedrock of authority in its possession of subject areas.

Because of the logic and momentum of the individual disciplines, subject expertise has an expansive dynamic of its own. It keeps rolling on. Overall coordination is shaped by this expansion, having to accommodate to what in purest form amounts to home rule by professionals.

Expansion of Central Collegial Bodies.   There is an increase in the number and strength of central bodies manned by professors and/ or institutional representatives, and an increase in their coordinative powers. This phenomenon is most noticeable in the support of research: the distribution of scientific funds in virtually every country much involved in research is heavily influenced by peer review among academic notables sitting on central science councils and commissions. More generally, the members of each discipline and subspecialty band together in national academic associations both to strengthen their own internal linkages and to act collectively on the larger stage. This line of segmented coordination grows stronger as the associations develop headquarter offices with full-time bureaucratic staff and political lobbyists. Academics engage in such strengthening of professional coordination in part as a defensive move, a counterforce, to the growth in the bureaucratic and political forms—and also to the actions of the bordering fields.

Psychologists had to look to their associational strength in recent decades in the United States as a defense against the actions of psychiatrists seeking state laws giving them primary control over mental institutions and therapeutic practice. In turn, medical sociologists self-consciously pulled together in defense against the new definitions and expanded jurisdictions of the psychologists that would have diminished the role of sociologists, both pure and applied. Associational linkage is particularly needed and used by academics in large, nonformal systems such as the American, British, and Japanese, in order to represent disciplinary interests across institutions without benefit of a line to a central ministerial office. But it is likely to expand everywhere as specialization deepens and consciousness of craft proceeds apace.

Institutional representatives also band together voluntarily in reaction to growing bureaucratic and political forces. All, or almost all, Latin American systems have a council of rectors (e.g., Chile), and some have two, one for private and one for public institutions (e.g., Brazil). National conferences of rectors became more active during the 1970s in Austria, Switzerland, and the Federal Republic of Germany. A Council of Presidents became a potent body for policy making in France. The national Committee of Vice-Chancellors and Principals (CVCP) in Great Britain has developed into a powerful organ to which the academic heads of all the universities belong. The CVCP became an additional central academic body to which the institutions could turn to have a collective voice in centrally determined matters. It, too, seeks to coordinate on "matters of common interest" through its own system of working parties, its own staff, its own deliberations, and its representation of the universities' views to the UGC and the Department of Education and Science.[46] So it is in many other countries, especially in those where campus headships have been weak traditionally and have emerged as important posts only in recent years.

Expansion of Faculty Interest Organization. There is an increase in the strength of comprehensive faculty bodies such as unions and associations. Old local collegial bodies have been replaced or supplemented by new forms linked to national organizations of professors: e.g., academic senates by local chapters of national unions. Faculties in sectors where they have historically had little influence have particularly seized upon union organization as a way of increasing their power. On behalf of an extended academic labor force, the professorial unions bargain with high levels of administration and political authority and thereby, as in the industrial domain, become tools of coordination, particularly in determining the conditions of employment and work.

In sum, professional coordination survives. It is alive and well in academia and not about to be done in by politicians and bureaucrats. Despite any and all opposition mounted against it, it is driven forward by the momentum of expertise. It sweeps upward from the bottom layers of systems, as academicians forge connections to one another—within and across disciplines, within and across institutions, within and across sectors—and seek hegemony in the system as large. Professional coordination is less obvious than bureaucratic and political forms, but it is always operative and often potent.

MARKET COORDINATION

As an ideal type, the fourth form of coordination is radically different from the bureaucratic, political, and professional forms, all of which have formal locations. Market coordination works with-

out benefit of a superstructure: unregulated exchanges link persons
and parts together. As noted earlier, political economists have
explained, in modern terms, the ways in which market interaction
coordinates the behavior of individuals, groups, and organizations.
It is not necessary to slip off into the mystery of an invisible hand that
leads individuals to promote larger ends. "All social controls have
elements of the automatic, unintended, and unconscious"; and, in
market life, people "are deliberate and conscious; but their acts
accomplish feats of coordination of which they are not necessarily
conscious and which they do not intend."[47] For example, one coordinating function of a market system is constant occupational reas-
signment, with consumer preferences and occupational preferences
reconciled in a reshuffling of labor from one field to another, one
specialty to another. When students avoid Greek and Latin, would-
be teachers in those fields are "encouraged" to become something
else, even sociologists. "Exchange" is a basic form of interaction that
stands in contrast to authoritative command; it can be seen as a
method for organizing cooperation among people.

Lindblom's formulation of "the three-market system" points to
the major types of markets that we may usefully explore in post-
secondary education: the consumer market, the labor market, and
the institutional market.[48]

Consumer Markets. These markets are where people normally
exchange money for desired goods and services. In education, student payments to institutions are the clearest example: when we
hear the word *tuition* we are in the presence of a consumer market.[49]
Governments use such markets when they award scholarships and
other forms of financial aid to individual students that they in turn
can choose to spend at various institutions; or governments use such
markets indirectly when they allocate money to institutions according to the number of students attracted. The central feature is
consumer choice. In some systems such choice is extremely wide not
only because diversity is present but also because governmental
policy keeps costs to the student extremely low or gives funds to
students to spend where they please. Choice may be very wide in
those systems that permit institutions to compete for students, engaging in claims of "product differentiation" as a way of attracting
consumers and thereby building a dependable base of support in a
hived-off segment of the market. And, of course, consumerism

takes place within as well as among enterprises, as students initially select fields of study and later move around among them. Here again choice can be very wide, even in "state systems," when students can select their major subjects without limit of quotas and/or can easily transfer from one field to another. Even in the most heavily socialized system of higher education, students have some capacity to vote with their feet, flowing from unattractive to attractive parts, within and among institutions, thereby promoting one component at the expense of another.

The great extent to which the consumer market reaches into areas of decision making normally thought to be in the hands of bureaucrats, politicians, and professors is indicated in the way budgets are heavily constrained by what one might call "the enrollment economy," the linking of financial support to student attendance.[50] In an outstanding analysis of budget making in American universities, Michael D. Cohen and James G. March stress that large parts of the budget "are embedded in the long-run complications of the enrollment cycle [and hence involve] a process that is heavily constrained by 'market' factors"[51]—by the fact that resources typically come to a university because of student enrollment, with the rate and pattern of that enrollment in departments and in the university as a whole dependent not only on the gross level of demand for education relative to the supply but also on educational programs, reputations, and competitors within and without. In private institutions, the enrollment cycle flows through direct tuition charges to students and their families; in public institutions, it flows through central officials reacting to the number of students enrolled. In the typical American university, the enrollment market dominates budgeting, sharply limiting the discretion of the president, other administrators, and the trustees. The budgeting problem is then "one of finding a set of allocations that produces an educational program that attracts enough enrollment to provide the allocations."[52]

Whenever we probe intensively into budget formation, we are likely to find enrollments—hence student demand and choice—entering heavily into allocations to sectors, enterprises, and operating units. The enrollment criterion is so simple, compelling, and often deeply institutionalized in long-established categories and procedures that it can dominate decision making, even in authoritarian states. In his study of the relation of universities to the state in

Mexico, Daniel C. Levy revealed a surprisingly high degree of *financial* autonomy.[53] Universities received their allocations mainly on the basis of enrollment size, and went on doing so even when government officials might have wanted to punish them financially for causing trouble. Allocations increased generally in line with enrollment expansion and did not vary on the basis of angry response and authoritative dictate. Hence, consumer demand and its direct representation in enrollment, in effect, determined order and continuity in the system at large.

Thus, whenever we note an increase in the capacity of would-be students to afford the costs of higher education, the consumer market has been extended. Whenever there is an increase in the capacity of students to choose among sectors, institutions, or disciplines, the consumer market has been strengthened. This form of market surely has been extended as a coordinating force in a large number of national systems in recent decades as they have become more accessible and more complex. Government officials and academics cannot allocate *that* much, control *all* that traffic, make *all* those decisions for students. Besides, it would be "undemocratic." Thus, increased consumer sovereignty is a fundamental way through which market-type coordination is extended.

Labor Markets. These markets are those in which people offer their capabilities and energies for money: hence, faculty and administrative employment constitute such markets within the higher education system. Here again, this form of market is used heavily by some systems and lightly by others, but it always exists to some degree. Nowhere is the state allocation of persons to academic positions so complete as to eliminate faculty and administrative choice. But there are major differences in degree and range of choice and the extent of mobility, differences that are determined not only by uniformity of the system, civil service restrictions, and firmness of regime control but also by such factors as the extent of control by academic barons and cultural traditions of lifelong employment in single institutions. Academic barons in traditional national systems, each controlling a personal and limited system of placement, as in Italy, have often greatly impeded the free flow of young faculty from one place to another.[54] The Japanese tradition of long, even lifelong, employment has reduced academic mobility in that country.[55] In contrast, much mobility can be found in the

United Kingdom, Canada, and Australia, as well as in the United States, systems in which institutions hire on their own and stress individual achievement as the basis for aggregate prestige. The United States undoubtedly remains the extreme example of academic labor mobility, among systems with mostly full-time personnel, even though the depression and high supply of the 1970s seriously dampened the job market for young academics.[56]

The coordering effects of the academic labor market are major. They are intertwined with those of the institutional market, in which, as emphasized later, reputation is the currency. And such functions as high-quality research seem heavily dependent on the way this type of market operates. The most powerful hypothesis in the comparative sociology of science remains the one advanced by Joseph Ben-David and Abraham Zloczower in 1962: that is, national systems that are decentralized and competitive are more conducive to scientific progress than are centralized and noncompetitive ones, in large part because of the opportunities thereby given to promising young academics to move from less to more attractive settings for the development of their ideas.[57] Scientific productivity is only one desired outcome in many national systems, but it is a highly important one that seems much affected by the structure of the academic labor market.

Institutional Markets. These markets are where enterprises interact with one another, instead of with consumers or employees. This form of market looms large in those economies where business enterprises are free to buy from and sell to each other and thereby produce a large volume of unregulated exchange. Planned economies seek to disestablish this type of market. Academic systems are not directly analogous, since there are no retailers, wholesalers, and manufacturers busily engaging one another. Instead, the relations among institutions are determined largely by the nature of their consumer and internal labor markets and the positions that the institutions then assume. Reputation becomes the main commodity of exchange; and relative prestige not only guides the consumers and workers but also institutions. Highly valued institutions may come to sit astride the whole structure, and, as they do so, they commonly generate the tides of academic drift, whereby enterprises imitate and converge, as well as heavily guide the choices of consumers and personnel. Some academic drift is likely everywhere, toward institutions and sectors whose higher prestige brings an assorted set of higher rewards: better students, better work conditions, higher personal reputation, and more generous financing.

Institutions frequently attempt to carve out a protected niche in the consumer market, and whole sectors engage in interplay in that market, in planned, semiguided, and unplanned ways. The Japanese government planned to have a small set of imperial universities elevated above all others, and this in effect give them a near-monopoly over the choicest part of the consumer market. But the government also permitted the existence of a private sector, and then, after World War II, allowed that sector to shoulder the burdens of expansion into more accessible higher education, to soak up high consumer demand by competitive absorption. Thus, the consumer market became divided between the public and the private, and subtypes of each, by a combination of planning, guidance, and uncontrolled competition. The state clearly and strongly shaped the dimensions of the consumer market by manipulating the reputation of institutions, placing Tokyo as number one and Kyoto as number two, but then left a good share of the market open for competitive determination. In contrast, the state in most European countries in effect planned the private sector out of existence, establishing a public-sector monopoly, and then sought to equalize the reputation of the public institutions within several sectors, or even in the system as a whole, by nationalizing the awarding of degrees and by establishing related common courses and curricula. Market-type interaction among institutions was strongly suppressed.

The possible interplay between public and private institutional sectors in the consumer market is shown in the move of Latin American countries toward more accessible higher education. The state has not everywhere sought a monopoly for the public sector: private-sector enrollment as a percentage of the total varies among the Latin systems from almost zero percent to over fifty percent and has been increasing in recent decades in many of the countries. The state has often not been able or has not even wished to keep up with the rising expectations and enlarged cohorts of qualified secondary-school leavers by expanding the public institutions. Then, too, the public enterprises often have had a declining reputation, because of the apparently low quality of the education they offered or their political turmoil or both. Thus, private institutions were, in effect, left many breaches in the market to fill. As Mario S. Brodersohn notes:

> The spectacular growth of the university student popula-tion has prompted the establishment of private institu-tions designed to cover the market not satisfied by the government either because restrictions have been im-posed on access to free government education or because the quality of the education they offered was low.[58]

As the national system comes under pressure for "more and better" higher education, a differentiation is highly probable in which there will be a "residual market" for private sectors. If the public institutions are providing "the better," much of "the more" is likely to go into that residual market; if the public places carry the more, the residual market echoes with demand for the better; and when the public sector is not providing either the more or the better, government officials as well as multitudes of consumers are likely to support those institutions, new and old, that compete in that resid-ual market.

The sector differentiation discussed in chapter 2 thus allows for varying degrees of interplay and compensation in the institutional handling of the consumer market. When only one sector exists, its failures cannot be compensated for, other than through its own reform. When several sectors exist, especially as between public and private, the weaknesses of one can be compensated for by the activi-ties of the other. State systems have often been encouraged by the failures of private institutions—so called "market failure"—in not providing sufficient access, low-cost education, secular education, etc. In turn, private-sector representatives are encouraged by "state failure" in the various forms described above.[59] Then too, as in Brazil, government officials may become fond of private-sector activity in much of the consumer market because they are thereby relieved of the burden of providing the capital for expansion and do not need to feel compelled to respond to enlarged and contradictory demands. Funding can be turned over to tuition, which customers pay as they go. In that case, adjustments are indeed made by "the market," instead of by government allocation, as consumers and institutions interact and institutions wax and wane. As noted in Japan, the private sector may serve as a shock absorber for govern-

ment as well as for the system.[60] If, with expansion, national funding
does not inflate at the same rate, then higher education as a whole is
somewhat freer of the financial constraints that occur when government attends to high cost. The political temperature is lowered;
the political issue-importance of higher education in government
itself, set primarily by costs, falls. Institutional markets that are
relatively free of governmental controls thus find support in the
everyday interests of politicians and bureaucrats.

Finally, institutional markets are not necessarily and for all time
more squeezed and regulated within large, encompassing state systems. Creeping centralization has been widely observed, but gradual
unobtrusive decentralization also occurs. Students of centralized
political regimes have noted that such regimes are likely to be subjected to a creeping decentralization as the sectors they attempt to
manage increase in size and complexity (for example, the industrial
sector of the economy of the USSR).[61] From a study of public higher
education in California, Neil Smelser generalizes that

> as a system grows and becomes more complex, it becomes
> progressively unmanageable if day-to-day authority con-
> tinues to rest with the central agency; although ultimate
> authority may still continue to reside in that agency, it
> becomes imperative to delegate operative authority to
> lower levels. Often, however, the decentralization lags
> behind the realities of growth.[62]

Rune Premfors noted at the end of the 1970s that decentralization
of operative authority had been considerable during that decade in
Continental systems of higher education as national policies became
increasingly comprehensive and ambitious.[63] The center cannot
hold to the integrated control it might exercise over a smaller,
simpler system. Planned or otherwise, authority slips off to the
operating organizations, restrengthening market forces in the sense
of interaction among enterprises that are semiautonomous in competing for personnel, clientele, financial resources, and prestige.

Such "market creep" has a low threshold for its occurrence in
higher education since tasks are so esoteric and complicated and the
whole enterprise ambiguous. No central group can know enough to
coordinate effectively so many disparate tasks and issues that are
subject to so much local variation. No group at the center has the

tools for tight integrative control, and this becomes apparent by experience if not by forethought. As noted, even a system as small and as planning-minded as Sweden's may turn away from central administration in an effort to strengthen regional and local adaptability.[64] And what is done in Sweden by proclamation is often done in larger and more complex societies by unofficial drift. Everywhere universities and colleges may creep away from the formal controls of systems, leaving coordination to looser linkages and even to market interaction.

Market coordination expresses a bias that is fundamentally different from political and bureaucratic forms. When an activity is transferred from market contexts to state control, it comes under a bias for aggregation.[65] Things are to be added up. The expectation grows within and without the government that someone will deliberately pull things together and otherwise systematize. When an activity stays in the market or creeps away to a more marketlike context, it comes under a bias for disaggregation. Things are not to be added up in one heap, in one place; they are to be left in their piecemeal state. "System" is then an altogether different matter. And officials and academics are not the only ones affected by these fundamentally different biases. For example, student protest is aggregated in nationalized systems. It heads for where the power is, and that is at the national center. Protest leaders are strongly inclined to think of changing a whole formal system. But protest is disaggregated in such a marketlike system as the American, more locally focused and heating up and cooling down in a disconnected fashion. The state system thereby encourages a student class consciousness; the market system restrains it.

* * * *

Markets, then, are increasingly shaped by state-sanctioned authority and policy. Basic is the controlling of competitive interaction by official segmentation of the primary markets. When a national educational system has different types of secondary schools, some of which block entry to higher education and others lead to different sectors or faculties, it has segmented the consumer and institutional markets. When a state master plan allocates students among universities, four-year colleges, and two-year colleges, it has decisively divided the consumer market and heavily shaped the institutional and labor markets. But, in turn, such blueprints are much affected by the traditional position and power of existing segments. Privileged institutions that possess the most desired parts of the markets commonly have sufficient influence to protect at least the core of what they already have. Thus, where there is a high degree of controlled competition, the institutions already sitting astride the market are likely to have more influence than government officials in determining formal agreements. Monopolists and oligopolists exist in the markets of higher education, aided and abetted by the state. The writing of their position into state law is a basic way in which enterprises possessing various degrees of autonomy fuse with state authority in determining the nature of what is normally taken to be a state-dominated system.

Also basic is the extent and nature of state subsidies, since the nature of exchange in consumer, labor, and institutional markets can thereby be decisively shaped. Subsidy by means of grants to individual students strengthens the hands of consumers: it helps more of them to come into the market and to choose among institutions. This method of spending state funds is the antithesis of institutional aid, where monies go directly to institutions in either block or restricted form. Institutional subsidy strengthens the place of institutions in the consumer market, freeing them somewhat from dependence on consumers. The swapping of dependencies, as between state officials and consumers, is involved in the choice between these two basic forms of state finance. Institutions naturally lobby for the one that promises the most resources and scares them least in the threat of loss of control.

State subsidy of markets also occurs in the common practice of basing funds on enrollment. Institutional income is then determined by the number of consumers attracted; any major falling off in attraction will concentrate the attention of the institution on reinvigorating its place in the market—not as much as when students come with grants and tuition payments in hand, but still enough to cause concern about what potential consumers might want. On the other side of the coin, sustained enrollment helps to free institutions from the dictates of government officials. Routinized enrollment-based financing minimizes financial restrictions on autonomy. Strong institutions, secure in their "brand-name" position in the consumer and labor markets, feel secure. Ambitious institutions know they can rise by growing in size. Only the small need to tremble before the officials of the state, fearing any loss of enrollment that would push them below official expectations on minimal size. Thus, interaction between institutions and consumers penetrates deeply into the basic aspects of state authority. Institutions manipulate the state as they maneuver in the consumer market.

INTEREST-GROUP CONTROL

What we have learned about the forms and processes of integration may be extended and placed on a different axis by turning, in summary fashion, to the question of group domination. The idea that politicians set policy, bureaucrats administer, and professors carry out the work is by now long behind us, a myth that was always at great variance with reality. The idea that bureaucrats proceed according to hierarchical dictate has also been put to rest. Instead we see new and old groups of various sorts in complicated interplay. Three patterns summarize much of what now obtains in reality but is underplayed in traditional theory. In pure form, they are a corporatist system, a guilded one, and one governed by a power market.

Corporatism refers to a relation between government and supposedly "outside" organized groups, in which the groups have formal rights to influence governmental decisions. Corporatism was given a bad name by fascism but has spread in democracies since World War II and has begun to acquire such neutral labels as "integrated organizational participation in government."[66] Modern states are inclined to include certain external groups in governmental decision making, with a related exclusion of others. The outside groups are formally organized as associations, unions, councils, and the like, and the government legitimates the organizations as representatives of certain bona fide interests. It comes to be understood in particular that certain economic organizations have the right of representation in national decision making.[67] As Samuel Beer notes: "The welfare state and especially the managed economy of recent decades simply could not operate without the advice and cooperation of the great organized producers' groups of business, labour and agriculture." Beer identifies a "new group politics" in Great Britain as a "system of quasi-corporatism bringing government and producers' groups into intimate and continuous relationship" in framing, applying, and legitimating state policies.[68] This relationship has not yet developed strongly in British higher education, since robust department bureaucrats and academic oligarchs have stood in the way, but one can anticipate gradual increase in its strength.

This phenomenon, however, has been striking in Sweden, where the government has worked long and hard to develop an inclusive democratic corporatism. During the 1970s, the three major Swedish trade union federations and the main organization of Swedish employers came to be strongly represented in the membership of planning and decision-making bodies in higher education at national, regional, and enterprise levels. "Several hundreds of representatives of interest organizations participate in formal decision-making bodies in higher education, from the board of management of the National Board of Universities and Colleges down to councils of admission in local institutions. . . . Simply put, the big interests of capital and labour have stepped in."[69]

Corporatism shades off into ways of relating interest groups to governmental decision making that are less explicit and less systematic in the interpenetration of government and group. In a number of societies (for example, the United States), a muted or partial corporatism is involved in the systematic access of organized lobbies to legislative and executive circles. Such representation is increasingly organized within the outside group itself *and* in its penetration of government. But the crucial matter is whether the outside group has privileged access to the point of reserved seats in decision-making bodies. As long as a board in higher education has no such reservations, but freely invites in or has appointed people who bring certain skills or represent different points of views, then the cooptation struggle tilts toward the board. It is positioned to use others more than it is used by them. But when a board has two members appointed by this manufacturers' association, three from that union, and so on, then the state system becomes a corporatist system in which the outside groups are positioned to coopt "the government." A tilt toward such cooptation occurs in an increasing number of countries as effective representation continues to shift from geographic entities to occupational groups, *and* as such groups find higher education too important for their own interests and ideologies to leave to professors and bureaucrats.

A guild system is one captured by inside professionals, a widespread tendency of which we have taken much note. To some degree, such capture can hardly be escaped anywhere. Professionals en masse are absorbed into the state machinery but in a highly balkanized fashion around specific areas of activity—wheat production, railroad transportation, mental health, space research, timber management, regional development, banking regulation, taxation policy, welfare for the poor, and so on. The number of these professional interests seems unimaginable until one becomes aware of the many agencies and subagencies of modern government and the hundreds and even thousands of professional categories that they involve.[70] The professionals find a community of interests with others of similar identity, at other levels of government and outside of government, and they find it difficult to cooperate with other types of experts in other bureaus. Thus, horizontal integration is difficult to effect—a defensive battle fought by generalists and higher chiefs who are supposed to be in charge—but vertical integration grows naturally along the many professional segments that extend from the top, like stakes, right down into the ground. The phenomenon has become so widespread that we can speak of it as a new general form of representation in government, in which (1) representation is by occupational group, and (2) the group is already inside government.[71]

As state authority expands over education, this form of representation grows. Higher education people, segment by segment and as a whole, penetrate the bureaus that fund them and may control them. When they are successful, their guild has coopted the government. The clearest cases of such cooptation are found in national science agencies that fund research.[72] The cooptation is indexed by the strength of peer review—the collective judgment of a body of experts brought in from the field—compared with bureaucratic judgment and political dictate. Such peer review is widespread throughout the scientific agencies of government in developed societies, a model thus likely to be imitated in less-developed countries as they seek competent judgment. The cooptation is also indicated by the way such agencies are substructured so as to reflect the understructure of the higher education system. For example, the National Science Foundation in the U.S. government is not only permeated with peer review but is so organized internally that its departments reflect the departmental divisions of the natural and social sciences in the American research university.[73] Likewise in similar bodies in the United Kingdom, West Germany, France, Italy, and Japan. In addition, the persons occupying the nominally bureaucratic posts in the agencies are often themselves professionals who have achieved the highest degree in a specialty, who have some scholarly standing in that field, and who even may be serving on short-term rotation from a university position.

As seen in the case of academic oligarchy in Italy, such capture need not be limited to scientific councils. Systems that have extensive state authority typically have extensive "advising" by professors in and around the state apparatus. The advisory bodies tend to accumulate considerable influence—when a minister has to "carry the field," he must first carry the advisory bodies—and are often normalized as a top channel through which requests must pass for approval. Thus, the commonly found body called the "superior council of public instruction," or words to that effect, involves itself in debates on expansion policies, curricular decisions, and key personnel appointments, superintending national competitions and appointing professors to the selection committees or arranging for them to be elected by their peers.

Thus, state systems may be as much guilded as bureaucratized or politicized: only awareness of what goes on behind the bureaucratic mask will tell us *how* much in a given case. Two points are certain. To the extent that the state system is guilded, its apparatus will be so organized that aggressive planning and direction will be practically impossible.[74] And in guilded systems, the dominating interests of educational and scientific elites will readily be portrayed as representing "the public interest." The professional constituency will be dressed in the clothes of government, even vested by law. Naked self-interest thereby does not need to appear in public.

Finally, but far from least important, is the play of power through the halls of central administrative agencies. Cadres of officials tend to develop prerogatives in their own specific bureaus and offices but then must fit themselves into larger administrative domains by respecting one another's monopolies, or by competing for jurisdiction and funding, or some of each. Bureau isolation and competition have widely been noted within ministries of education, and between the ministries and other departments involved in education.

Mexico offers a case that is again fascinating, since a political regime labeled "authoritarian" by political scientists supposedly would have the will and the muscle to pull things together. Yet observers have noted that lateral cooperation between departments within the huge Mexican Ministry of Education is extremely difficult: "All departments work totally independently one from the other and take no interest in what others are doing. . . . The Ministry is an archaic structure which can be described as a series of independent empires, each inviolable, with long traditions and rights that no minister is going to be able to alter."[75] Research on higher education in Thailand has noted extensive bureau isolation and competition, with different universities and colleges belonging to different central agencies.[76]

> Even now [1979], although universities have more independence, the ruling bureaucrats establish the general policies of the universities, directly appoint the highest university officials, and review all faculty appointments. . . . The struggle over university control occurs primarily within the bureaucracy, reflecting several decades of conflict between military and civilian factions.[77]

The Thai case is an extreme example of the tendency for state patronage of higher education to become bureau patronage of segments of the system. As is common in Latin America, for example, vocational training is typically handled by the ministry of labor or a bureau other than the ministry of education.[78]

In highly developed societies, the more modernized structures of governmental supervision of higher education hardly exhibit a lower degree of bureau balkanization, protectionism, and competition. In Australia, historically, in each state except New South Wales, "a single university [has] related directly to its state government, while teachers colleges, institutes of technology, technical colleges, agricultural colleges and similar institutions generally came under the direct control of a particular state government department."[79] In Great Britain, France, and Sweden, "departmental compartmentalization" in higher education is "a hindrance to comprehensive planning."[80] Research on planning in advanced nations generally has found that planning must be reconceptualized to refer to bargaining and negotiation, within and without government, necessitating an analytical vocabulary of "negotiated planning" and "planned bargaining." "Planning's problem is that it can only deal manageably with concentrated sectors": the academic system is distinctly not that.[81]

Thus, higher education is subjected to what may be called power markets, markets composed of units struggling against one another within the broad frameworks of state authority. This, too, is a form of coordination. In a classic essay, Norton E. Long points to "competition between governmental power centers" as a—perhaps *the*—most effective instrument of coordination in complex government. He notes:

> The position of administrative organizations is not unlike the position of particular firms. Just as the decisions of the firms could be coordinated by the imposition of a planned economy so could those of the component parts of the government. But just as it is possible to operate a formally unplanned economy by the loose coordination of the market, in the same fashion it is possible to operate a government by the loose coordination of the play of political forces through its institutions.[82]

Recent work in political economy has richly portrayed the division of state authority among a plurality of officials and offices. Interdependence among these authorities requires mutual adjustment among them—witness the hundreds of interagency coordinating committees in the British and U.S. governments—and that adjustment carries much of the load of coordination. As reciprocal obligations develop, mutual control among officials becomes as intricate as officials' control over the population. In sum, "large-scale politico-economic organization is possible either through unilateral coordination in hierarchy-bureaucracy or through mutual adjustment among authorities who practice an extended use of their authority in order to control each other."[83]

Such reasoning applies strongly to administrative pyramids in academic systems that typically have no definitive apex but instead have, at the top, a variety of boards, bureaus, commissions, and committees; that are loaded with diverse experts possessing arcane knowledge and authority rooted in their expertise; and that must serve as frameworks committed to encompassing a good share of the increasing body of specialized knowledge, skill, and lore of modern society. There remains little wonder that we know so little about how the actions of persons and organizations in higher education are concerted when we look only to formal plan and hierarchy. Beyond the concerting actions of the professional oligarchy and the many exchanges of the consumer, labor, and institutional markets, there is the struggle and adjustment of officials within the state apparatus itself. Bureaucrats are partisans; they are themselves interest groups. Their interest-driven efforts become a form of organization and coordination, one in which they provide linkage not through command and enforced cooperation but by competing for resources and reputation and adjusting to one another's authority.

THE LIMITS OF STATE CONTROL

The primary characteristics of higher education systems amount to a veritable catalog of reasons why they stubbornly resist state control. It is not simply a matter of individual scholars believing in freedom of research and teaching. Such beliefs are potent, but if they were the only source of resistance, they could readily be overcome by those who would seek to command from the top. Instead, the sources are multiple and firmly rooted. The expansion in the scope of the university in the nineteenth and twentieth centuries has brought with it an increased complexity of curricula that in itself has served to limit intervention. The arcane knowledge of the basic units is difficult for higher-ups to penetrate. The wide range of those units makes the curriculum a thicket for generalists and amateurs who would plough through it simply and authoritatively. The guild mentality spreads, with each esoteric cluster oriented to self-control. The segmenting of such groups leads to a related compartmentalization at the top. Even such ostensibly unified and neat coordinating devices as the British University Grants Committee become a maze of subject subcommittees in actual operation. To take a look at physics at York, you had better send some physicists.

Thus, the bottom-centeredness of academic systems does not relent in systematic resistance to top-down surveillance and control. Even as the formal devices of managerial control become more powerful tools, it does not become easier for "the state." To the contrary, it becomes only more difficult. And as complexity increases, the price of centralized control goes up.

Some of the limits of state control can be explored by surveying several successively more severe attempts to exert state control: centralized systems in Western democracies; centralized systems in Latin American authoritarian regimes; centralized systems in Communist societies; and the German universities under Nazism. As indicated earlier, centralized systems in Western Europe, such as those in France, Italy, and Sweden, have been increasingly prompted to devolve authority and administration to regional and institutional levels as they have grown larger and more complex. The national center, objectively and subjectively, becomes overloaded and/or too remote as the system widens and deepens. Observers in such countries increasingly claim an inverse correlation between centralization and "innovative capacity."[84] Of course, any significant degree of loosening of central state control is difficult to effect: those favored by central control do not readily give it up. But the sentiment grows that the limits have been reached.

The experience of academic systems under authoritarian regimes in Latin America is also instructive. Here the cases vary from mild or benign authoritarian control to heavy-handed and even brutal repression. In the mild case of Mexico, the relation is one of negotiation and routinized allocation rather than command. The university has power and the state must bargain with it. When the state moves arbitrarily and even with military force, as in the 1968–1970 repression of student protest, a heavy price is paid, right down to destabilization of the entire political system.[85] In the heavy-handed cases of Argentina and Chile, regime repression has led to a demoralization of the academic system, including a severe migration of talent.[86] Here the limits of state control are clear: a heavy price in a lowering of competence in science, scholarship, and professional preparation.

In the case of the USSR, policies of control of the post-1917 Communist regime have vacillated between the wish for strict political control and the need to accommodate to the nature of science and scholarship. Loren R. Graham has shown that the successful effort of the party and the regime to gain control of the Soviet Academy of Sciences under the first five-year plan (1927–1932) caused Soviet natural science to suffer "genuine and serious damage," with effects in the social sciences and such fields as history and philosophy bordering on the calamitous. But the effects were selective. The state was also attempting to improve the material conditions of science, laying the groundwork for later major expansion. Strangling political control was opposed by invigorating material assistance, and the scientific and scholarly establishment was resilient: "it grows around its wounds, seeks other paths to its goals, and continues its development as long as it can find minimum sustenance."[87] The underlying dynamics of knowledge organization are difficult for the state to contain.

In the Communist societies of Eastern Europe, regimes have learned the hard way about the self-defeating effects of strict top-down control. One example is precise manpower planning, in which universities are told by central state officials how many students they can admit, field by field, on the basis of projected manpower needs—fifty-seven pharmacists, etc.[88] The boomerang effects are then considerable, as the interests of students and professors are narrowly constrained within the academy and in the later employment and reemployment of graduates. Occupational straitjackets do not accommodate changes in occupations and individual preferences. These systems have also seen their academic staffs demoralized and demotivated, as well as undergo a serious loss of talent, when political criteria have been used to crack down sharply on dissidents. How far can the system go in emphasizing loyalty and political dependability before valuable competence is lost? The success of such regimes in the medium and long run depends on the productivity of the nation as compared with sister nations in the same bloc as well as with "capitalist" powers only a few kilometers to the west.

Finally, there is the extreme case of German universities under Nazism, where repression was hard and sustained. In retrospect, several outcomes stand out. The loss of talent was extensive, as scholars and scientists were forced out of the university on political grounds and many fled the country. Then, too, when political groups took over segments of the university, such as the student associations, they soon had empty structures on their hands.[89] Students in general and good students in particular found the compulsory political classes and meetings so boring and sterile in intellectual content that they withdrew their energies, sinking into passivity or exiting to other places and pursuits whenever possible. The segments most under control became the least attractive for students and faculty alike.

Many segments, however, were not effectively captured: they remained considerably in the hands of academics trying to use normal apolitical criteria of judgment.[90] Science, engineering, medicine, economics, and certain other fields of study were needed to galvanize the kind of state and nation that the leadership of the Third Reich wanted. Conditions of high productivity had to be allowed for: some science faculties had to be given significant resources and some leeway to pursue research and training based on their autonomous expertise. Professors also learned to turn in, even more than usual, on their own disciplinary clusters, in effect hardening the operating structure and making it even more difficult for political criteria to be decisive across the board. As Arye Carmon notes, the regime "had the power to vulgarize the University, but it was not powerful enough to generate a complete transformation of the devotion to *Wissenschaft*. Small pockets of academic integrity survived under the surface, while on the surface, ideology and mediocrity prevailed."[91]

Overall, the German university system under the Nazi regime was extensively reshaped. But the ultimate high price paid by the state came from the surviving value of the many segments of the system, as determined by competitive development in other countries. The crucial outcome was the fate of German nuclear science as emigré scientists took their talent to Britain and the United States; others who remained behind silently refused to develop further what they already knew; and, crucially, state officials and the scientists dealt with one another in ways that in effect sabotaged a maximum joint effort, with nothing approaching the effectiveness of the American Manhattan Project.[92] In the development of nuclear fission, German science, centered in the universities, was ahead as late as the mid-1930s, and on a par with the Allied effort as late as 1942. After that, it fell behind. As David Irving summarizes:

If one compares the parallel courses of German and Allied atomic research after the parting of the ways in 1939, it is clear that for both parties the turning point had come in 1942. Up to then, both sides had covered much the same ground. . . . After the middle of 1942, Germany virtually marked time until the end of the war, gaining in those three years knowledge that could have been won in as many months had the will been there. . . . Germany's nuclear scientists failed to win the confidence of their government; and were left stranded on the shores of the atomic age.[93]

The costs of strict state control and governmental mismanagement under the Nazi regime include the substantial probability that Germany thereby lost the opportunity to be the first nation to develop the ultimate weapon.

SIX

CHANGE

A leading American educational statesman of the 1960s and 1970s, Father Theodore M. Hesburgh, has remarked that "the university is among the most traditional of all the institutions of our society and, at the same time, it is the institution most responsible for the changes that make our society the most changing in the history of man."[1] How can it be that the university, and indeed the higher education system at large, is sluggish, even heavily resistant to change, but somehow also produces virtually revolutionary change? The contradiction may be nominal, born of the words used, but there is a good case that it is real. There is so much observable inertia that we need a theory of nonchange. But there is also so much change in higher education itself, and change generated by it for the rest of society, that we need a systematic approach to change. At least we should solve the "Hesburgh paradox," and go beyond, since there is much more that is contradictory about academic change.

Systematic approaches are hardly at hand: change remains the most recalcitrant subject in the social sciences. The term itself is variously used, referring to alterations that vary from simple reproduction to radical transformation. Those who search for the causes of specific changes in different institutions soon bog down in the complexities of history, perplexed by conditions and trends that converge and separate in seemingly accidental, unpredictable ways. The search hardly becomes simpler when we turn to academic forms, since there, as we have seen, the encompassing systems are particularly complex and ambiguous. But while analyzing patterns of work, belief, authority, and integration, we identified a number of basic directions of change, e.g., the proliferating of academic disciplines, the adding of levels of student passage, the strengthening of state authority. The task remains to place these and other changes in a framework that will order our understanding.

It helps in the beginning to keep in mind the difference between the emergence of an educational system as a major form of change and the alteration of a system once it is in place.[2] While separating from other segments of society (family, church, community) to become a distinct sector, an educational system must be heavily a product of its environment. It accumulates interior segments from those existing already in, say, the church, and sometimes it has much structure laid down upon it for coordination by exterior bodies. At the outset, it has little structure and culture of its own to guide interaction and change. But as a system develops, it builds its own sources of continuity and change. It grows larger and becomes more complex; it acquires structures of work, belief, and authority. Budgets become entrenched, personnel fixed in categories, costly physical plants turned into sunk costs. Institutions and subsectors become rooted, powerful interests with their own traditions and rationales. The system becomes deeply institutionalized, we say, which means in effect that constraints upon change and imperatives for change are increasingly located in the system. Sectoral hegemony develops: inside bureaucrats and professionals have heavy influence; outsiders have trouble in grasping the levers of control. The mature social system compared to the emerging one is like the adult compared to the newborn or young child: it has greater stability of character and hence of response; it is much less dependent than when recently emerged from the womb (of society).

Thus, developed systems will be full of constraints upon change. In their systematic study of the British system of higher education, Tony Becher and Maurice Kogan conclude that

> many changes, including those generated from within, fail because they are unable to accommodate to existing structural constraints. Academic structures and regulations for the most part evolve to protect the legitimate interests of researchers and teachers. They help to define, and also defend, the main areas of professional concern within an institution. But once established, they can prove surprisingly intractable.

The conservatism of higher education is contextual. "The main constraints on change are social, not psychological: they depend more on the way the system operates than on the particular stand that its individual members choose to take."[3] Similarly from American research, after intensive analysis of a major reform effort at the Buffalo campus of the State University of New York, and extensive review of the literature on innovation, Arthur Levine points to "the centrality of organizational facts of life in shaping change."[4]

Yet, in the face of all the barriers to innovation, academic enterprises and systems can themselves be surprisingly adaptive. Mature academic systems may be like many old organizations. As observed astutely by Herbert Kaufman, old organizations "must either have been created with a very successful adaptive mechanism or have acquired one" to have gotten past all the dangers from environmental changes along the way, and still maintain a continuous identity through generation after generation.[5] Old organizations have at least proven their capacity not to go gently into institutional eclipse. As put succinctly by Anthony Downs: "The older a bureau is, the less likely it is to die."[6] Arteries may harden and niches may solidify, but it is also possible that mature academic systems know something about adaptation and evolution that new enterprises and systems must learn.

Basic to the analysis of academic change, then, is the simple principle that existing structures have response sets that shape what follows. As put by Margaret Archer, "once a given form of education exists it exerts an influence on future educational change."[7] Hence, analysis of change can begin with the forms that are in place at a given time and then search for the difference those forms make in the period that follows. We put change in context when we concentrate on the immediate structural setting. The forms of that setting embody the momentum set by historical evolution. The forms allow us to predict future behavior of the system from present-day tendencies—similar to the prediction of individual behavior from established personality or character. Structural predisposition not only tells us about systematic resistance to change but also about imperatives for change, since social systems, more than individuals, contain complex interactions that lead on to altered states. We need to know how change is conditioned by "the way the system operates."

The value of this approach is shown by the weakness of the hypothesis about academic change that was paramount in international thought in the late 1960s and the 1970s: that European systems of higher education would follow the evolution of the American system. Concentrating on the environment of higher education, analysts saw the systems as inevitably pushed in the same direction, converging as they all slid down the same evolutionary path from elite to mass to universal. All systems were seen as subject to the same set of trends and demands: democratization, rapid economic growth, expanding knowledge, increased political management of education. "There is almost certainly going to be a continued popular demand for an increase in the number of places in colleges and universities"; "there is the pull of the economy, marked particularly by the continued growth of the tertiary or service sector of the society"; and so on, through other forces in common and trends "that we can reasonably expect to continue for the rest of the century."[8] The external trends were in the saddle, since "the dynamic processes of growth that had been set off in Western Europe during the 50's and 60's would have a life of their own, and would exert an autonomous pressure on those societies for a continued expansion of their systems of higher education." Inexorably, the European nations would make "the institutional changes that such an expansion required."[9]

But the various national systems were not about to converge to the degree predicted. As Martin A. Trow later commented on his earlier prediction: "My analysis of the movement of European systems toward an American-style system of mass higher education [was] simply wrong in the light of what has happened since 1973."[10] Analysts had overplayed demand and underplayed response. One lesson of the 1970s was that the existing forms and beliefs of secondary and higher education determined considerably whether systems stopped expanding at ten to twenty-five percent of the age group or relentlessly continued on to forty to fifty percent or more. The capacity as well as the willingness to keep expanding varied greatly in sectors and in each national system as a whole. In effect, the "supply" side, consisting of institutions and their responses, heavily determined what trends and demands would be effective. The existing systems of France, West Germany, Italy, and other countries shape demands differently, and thus clearly need not respond the same way as the United States to seemingly common demands. As Roger Geiger has judged the Belgian case: "The enrollment stagnation that suddenly struck Belgian universities was not an avoidable accident, but rather an inherent consequence of their nature and their recent history. . . . The maintenance of rigorous academic standards . . . has had the effect of limiting university study to a relatively small portion of the population"—about ten percent in the mid-1970s—a share that seemed "to represent a kind of natural limit of the system as it is presently constituted."[11] The limits come not from a genetic pool of talent but from the organized subsystem and its related beliefs. It is the immediate institutional conditioning of action and reaction upon which we need to focus.

The analyses that follow focus on the structures identified in previous chapters with the purpose of summarizing how they systematically condition change. A second section then views change from the standpoint of tension between order and disorder, pulling out of the earlier analyses four dimensions along which order and disorder contradict one another in academic systems. Since the primary flow of change is toward complexity, a third discussion moves to a theoretical explanation of why differentiation is a fundamental process in modern academic systems. The sociological perspective developed here permits us to grapple anew with issues of power and economy. A fourth section switches to an intersystem perspective in order that we might consider the transference of academic forms and beliefs from one country to another. International transfer is a major route of change that should not be overlooked, even if little research on the matter has been done thus far. Our discussion concludes on the note that change in systems organized around bundles of knowledge and their carrying groups will remain uncommonly disjointed, incremental, and even invisible, despite the imposition by modern governments of vast superstructures of control.

STRUCTURAL PREDISPOSITION AND ADAPTIVE CAPACITY

The fundamental adaptive mechanism of universities and larger academic systems is the capacity to add and subtract fields of knowledge and related units without disturbing all the others. As we have frequently noted, scholars in one set of disciplines hardly need to care when, in another part of the system, other scholars are revamping or giving birth to other disciplines. For example, who has to pay any attention at all in literature or sociology to the emergence of biochemistry? Some biologists and chemists have to care, even be involved in an interest-group struggle. But such struggles are localized; the interests of most groups are not involved. With a variety of semiautonomous cells and cadres, one part can also deteriorate without affecting all the rest. Units can independently prosper or burn out, survive or die—with the latter usually coming about by slow attenuation over a long period of time, turning a once-vibrant organism into a mere shell of its former self. Adaptability, in short, lies first in the internal variety of amalgamated, conglomerate organization. It is the peculiar internal constitutions of universities that allow them, in Durkheim's phrase, to "bend and adapt themselves to a whole variety of circumstances and environments," thus producing diversity among universities ("in no one place [are they] identical with what [they are] in any other") and, at the same time, to maintain an appearance of similarity that allows us to recognize them "in all the guises which [they] take."[12]

But the capacity to "bend and adapt" is clearly aided or restricted by the specific forms institutionalized in national systems. Some forms favor adaptation to the requirements of expanding knowledge, for example; others resist it. Some forms are thereby successful in negotiating change, and therefore are likely to continue through it. Others are not successful but instead become cases of *form failure*, thereby stimulating efforts to discontinue them and develop alternatives. We need to turn to key structural features and note their particular ways of influencing change.

WORK STRUCTURE

Chapter 2 compared national arrangements of work according to horizontal and vertical differentiation within and among enterprises. What differences do the various kinds of sections and tiers, sectors and hierarchies, make in constraining and facilitating change? What changes are occurring in these structures themselves?

Section Effects and Changes. In determining change, it matters significantly whether a country has a chair or department structure at the operating level. The adaptive capacity of the chair structure is restrained by the capacity and inclination of a single chief, providing a narrow base for comprehending and managing a modern discipline. As chairs multiply to accommodate more bundles of knowledge and larger clienteles, they also fragment and balkanize disciplines as well as faculties and universities. A common characteristic of chair systems undergoing expansion in modern times is that the chairs become too burdened, responsible for more programs, assistants, and students than a single person can supervise effectively. Overload is the operational dynamic that undermines the legitimacy of the chair and gives increasing credibility to the argument that chair power is dysfunctional as well as undemocratic.[13]

Because of such failure of form, an evolution from chair to department organization has been taking place during the 1960s and 1970s in Continental systems.[14] The Swedish system, while retaining chairs, strengthened its departmental organization and has attempted to manipulate task assignments by altering the purposes and domains of the departments.[15] The French system, following the 1968 crisis, has sought to group academic personnel, senior and junior alike, in new units of teaching and research (*unités d'enseignement et de recherche—UERs*) that would replace or sometimes simply rename the traditional faculties; these could contain departments or also serve as departments that would replace chairs.[16] Much movement away from chairs has occurred in Latin American nations (e.g., Brazil), in old institutions and sectors and especially in newly created ones.

The system in the German Democratic Republic (East Germany) went through wholesale top-down reform in the 1960s that, in the universities, replaced a large number of chairs and institutes with a fewer number of departments:

> The traditional German subdivision of the university into a handful of Faculties (e.g., Philology, Mathematics and Natural Sciences, Medicine, Law and Economics, Theology) was reshaped into more manageable units known as *Sektionen* comparable to the departments of British and American universities. The innumerable institutes, built around a professional chairholder and often unhealthy centers of patronage and sycophancy, were abolished and likely merged into departments. In round numbers, some 190 departments [in the entire national system] took the place of 960 institutes. Berlin's

Humboldt University, for example, now has 26 departments where formerly it comprised 169 institutes and 7
faculty.[17]

This was no minor change:

> The introduction of the *Sektion* was the most radical
> reform to take place in any of the Eastern European
> systems of higher education. It was also one of the most
> successful, and attempts to imitate the East German
> innovation have been detectable in the universities of
> other Socialist countries.[18]

As a general form, the department has not been under such
pressure. It has been assaulted mainly by general-education or
liberal-education proponents, chiefly in the United States, who see it
as a narrow base for such programs.[19] The department is clearly
weak in this respect. College organization, as typified at Oxford and
Cambridge, is more successful in the support of undergraduate
education that, formally and informally, becomes something more
than disciplinary specialization. Also, the department alone cannot
handle the increasing complexity of academic specialties, and without much fanfare it is increasingly supplemented in advanced systems. We noted earlier that there is much matrix structure in
modern universities, with professors and students participating in
area-study centers or problem-focused institutes or undergraduate
residential colleges as well as departments. One can even observe
"triple-matrix" arrangements: for example, a professor serving
simultaneously in a history department, a Far Eastern center, and a
comparative research group focused on science or education or
some other societal sector that cuts across departmental interests
and geographical-area clusters.

Everywhere the sections of universities expand in number. Departments, institutes, and chairs multiply to keep up with the larger
scale of operations as well as the increased specialization of knowledge. The countertrend of promoting interdisciplinary programs
and problem-centered units ironically also produces additional
units of specialized commitment, e.g., a child-study center or an
energy research group. Thus, the horizontal base of universities
and higher education systems becomes wider with every passing

decade. Departments may soak up the parochialisms of chairs and provide more suitable coverage of disciplines, but the proliferation of departments and counterpart units fragments the base of the university to an ever greater degree. As institutions and systems grapple with this problem, usually in an incoherent fashion, two responses are common: to increase the administrative capacity of the university or college to coordinate itself, with more oversight and formal linkage; and to elaborate levels of education, the lower of which may offer broader programs that bridge specialties. This brings us to tiers.

Tier Effects and Changes. As developed in chapter 2, the characteristic form of academic system around the world has provided essentially one organizational tier devoted to work of the first professional or academic degree, with more advanced work consisting of students staying on with a professor to do research and write papers and dissertations. In contrast, the U.S. model evolved a vertical differentiation in which a second major tier of professional schools and a graduate school in the arts and sciences sits on top of the undergraduate college.

The U.S. model has proven that it has adaptive capacity. The second tier provides for new interests that bypass the interests long rooted in the first. The old-time professor—Mr. Chips in the extreme—could still retain the student for up to four undergraduate years, time enough to provide an education defined as general or liberal and still guarantee such academics a clientele, a curriculum, and an enduring domain of jobs. The new professional training, and advanced research, did not directly intrude upon and compete for this time and space. Instead, operating somewhat in a world of its own, it became particularly responsive to emerging professions and would-be professions. Indeed, as put by Robert H. Wiebe, an American historian, the U.S. universities did not simply respond to emerging professions but helped to initiate them:

> The universities played a crucial role in almost all of these professional movements. *Since the emergence of the modern graduate school in the seventies* [1870s], the best universities had been serving as outposts of professional self-consciousness, frankly preparing young men for professions that as yet did not exist. By 1900 they held an unques-

tioned power to legitimize, for no new profession felt complete—or scientific—without its distinct academic curriculum; they provided centers for philosophizing and propagandizing; and they inculcated apprentices with the proper values and goals. Considering the potential of the universities for frustration, it was extremely important that higher education permissively, even indiscriminately, welcomed each of the new groups in turn [emphasis added].[20]

There was something about the second tier in the American structure that caused it to expand, "permissively, even indiscriminately," to include an unusually wide range of professions and specialized fields, overcoming "the potential of the universities for frustration." Four interlocking sources of permissive expansion are evident. The first is the clear organizational separation itself, which cut loose those devoted to specialized professional training from the power of those, long entrenched, whose commitment was to general or more elementary preparation. Professionalization was given a distinctive home, one juxtaposed against the values of the first tier, the level of college education. The second cause is found in the administrative tools provided. Administrative positions were created, the dean of the graduate school and the deans of the professional schools, that were committed to the building of this level and its major parts. Third, the graduate tier provided special protection for research and research-minded faculty members. The research imperative rules this roost, in contradistinction to the teaching imperative in the first tier. The test is that as soon as the second level is eliminated, as in the American four-year or two-year college, the rewards for teaching heavily dominate. Where the American system has managed to couple research and teaching, it has done so by formally separating two tiers but then linking them together by having departments and their faculty members simultaneously serve each. The institutional bills have been paid largely by income, public or private, generated by the teaching function of the first level, income that then has helped to subsidize those professors who, best at research, manage to tilt their work load toward light involvement in the first tier and heavy involvement in the second.

Fourth, these intrainstitutional sources of dynamic and permis-

sive expansion at advanced levels of training are set within the
interinstitutional characteristic of competition. Institutions have
been free to interact individually with the "demands" of the labor
market, starting up a law school or a school of business or a school of
architecture whenever it appeared viable. If Ivy League universities
were stuffy about granting their approval to occupations less noble
than the top half-dozen professions, other universities were not.
There were always some universities and colleges that were formally
free of those who would exercise the potential for frustration. Thus,
a university might react sympathetically to even the claims of real-
tors and give them a foothold in the evening division for training in
"the real estate profession," as well as respond more fully with
regular professional schools to the claims of such semiprofessions as
engineering, education, librarianship, nursing, and social work.
The dynamic of institutional aggrandizement in an open and competitive arrangement of institutions, a topic to which we will return,
became a basic source of the expansionist tendency in advanced
training.

In contrast, the British system, more undergraduate-centered,
has had more difficulty in supporting advanced work. Becher and
Kogan note that

> postgraduates are another group who, although they
> apparently enjoy at least the limited participatory rights
> of students, are marginal to the enterprise in much the
> way that we have observed full-time contract researchers
> to be. . . . The institutional provision for doctoral stu-
> dents is much more limited than that for undergrad-
> uates. . . . This state of affairs is a relic.[21]

In the broad spectrum of national systems, the British and American are, in many characteristics, close to one another. But they differ
significantly in tier structure, with the British emphasis on the first
degree, and not the Ph.D., reflected in weaker organizational support for the latter.

Because multiple levels provide a more flexible and adaptive
structure for varied tasks and changing demands than does a single
one, we can predict increased pressure in national systems to differentiate as many as four and five levels marked by degrees. The

American system already has four: the two-year Associate in Arts degree, available primarily in community or junior colleges; the four-year Bachelor's degree, available in both colleges and universities; the five- and six-year Master's degree; and the eight- to ten-year Ph.D. degree, and the six- to eight-year professional degrees, available in universities primarily. Postdoctoral training constitutes an emerging fifth level, already institutionalized in biology and some of the other scientific fields. As a single tier buckles under the burdens of expansion, systems innovate with first, second, and third "cycles," as in France, or new national testing devices, as in West Germany, or various other ways of establishing new hierarchies of sequence and selection in order to cope with the tensions of mass entry and selective training, general and specialized education, and teaching and research. More program levels are created, with attached degrees, and, however reluctantly, separate organizational levels are created to underpin those programs and degrees. For example, during the 1970s, the Japanese system sought to create more graduate schools, and the rapidly expanding system of Brazil has built an important graduate level.

Helping to stimulate the development of tiers is the growth and proliferation of sections specified earlier. A more general first tier offers some integration within and across disciplines. In the French reform, the first cycle attempts a more general approach to a discipline or profession, an introductory bridging of subspecialties that offers some possibility of an integrated foundation for later specialization. In short, the expansion of tiers permits not only more specialization but also some consolidation of subjects within sections and among them, thus serving as a partial counterforce to the separation of academic specialties. Tier expansion provides more organizational space.

Sector Effects and Changes. The principle that diversified structures facilitate change applies even more strongly to the division of labor among institutions. Chapter 2 described how national systems vary from one institutional type under single state authority to many types under market conditions. The multiple-type systems on the whole have been more adaptable, and the direction of change is away from homogeneity. As those in the Italian system have been painfully finding out, the nationalized public university alone cannot zig and zag in all the many directions called for by increasing heterogeneity of function. It does not adapt well to new types of students, new connections to labor markets, or new academic fields, especially when they appear to be of lower status; tradition is institutionalized in ways that rigidify the entire system; the single form, the university, becomes overloaded and risks a loss of concentration of resources and attention upon its traditional activities. Everyone then feels caught in a difficult situation, leading to a sense of continuing crisis. Some groups then develop an interest in new forms, or at least new units that bypass the old units. If they are stymied from adding new enterprises and new sectors, they try to add a department here and an institute there, under municipal sponsorship or private support, especially as the rigidity of the old nationalized system weakens its capacity to prevent such initiatives from taking place. Structurally simplified systems lose legitimacy through repeated failures of response.

Separation of sectors is a critical persistent issue. The search for fair shares on the part of institutions and their staffs, and for equality of treatment and outcomes for students, pushes systems away from binary, tripartite, and other multiple-sector arrangements. Thus, national systems still actively seek a way to *de*differentiate. The label of "university" is generously passed around, as in many American states. New definitions tell the public there is going to be only one type of institution, the comprehensive university, with everything made a part of it, as in the Federal Republic of Germany and in Sweden. Then the all-embracing unit must be exceedingly diverse internally, acting as a holding company that blesses everything with a single name and allows fundamentally different enterprises within it to have different clienteles and different types of faculty, even to serve different levels of higher education and to give different types of degrees.

The modern comprehensive university in some countries represents an effort to have it both ways, to allow for differentiation of major parts and, at the same time, assign a formal equality that hopefully will keep down invidious distinctions. But this form appears unstable, especially in large systems, as the more prestigious parts resist the lumping together of everyone and as attentive publics as well as insiders perceive real differences and attach different values to the parts. Thus, the German effort in the 1970s to develop completely new comprehensive universities and fashion ones that bring together technological schools with old universities has not been well received by university professors, whose resistance alone appears capable of stalling or severely attenuating the development of this form. Explicit sectors thus seem to be the chief answer to the macro organization of an evermore extended division of academic labor. The crucial process of change from implicit to explicit is the legitimation of roles for different types of institutions, a topic to which we return in due course.

Hierarchy Effects and Changes.   Institutional hierarchy, we established earlier, ranges from dominance by one or two universities, or a relatively small elite sector, to modestly steep but open institutional ranking, to little or no difference in prestige. Forms of hierarchy have great persistence. The peak of the French, Japanese, and British systems has exhibited great capacity to maintain its standing and dominance, to the dismay of reformers in general and egalitarian-minded ones in particular. The somewhat less steep and more open hierarchy of the U.S. system also sustains itself, never moving significantly toward the "peakness" of the three systems described above or substantially toward a general parity of esteem. Research universities remain the dominant sector. Within that sector (and each of the other sectors), some institutional mobility is noticeable: e.g., Stanford University and the University of California, Los Angeles (UCLA), moved upward in the status hierarchy in the three decades between 1950 and 1980. But individual position is typically stubborn, with strength begetting strength and weakness a vicious circle, over the long as well as the short run. And the formal institutional equality characteristic of the university component of the German system and all of the Italian one also persists, without any rapid movement toward greater hierarchy.

The most hierarchical systems continue to serve relatively well in selecting and training talented people for public administration, their grand historical contribution. But against growing claims for equality and fair treatment they appear to many as examples of failure of form, not sufficiently adaptive, and hence face mounting pressure to change. Clienteles are joined by "have-not" sectors and second-best institutions in pressing for more equitable shares and

less invidious distinctions. Increasing numbers of British universities become so good in certain educational programs or research
fields that they become attractive alternatives to Oxford and Cambridge for students and faculty alike. The polytechnic sector struggles hard for parity with the university sector, with some favorable
results in such crucial matters as faculty salaries, teaching loads, and
the right to do research. Leading private universities in Japan have
become known increasingly for their quality, almost overlapping in
prestige rankings with the public universities. Even in France, the
small and narrow peak comes under increasing criticism. The move
into more accessible higher education erodes the legitimacy of such
a high degree of concentration.

The other two forms of modest and low hierarchy are also under
pressure to change in character. The middle ground of hierarchy
characteristic of the United States is also challenged on grounds of
privilege, since it correlates with social class and racial differences in
access, contains large differences in financial support per student or
faculty member, and exhibits important differences in job placement and life chances. A relatively flat hierarchy such as the Italian
structure is challenged by *its* deficiencies: an inability to differentiate
and support "nonuniversity" forms of education and training; the
lack of institutional focus for the selection and training of competent
civil servants. Minimal differentiation means that centers of excellence are in short supply.

In short, forms of hierarchy persist, but each comes under pressure to evolve as changing definitions of interest in higher education
point to defects. We shall return to the issue of hierarchy in chapter
7, since it is made problematic everywhere by the contradicting
values brought to bear on modern higher education, placing the
question of sectors and their respective statuses in the forefront of
policy deliberations.

*   *   *   *

In general, across sections, tiers, sectors, and hierarchies, simple
arrangements constrain spontaneous change whereas complicated
arrangements facilitate it. As they face increased complexity,

national systems will tend to move toward variety along some combination of two or three or all four of these dimensions.

As explored in chapter 3, various bodies of belief are closely intertwined with the work structures of academic systems. Hence, ideational constraint and facilitation are involved in the effects of those structures. More generally, the symbolic side of academic organization guides change by (1) defining the legitimacy of knowledge contents, hence the claims of new fields of teaching, research, and service, and (2) defining the legitimacy of position, that is, how changes will affect the interests of established groups.

What is acceptable change in the sense of decent and appropriate activities for academics? Disciplinary cultures help define the acceptable; as reviewed earlier, computer science more readily makes its way than ethnic studies because it is more accepted by bordering established fields. Enterprise doctrines may define the acceptable quite narrowly, as in an intensely religious college of a Protestant sect or a "university" specializing in one or two fields; or broadly, as in the modern comprehensive university that has trouble knowing where to stop. The profession as a whole has its own definitions of academic work, typically frowning upon changes sought or enacted by state officials that restrict academic freedom. Traditions of the entire system in regard to access and graduate employment powerfully affect what can and will be altered. Notably, each of the major sources of belief goes on elaborating doctrines that seem appropriate to evolving work commitments. For example, an emerging discipline strives to create a new common vocabulary for its members that helps define the field and set it off from others.

Beyond such definitions lie the interpretations of academic groups of how specific changes will affect them. In terms of the decency of the subject, it may be legitimate to form an American Studies department in an American university. But the sociology and history departments may see the matter otherwise and readily interpret the move as one that will injure them by drawing students away and by reducing their claim on faculty positions. Subgroups within a discipline battle vigorously for control of resources to the extent each believes that, with its group ideology, it possesses the best perspective. True believers help a new perspective gain a niche in settings where those of other persuasions would shut it out. Thus, in sum, academic groups perceive changes and respond to them as guided by their definitions of what is legitimate activity and their sense of how their own work, identity, and tradition will be affected.

The beliefs of established academic groups operate in a similar fashion in filtering external changes and demands. As highlighted in chapter 3, there is no simple stimulus-response between such external changes as population expansion or economic growth and adjustments in higher education. Beliefs, fixed or changing, intervene to define what the external flows mean, and should mean, for the functioning of the many parts of the system. The belief, deeply institutionalized in the U.S. system, that universities and colleges should competitively seek to improve themselves in ways that bring higher status helped to produce the contradiction of some institutions becoming more selective at the same time the system as a whole moved toward admitting everyone without regard to merit. Elsewhere, departments and faculties within universities individually adjust to rising and falling consumer demand, with some, in a time of falling demand, tightening their own selection and others becoming friendly toward applicants they formerly would have rejected.

Chapter 3 concluded that there were fundamental trends occurring in belief systems. The first is a general symbolic disintegration, with the beliefs of the enterprise, the academic profession, and the national system increasingly pluralistic and fragmented. This trend followed from the dynamics of the underlying disciplines that cause them to split and multiply, producing additional arcane patterns of thought and definitions of proper behavior. The second is a countervailing trend toward integration promoted by systemwide standardization and common attachment to such general values as objective inquiry and individualism. Both types of change, widely evident, are inescapable. Change in beliefs thus has a built-in contradiction, one that is tolerable in part because each type of change proceeds on a separate axis. The trend toward symbolic disintegration proceeds primarily in the division of bodies of knowledge and their related cultures. The trend toward integration moves along the line defining common membership and identity in large systems. Between matrix-type linkages, standardized categories, and diffuse common values, academic systems apparently will not fall apart, no matter what their future huge scale and astonishing complexity.

AUTHORITY AND INTEGRATION

The forms of work and belief are paralleled in complexity by the variety of forms of authority and the means of integration discussed in chapters 4 and 5. Here, too, the contest between "forces" of nonchange and "forces" of change is inordinately complex. But certain predispositions are clearly evident as we review the types and amount of authority possessed by different academic groups and the alternative ways of concerting academic activities.

Following Margaret Archer, we may say that centralized structures of authority tend to remain centralized, and decentralized ones decentralized.[22] There may be some drifting of each upon the other, but convergence can readily be exaggerated as a trend as we observe in the short run the efforts of some centralized systems to decentralize and decentralized ones to unify. There is reason to expect that the French educational structure, let alone that of the USSR, will remain centralized. "Bureaucratic indispensability," as Ezra N. Suleiman has shown, remains extremely high in French government generally.[23] In the most highly bureaucratized state among the Western democracies, power remains with, and keeps rebounding back to, the central bureaucratic elite, whose members invariably attended a *grande école* prior to recruitment into one of the *grand corps*. The French institutions of centralization have much stability and endurance. They are resistant to shifts in power of the political parties since the parties have similar bureaucratic elements. And such mildly decentralized systems as the British, and the radically decentralized American system, are not about to approximate the French let alone the Communist model, even as they become more centralized. Too much power, with related traditions, is fixed at lower levels. The hands of history felt in present-day arrangements will continue to hold British universities away from central ministerial control in a way that makes the British system qualitatively different from the French mode. Much of the funding of U.S. institutions will remain at the level of the individual states, protecting state power and long-standing traditions and understandings. As corporate entities, private institutions will continue to be highly resistive to control by central officials, in ways not to be imagined in the centralized mode even as slices of their operations become government-dependent. Here again, the constraint side of structural predisposition is impressive.

But a balanced account must leave the matter open and look also to the inducements for change, which lie in part in failure of form. Each national mode of authority distribution contains weaknesses that stimulate compensating effort. Thus, in the Continental mode, identified in chapter 4, reform has sought to pull authority from the top and the bottom in order to strengthen the weak middle levels of administration, that is, administration at regional and institutional levels. In the German federal variant of this mode, reform has attempted also to move authority upward to an explicit national level of coordination, simultaneously strengthening coordination below the *Länder* ministries. In the British mode, reform has sought to develop a superstructure responsive to central policy in order to strengthen the top level of coordination in what was previously, in formal terms, a nonsystem of autonomous institutions. Similarly in the American mode, reform has appeared in the shape of more administered order, in a complicated arrangement of at least three levels of coordination (multicampus, state, national), in an attempt to strengthen coordination and direction in the largest laissez-faire system ever developed in the history of higher education. In Japan, authority has been drifting upward to the national level as the huge sprawling private sector has come under greater governmental guidance as the price of public financial assistance.

In sum, in mature academic systems (1) the historically set distribution of authority will tend to perpetuate itself, and convergence among national systems will be limited; (2) but each national authority structure will contain weaknesses that call for compensating effort and thereby help set the direction of conscious reform and unconscious adaptation.

Within these broad patterns of resistance and inducement we can observe also some effects of bureaucratic, oligarchic, political, and market forms of system integration. Each has standardized ways of promoting change as well as characteristic constraints. Bureaucratic order facilitates change by means of planning and administrative implementation. Of the four types, it carries with it the clearest model of rational hierarchy, an administrative scheme whereby ideas can flow to the top, there take the status of plans, and then be implemented back down through a set of offices. But as is well known, bureaucracy ordinarily brings with it a plethora of constraints upon change. Rigidities set in around traditionalized roles and procedures; the internal struggle for resources leads to a zealous guarding of turf that saps new ventures; and norms of fairness encourage uniformities that block experimentation and special ventures that appear out of line. Thus, under bureaucracy, the hope for change lies in effective planning and change-oriented administration; the resistance to change lies in normal processes and procedures of large administrative entities and in the ways that such entities, over time, turn means into ends in themselves.

Oligarchy can facilitate change through personal initiative and collegial planning. A professor holding baronial power can move ahead rapidly, ignoring the wishes of bureaucrats, senior colleagues who chafe against his authority, and voiceless junior staff. In systems characterized by interlocking rigidities and high resistance to change, one can find personal breakthroughs, even breathtaking and dramatic advances, made possible by the power of a leader to move virtually as he pleases. The great development of physics in Italy under Enrico Fermi in the 1930s is a good example.[24] A preceding powerful professor helped Fermi to gain baronial powers, bringing him to the most important chair in physics in the country, arranging resources, and protecting him against those who would limit his work and influence. Fermi himself then soon developed the capacity to maintain and enlarge his powers, using them to bring together an enormously creative cluster of physicists whose work lifted Italy to the first rank in the world in this particular discipline.

Such personalized change is idealized in the guild model of academic organization and is part of the rationale behind the chair system: with carefully guarded selection, the most highly competent academics will be given great influence with which to mold the activities of their fields. While the notables each utilize personal power to advance the work of their respective domains, they can also come together as a small group, free of petty bureaucratic restraints and the slow processes of democratic deliberation, to effect change in the more general domains of faculty, university, and system. Collegial planning has widely been used to change the work of

departments, institutes, faculties, and colleges, even when the group
has been heavily oligarchical. The important condition is that the
rewards of the system become translated into local incentives for
change, e.g., the rewards of research productivity translated into
prestige and honor for the group as well as the individual, encouraging local clusters to seek and to maintain high rank in their field.

The facilitating conditions, however, are so often submerged by
the constraining tendencies of academic oligarchy. Personal power
becomes deeply entrenched, producing a closed system around the
baron. As external scrutiny is walled off, privilege is localized. The
master and his journeymen and apprentices are then protected
from the sanctions of the discipline as well as those of the bureaucracy and the political officials. Then the incentives for change wind
down. Similarly, the collegial group, if long possessed by oligarchical
powers, can develop all the ills of closed systems—walling off internal demands, ignoring changes in environment, and substituting
local and particularistic criteria for general and universalistic ones in
judging performance. In general, oligarchical forms tend to become
heavily resistant to change as guildlike groups guard local, fragmented guild territories. It has been a long time in history since
guild monopolies served well the evolution of habits and practices at
work. But as chapter 5 made clear, guild forms have been effective
in the past, and continue to play a part today, when combined with
bureaucratic, political, and market arrangements.

Political forms of coordination facilitate change by means of
interest-group struggle and domination by party and state officials.
As top state officials, external interest groups, or emerging internal
constituencies enter the power arenas of higher education, they
generally seek changes that seem favorable to their own interests.
Thus, the emerging corporatist relation of "big labor" and "big
business" to the academic system in Sweden has been used to favor
curricular changes that make higher education more vocational-
minded, focusing on linkage between training programs and the
changing job market.

The essentially political demands for more "participation" that
have been so extensive in advanced systems during the 1960s and
1970s have involved a host of sought-after changes, from different
curricula to a permanent redistribution of power. In authoritarian
states, where interest groups are suppressed or absorbed by the

interlocking apparatus of the party and the regime, the political sources of academic change, if they exist, lie more in the political apparatus itself. The domination of top party and government officials can then be a powerful lever for change, especially in post-revolutionary stages, when, for a time, a few can sweep all before them. Then one can accomplish top-down, root-and-branch over-hauling, as was done in the USSR in the 1920s, in Eastern European countries in the late 1940s and the 1950s, and in Communist China and Cuba still more recently. A regime may even for a time elevate a political ideology over widely shared norms of academic selection and competence (as China did in the early 1970s), so that party loyalty (along with worker/peasant background) weighs more than ability in selecting students, and professors and students alike are sent away to work in the fields in order to put them in touch with the masses and attenuate any elitist tendencies they possess.

But politics, too, settles down as it settles in. Regime norms become great uniformities, severely undermining the conditions of initiative and adaptation at all lower levels. External groups, internal constituencies, and segments of political officialdom closely guard those activities of direct interest, enlarging and making still more complicated the web of veto groups. So where new interests are forces for change in one decade, they become, according to their success in achieving power, sources of rigidity in another. The political aspects of direct coordination share with bureaucracy and oligarchy the tendency for deliberately organized social forms over time to vest self-interest, accumulate tradition, and fix on routines.

Market forms of coordination facilitate change by means of com-petition among enterprises and extremely loose coupling that allows enterprises and sectors to move disjointedly in various directions. Overall controls are abated, releasing and even demanding local initiative and adaptation. Enterprises that need to make it on their own have to be attractive to some clientele and personnel and responsive to their changing wishes. Market conditions can make for very open and expansive systems, as in the way the private sector of Japanese higher education served as the main vehicle for the shift of that country into mass higher education, with consumer demand in the saddle.

Under some conditions, however, loose marketlike linkage can be heavily retarding. Chief among the constraining conditions is a

near-monopoly of prestige by one or two institutions or a single
model, for then, despite the freedom to experiment, wander, and
diversify, enterprises voluntarily imitate the established type. This is
an important restraint on institutional diversity in Japan, where
imitation takes place up the hierarchy, including by autonomous
private universities. Then, too, institutions can settle down in a
mutually acceptable division of labor, enjoying the comforts of protected niches. Thus, how much and in what ways market conditions
facilitate change is very much dependent on the balance of incentives in the market for institutions to stay as they are, try to squeeze
into the main niche, or seek individual roles.

Among the major types of order, the market form seemingly has
the strongest adaptive capacity, helping to account for the high
adaptability of the U.S. and Japanese systems. But the matter is
complicated, with each form having its own ways of facilitating and
constraining. The problem of balancing forms of order, raised at
the end of chapter 5, is thus in part a problem of appropriate balance
for facilitating and constraining change. No one form apparently
will give even satisfactory results, let alone outstanding ones, despite
the claims of partisans of each. Much further study is needed of how
these forms operate in combination and under the various conditions that we observe in different countries, including finally the
special features of history and context that make each national
system unique and turn purported generalizations into tendencies
and possibilities rather than iron laws. One likelihood is that the
effect of each major form of order upon change will vary over time,
facilitating in one period and constraining in another.

The market form appears least susceptible to such variation, and
hence the form most likely to keep a system open to change and
adaptable to new environmental demands. But the matter is hardly
settled, since we can observe how much established academic enterprises voluntarily settle down, subject to their own internal processes
of institutionalization and the tendency to leave well enough alone
when the payroll is being met. But in any event, the question of
balance clearly has a time dimension. When central state authority
has been in the saddle, then the opening up of the system to change
may depend on some combination of forms incrementally adjusting
that authority internally, devolving some power to lower levels, and
strengthening the marketlike interactions of students, professors,

and institutions. Or where the market aspects have predominated and caused stagnation, there political and bureaucratic interventions can be vehicles of change. To know that no one form is forever dependable, for either the conservation or renovation of such an important public good, is to encourage an evolutionary perspective. The hero of one era may be the goat of the next, for coordinating structures as much as for individuals.

The Contradictions of Order and Disorder

We have thus far studied change through the lenses of constraints and impulses of established forms, identifying features that, on one hand, make for constancy, even rigidity, and those, on the other, that stimulate alteration, even headlong change. The pulling and hauling upon academic activities is mind boggling, with natural tensions increasing with growing size and complexity. Those tensions can be fruitfully viewed as contradictions between the ways of order and the ways of disorder. Throughout we have stressed how much, in academic systems, disorder holds out against the establishment of order; but also, in reverse, how order is achieved in the midst of uncommon disorder. Four categories of contradictions can be established: those caused by differences between the disciplinary bottom and the administrative top; those promoted within the superstructure itself; those characteristic of the lower ranks; and the evolutionary reversal of orderly and disorderly tendencies.

CONTRADICTION BETWEEN DISCIPLINE AND SYSTEM

The different major levels of system organization contain different predispositions. We may clarify the analysis and not lose much information if we reduce the six authority levels used earlier to three: the understructure, or essentially disciplinary level; the middle structure, or enterprise level; and the superstructure, or system level. The understructure consists of the many operating units found within individual universities and colleges, including the larger ones at the level of faculties, schools, and subcolleges; the middle structure is the university or college in its entirety, and hence includes the campus and multicampus levels; and the superstructure is composed of all the system links that relate one enterprise to another. The three levels often march to different drummers, having different directions, sources, and vehicles of change. As between the bottom and top, they are often oppositely propelled.

The basic direction of change in the understructure is toward fragmentation and loose coupling. As the disciplines and professional fields become evermore specialized, they tend, as aggregates, to be evermore disunited. The sources of change lie in the interests, ideas, and organization of these disparate areas. Each field has important dynamics of its own. Each is an autonomous career: for example, that of physicist or economist or classicist. Each has organizational turf to maintain, defend, and expand. Each has a bounded body of knowledge, analytical approaches, and methods it can claim as its own, ideas that evolve slowly where the spur of research and criticism is weak but rapidly in an increasing number of fields in which research and criticism are heavily rewarded. The most scientific fields are highly dynamic, virtually racing ahead at breakneck speed in the advanced systems that emphasize research. Such leading cases as genetic engineering dramatize and clarify what is more humdrum and unclear in other fields and systems, namely that internal sources of change, at lower levels, grow stronger as academics professionalize the higher learning.

The principal vehicles of change in the understructure are found in the processes dictated by professional forms. As seen in chapter 4, the basic operating units are typically dominated by the personal, collegial, and oligarchical arrangements that academics themselves have constructed for use in such crucial activities as research, teaching, hiring personnel, and evaluating students. Critically, the primary links to "the environment" are specialty-based, with each disciplinary section of a university or college or institute possessing bridges of its own to groups outside the enterprise. The crucial linkage is to others in the same field, first within the academic system itself and then secondarily, in the professional fields and some of the arts and sciences, to members of the field located outside the academy. The relevant environment is reflected in the decision structures of departments and other operating units: e.g., if historians turn to others outside of their own institution for information, advice, criteria of judgment, and specific recommendations on personnel and program, it is first to other historians.

Hence, in the understructure, changes flow within disciplines, across enterprises, and thereby from the environment of the individual enterprise to its interior segments. Changes are propelled and carried by professional modes of linkage and authority, with the changing emphases, styles, and standards of each field at large, particularly as modeled in high-status units, exerting steady pressure for adaptation. The professional qualities of sectors and systems vary widely for reasons pursued below. But the general characteristic of segmented professionalism helps explain why such large environmental forces as "consumer demand" and "labor-force demand" often tell us little about the reactions of professors and the direction and magnitude of change in academic enterprises. As in the case of nineteenth-century Oxford and Cambridge, academics can sometimes virtually ignore the rest of society for decades at a time because they have obtained a high degree of self-control. They can do so also for the more widespread and basic reason that for them the most demanding part of their environment is other academics in the same field.

In short, the understructure is possessed by the logics of discipline, expertise, and professionalized disorder. Change is resisted on disciplinary grounds, but it is also thereby generated. There is a mutation and proliferation of disciplinary groups, a restless expansion generated primarily by commitment to research. This restlessness is more characteristic of some subjects than others, some enterprises than others, some systems than others. But it spills out from the dynamic centers to the more placid peripheries, along the functional lines that link together those having common membership in a field of study.

In contrast, groups at the top of academic systems have quite different directions, sources, and vehicles of change. As earlier noted, state-constructed administrative pyramids are the dominant form of superstructure in the academic systems of the world, with officials and citizens alike more inclined to take their chances with the failures of government than with the failures of the market. The state pyramid is possessed primarily by a logic of explicit coherence, essentially that of administration. The primary rationale is to impose order that will link together the otherwise fragmentary disciplines, enterprises, and sectors. Political and bureaucratic personnel who occupy the higher sites are responsible for "coordination" in the ordinary sense. They are mandated in their specific roles to take charge, to systematize and make more uniform what otherwise would be unsystematic and varied. Their own beliefs stress hierarchy and formal linkage. Their powers are used to make embracing formal systems and to fill in administrative levels: multiple university campuses made into a university system; university and nonuniversity sectors made parts of an encompassing state system; many state or provincial systems linked as a national one. The trend toward unity need not stop even there, since a set of national systems, as in Western Europe, may be partially pulled together by efforts to work out course and degree equivalences, common job rights and statuses, and so on. The strain is to unify. The golden rule is: systematize, systematize, don't let any exceptions escape your eyes.

As superstructures become larger, more complex, and more dense in linkage, many external trends and demands become operational in the system as a whole to the extent that they become "state demands." What consumers "want" and what industry, the professions, and the civil service are "demanding" is interpreted by political and administrative personnel and has to be processed through their offices—the shaping of laws in the legislative subcommittee, the juggling of issues and priorities in the chief executive's office, the fashioning of administrative regulations in the national or regional ministry. The officials themselves also come to expect that they will initiate changes, and they acquire staff experts whose interests and work professionalize reform. The vehicle for change is thus political and bureaucratic coordination, as opposed to the vehicle of professional influence, which is primary in the understructure.

The middle structure is indeed in the middle, often mediating between the natural flows of the bottom and the top. Those positioned at the university or enterprise level develop interests and beliefs that reflect the nature of the system both above and below them. Their natural direction of change varies accordingly. In a system dominated by the top state administration (e.g., the USSR), the university heads are extensions of that administration and are used to push the many parts toward integration. In a system where the segmented professionalism of the understructure triumphs over all, the enterprise officials are arms of their "colleagues," elected rectors and presidents who reflect the distribution of power at the operating levels.

The campus and multicampus levels have their most prominent role, as we have seen, in those systems where little or no formal coordinating machinery exists above them. Personnel at these levels—trustees and presidents and immediate staff—are then literally forced to act, to be responsible. Instead of being arms of the state, or representatives of the professors, they are, in pure form, the leaders—"captains"—of autonomous enterprises. In that case, their efforts on behalf of the welfare of individual institutions leads toward marketlike interaction in which competition is the catalyst for change.

The difference between the understructure and the superstructure in predisposition is thus great, especially with state pyramids predominating in the systems of the world and market interactions increasingly entangled in state guidance. If we look at the "bottom" of the higher education system, we see movement toward autonomous parts, even the "anarchy" part of "organized anarchy." If we look at the "top" of the higher education system, we see encompassing formal systems, evermore laced with administrative patterns. The logics of change are entirely different. Hence, it is always necessary, when speaking of a type of academic change, to specify the levels at which it operates, since an opposite disposition is likely to characterize the levels not directly in view.

CONTRADICTION IN THE SUPERSTRUCTURE

The logic of order in the higher administrative levels of systems, however, is not left in peace. Rather it is disturbed within its own roost by the counterlogic of bureaucratic differentiation and competition. We took extensive note in chapter 5 of evidence from a number of countries pointing to intra- and interbureau conflict as part of the normal way of doing governmental business, East and West, in developing and developed countries, as well as in such small, tidy systems as the Swedish and such larger, ungainly ones as the Italian and the American. The reasons are simple: the differentiation of parts is a trend that occurs within the top rungs as well as the lower parts of academic systems; compartmentalized groups struggle with one another in efforts to gain resources and effect their ends, thereby steadily creating disorder. There is no escape in any system from operational parts having representatives at higher levels. Someone at the center must speak for the nonuniversity sector; others support the universities. Someone must speak for the natural sciences, each in turn; others must push the cause of the humanities. Each of the professional areas of study will have its own center representatives, even, as we have noted, partisans in a sponsoring bureau separate from the ministry of education. We may call this parallel fragmentation, a sort of pluralism on high that reflects some of the pluralism underneath. And there is no escaping a bureaucratic and political struggle that is nearly the opposite of neat pyramidal order conveyed by the ideal conception of bureaucracy.

Hence, the tension between order and disorder also runs up and down the corridors of ministries. Central staffs are hardly more immune to it than professors, particularly since their beliefs tell them that matters should be orderly in their domain, and they live constantly with the fact that they are not. Such tension is expressed in part in the push-and-pull of subbureau striving, on the one hand, and efforts at unity, on the other: the head of a technical-education section doing all he or she can to promote technical education and the higher chief attempting to coordinate technical education with all the other higher education segments. Such struggle finds some accommodation in numerous mutual adjustments wherein bargaining officials learn to get along with one another, thereby establishing some order. But it can also be a source of change, since such adjustments are not set in concrete. Power markets, like economic markets, have a potential for instability, since someone in the future may find it in his interest to proceed differently. At least he or she will clearly not be restrained by the perfect definition of position and connection to others that the model of bureaucracy conveys.

CONTRADICTION IN THE UNDERSTRUCTURE

The logic of disorder that we portrayed as dominant in the understructure, as compared with the interests of higher administrators, is also not left in peace. It, too, is disturbed within its own roost, by the counterlogics of unified programs and integrated services. Amid the disarray of its courses, accumulated in an arbitrary manner by the specialty interests of faculty members, a department fashions programs. Some courses are related to one another as beginning, intermediate, and advanced; as cognate subjects; as chosen representatives of subfields that, taken together, constitute a departmental major or minor. Professional schools must fashion programs that turn neophytes into experts. Hence, there is a constant strain toward curricular order within a law school or medical school or even a school of architecture, at the same time that electives and nonrequired courses proliferate.

Some of the strain between disorder and order at operating levels of academic systems thus takes the form of a difference between the natural tendencies of research and scholarship and the requirements of transmitting and distributing knowledge. The first is the more anarchic, as individuals follow their own leads. The second is more integrative, as knowledge derived from specialties is pulled together in packages that can be taught to those who know little about the subject. While the first constantly disrupts established order, the second brings some order out of subject-matter anarchy. Change is involved: the pursuit of research and scholarship renders curricula out of date and in need of revision, which someone gets around to sooner or later; the pursuit of integrated materials for teaching programs suggests that endless fragmentation of scholarly interests is antithetical to teaching and learning, and that therefore some consolidations of interests in the department are appropriate.

Such tension is written large between institutional sectors that are variously discipline-driven and consumer-driven. Research universities are primarily discipline-driven. Research professors first answer the call of their research interests and only secondarily take note of what their student-customers would like to have. But teachers in community colleges and other short-cycle units march first to the tune of teaching programs fashioned for direct appeal to students. In this sense, research universities are inner-directed, guided by a multitude of disciplinary directives. Service colleges are other-directed, much more dependent on the meeting of consumer wishes. Sectors vary in their combination of the two styles; and, notably, individual institutions vary over time. When students are abundant, universities can afford to follow internal staff desires and place teaching and service on a take-it-or-leave-it basis. When students are in short supply, institutions think more about what attracts students and seek to discontinue esoteric subjects "too expensive" to continue. Outside a few quaint places, it is embarrassing in the arts and sciences and most professional schools to have more professors than students! Thus, the needs of teaching as defined by consumer interest promote at many levels and in many ways a counterforce to the happy anarchy produced by research and individual scholarship.

THE EVOLUTIONARY REVERSAL OF ORDER AND DISORDER

Perhaps the most fascinating of all the major contradictions is the way that disorderly approaches to system can lead to order and an orderly arrangement can produce disorder. A classic case of the first is found in the creation and spread of the graduate school in American higher education. The widespread adoption of the graduate school was neither planned nor instituted by an encompassing administration or any other particular body. Rather it came out of a disorderly competition as emerging universities faced the common problem of how to accommodate research and advanced training in a setting already occupied by the college, then a two-hundred-year-old form. Without system control and support, institutions were free to experiment in how to make these accommodations. Competition forced them to be alert to the successes and failures of others. Thus, Charles W. Eliot, Harvard's great president (1869–1909), was initially no great supporter of the new "research imperative," and certainly not one to bend the knee to upstart research-minded professors. But he changed his mind and his tactics in the face of the clear and present danger that renowned professors would move from Harvard to Johns Hopkins and other new universities or choose not to come to his institution.[25] The would-be universities were free to imitate whatever turned out to be the most useful, or at least useful, structure for accommodating the new tasks. As the graduate-school form spread, the new tasks became defined, organized, and standardized without benefit of administrative imposition. An orderly arrangement came about by the intertwined effects of competition and drift.

In contrast, order in the macro organization of administered systems has frequently led over time to much disorder in the handling of such new tasks. In Western Europe, as described by Joseph

Ben-David, "the new functions of science which emerged since the middle of the nineteenth century were grafted on the national systems of higher education which had emerged in the first half of the century."[26] Pure research had to be supported in the universities from the budgets of governmentally financed research organizations established ad hoc. Practical research was segregated in specialized research institutions, since it lacked the respect necessary to have established professors support it. An administratively ordered system had the effect that "a function which was implicit in the state of science in Europe . . . could not be properly fitted in the existing conceptions and organization of scientific work." As a result, "it developed through a variety of exceptions and improvisations," that is, in a disorderly fashion.[27] Development by means of exception meant that in the twentieth century science was not to have the secure foundations within the university that were provided by the emergent-but-widely-adapted graduate school in the U.S. system.

The disorder produced over time by efforts to order academic systems explicitly has become increasingly a problem as the rate of social change has accelerated. Italy and France, as we have frequently noted, are now classic examples of centralized systems accumulating rigidities of bureaucratic and oligarchical control that, in the face of rapid change, have helped produce overload, stalemate, and breakdown. The in-place structure could not adapt rapidly enough, heavily constrained by the interlocking controls and the ingrained forms that had developed over a long period of time. The resistance of the formal systems to rapid change led to disorder: the great breakdown in France in 1968 and the turmoil of the following decade; the semipermanent state of crisis characteristic of the Italian system since the late 1960s. One need not fully adopt the stalled-society perspective of Michel Crozier to recognize the heavy constraint on orderly evolution produced in those two major academic systems.[28]

Three causes loom large in producing disorder over time in deliberately ordered systems. One is the systemwide institutionalization of specific forms to the point where they are unconsciously assumed to be the right and only way for all. For example, in Italy in the late 1970s, after a decade of traumatic strife and perceived breakdown, professors were still attempting to give individual oral examinations as the key point of passage for year-long courses, an

enormously time-consuming procedure if done correctly but one
that had become increasingly arbitrary and capricious as professors
and their assistants raced through masses of students. But a simple
change to written examinations, common procedure in many other
systems, was not on the agenda of change. In a formally disordered
system, someone would have done it differently.

A second cause is the systematic vesting of interest in such common forms. The resistance to change is a matter of power for a large
stratum of people. When a possible change is admitted to consciousness and even debated, it is seen as a threat to that stratum's rights
and privileges. Thus, an attack on the oral examination becomes still
another threat to professorial control. Such resistance is generated
particularly by large plans aimed at correcting everything at once.
As noted by Arnold B. Heidenheimer in analysis of constraints
upon change in the educational systems of Sweden and West Germany, maximalist strategies bring out maximalist resistance by (1)
exciting the fear and envy of a greater number of advocates of
competing policy interests, and (2) increasing the number of decision-making sites in which opponents can rally opposition.[29]

The third source of administrative disorder is the balkanization of
interest and power in the superstructure, already noted, a fragmentation that precludes or heavily attentuates top-down change. Leaders cannot lead, despite enabling positions at the top, because they
do not have the power. The many offices, divisions, and bureaus in
the central headquarters protect specialized interests as much as do
the many chairs, departments, and faculties in the field.

Thus, academic systems steadily produce disorderly ways and
orderly operations that interact with and stimulate one another.
Academic forms condition change in part by setting and sustaining
their opposing tendencies. The contradictions are perhaps necessary to adaptive capacity, since the adaptive system, needing both its
disorder and its order, is kept from freezing in place by the resulting
tensions.

THE PROCESS OF DIFFERENTIATION

Elaborate structures, it seems, are more congenial than simple
ones to the support of modern educational work. Evolution is from
simple to complex. Can we now generalize about the causes of this

primary direction of change? In describing the elaboration of sections, tiers, sectors, and hierarchies, we have argued that changes stemmed from the efforts of a variety of groups, some new and some old, some specialist and some generalist, to protect and enhance their own operations. Pausing for a moment of theory, such observations can be generalized and related to a fundamental sociological approach to social change, that of differentiation. If propositions about differentiation can be made valuable in understanding change in academic systems, we shall be in luck, since there is nothing so practical as a good theory, particularly one applicable to education that does not avoid the role of power in social affairs.

Increased complexity in systems is related to an increasing complexity of tasks. The widening mix of tasks in academic systems, we have seen, is produced primarily by three proximate "forces." The first is the more varied array of students entering the gates when substantial expansion is allowed to take place. This diversification of consumers naturally has more remote causes lying behind it, e.g., a widening recognition of the value of higher education in personal advancement and a spreading ideology of educational equality. The second force is the widening of the labor market to which higher education relates, which has behind it general changes in the economy and the structure of the labor force. The segmentation of knowledge workers outside the academy acts directly upon academic systems by means of the actions of managerial, professional, and technical groups, who seek training and legitimation for their domains of work, and acts indirectly by altering the demands of the student consumers as they perceive future job opportunity and placement.

These first two forces are central components of the grand environment of higher education, ones that are commonly relevant and have to be taken into account. They are key "external transactions."[30] The third proximate force lies in the effects of the research and critical scholarship that take place largely within the academy itself: the emergence of new disciplines, the splitting of old ones into numerous specialties, the intensification of knowledge in the various fields, and the spread of the leading models of academic specialization within and among academic systems.

The three forces may operate somewhat independently of one another; e.g., consumer demand may increase greatly at the same time the pull of the labor market diminishes. But they may also converge to produce enormous pressure and seemingly explosive change, as happened in many national systems since 1960. A broad cause of crisis is the coming together of such potent forces for rapid adjustment in the way the academy is organized.

Central to the effects of such forces is the development and reforming of the self-interest of individuals and groups around differentiated specialties and the organizational parts that support and carry them. A more heterogeneous clientele means a wider range of types of students in personal characteristics who are interested in numerous semiprofessional as well as professional fields, who need more remedial as well as more advanced work, and who seek services and procedures congenial to different cultural, class, and ethnic backgrounds. Thus, in the aggregate, student interests attach to differentiation. Then, too, the increasingly segmented labor market of knowledge workers attaches the interests of management and labor groups, in the form of demands for relevant training, and the interests of students-in-progress and students-as-graduates to expertise in a wider range of academic specialties. Finally, driven by the commitment to research and critical scholarship, discovery draws the interests of academics toward the new, revised, and always-more-numerous cells of knowledge produced by inquiry. Thus, vaguely formulated forces are no longer so mysterious: they operate in processes of change by realigning the interests of participants. In knowledge-bearing systems, interest is largely attached to bundles of knowledge. As knowledge splits, so does interest, and vice versa, in interaction between the two.

We may connect differentiation and interest by setting forth six generalizations that together relate historical development and contemporary structure:

(1) *The historical production of academic organization centers in groups vesting their interests in specific, specialized forms for grouping academic work.* The motor power of development lies in new attachments of interest—of outsiders, students, officials, and especially the academic workers themselves—to emerging forms, to groupings of activities that are new claimants for place in the structure of tasks.

(2) *Existing educational structures distribute vested interests in their maintenance.* The motor power of stability and continuity lies in the ability of groups in power to defend what they have, and, in concert or accumulation, thereby to maintain the whole system as it exists.

As Margaret Archer notes, those already in office in the system may decide to transform it radically, but rarely do they do so. In reality, "structures distribute vested interests in their maintenance and it is the fact that groups do defend these which make patterns of inter-action and change durable in the long-run."[31]

(3) *The struggle between stability and change appears operationally within systems as a clash of old vested interests and groups seeking to vest new interests.* "Stability" has its agents, workers who knowingly or un-knowingly serve on its behalf. "Change" has its own agents, persons willing to serve in its cause, since they are thereby served. As put by Dietrich Rueschemeyer in a general analysis of social differentia-tion: "Resistance against differentiation is likely to come from offi-cials and organizations who have some share of power and whose jurisdiction would be subdivided. . . . Similarly, a division of roles and organizations will be favored by those who thereby gain in privilege, status, or power."[32]

(4) *The outcome of the struggle and hence the extent of change is deter-mined largely by the relative power of the stability agents and the change agents.* Existing structures effectively resist change, and even be-come immovable, entirely blocking or stalling change for a time, to the extent that the vested interests monopolize effective power. Such structures become open to change to the extent that old groups have only partial power and new groups are able to accumulate some influence.

(5) *Given the diffusion of authority in academic systems to an array of expert groups, it is difficult to transform the organization of those groups against their wishes. Their capacity to oppose change favors development of new organizations, rather than the transformation of existing ones.* Put more generally: "When opposition to differentiation from vested interests in established organizations is considerable, more complex organizational forms may develop more easily in new organizations than through the transformation of existing ones."[33] The historic compromise in academic change is that new units bypass the old, and yet the old ones survive.

(6) *The amount of power normally possessed by various groups in an established arena of action, such as an academic system, is determined primarily by the legitimacy of group activity and ideology.* The power of history professors in a university depends largely on recognition by others of the central value of teaching history and their acceptance

of the arguments put forth by historians to justify a secure and
central place. As mentioned earlier, a new field like biochemistry
rapidly wins its way in entering academic systems as bordering
vested interests value its activities and accept its claims, whereas
other new fields, like women's studies or black studies, remain problematic, as established interests remain doubtful or even decidedly
dubious about their coherence as fields and the cogency of their
claims as bona fide areas of study. Such new fields "make it" to the
extent they are able to form a legitimacy, using events and whatever
influence they can muster to educate others to new perceptions and
definitions.[34]

Thus, the elemental linkage, leaving aside the back-and-filling of
interactions, runs as follows: much change occurs through differentiation; differentiation is driven in the immediate setting by the
rearrangement of interest; interest is basically divided between
those already vested and those seeking to become vested; the outcomes of the interest-group struggle are determined by relative
power; and power is rooted in respective legitimacies.

This simplified chain connects educational change to basic sociological thought on the causes of social differentiation and the evolution of institutional forms. It finds resonance in the classic argument
of Emile Durkheim on the motor power that drives the division of
labor in society. Durkheim placed high among the causes of differentiation the mutual interest that groups have in protecting themselves.[35] If somewhat similar units are in conflict, or sense that
conflict is imminent, they can avoid direct confrontation, and possible defeat for one or the other, by specialization. In separating
tasks, specialization pulls apart groups that otherwise may have to
fight it out:

> The struggle between two organisms is as active as they
> are similar. Having the same needs and pursuing the
> same aims, they are in rivalry everywhere. . . . It is quite
> otherwise if the co-existing individuals are of different
> species or varieties. . . . What is advantageous to one is
> without value to the others. . . . The occultist does not
> compete with the psychiatrist, the shoemaker with the
> hatter, the mason with the cabinet maker, the physicist
> with the chemist, etc. Since they perform different ser-
> vices, they can perform them together.[36]

Biochemists and chemists do not have to fight over turf within a chemistry department if biochemists can develop their specialty to the point of a separate department. Historians of medicine reduce conflict with historians and/or professors of medicine as they pull away in new departments devoted entirely to the history of medicine, in either the liberal arts or the medical school. Both parties avoid the dilution of their resources that is likely to occur if they remain in the same budgeting unit. Increasing everyone's claim on funds by splitting into more operational units is a practiced art in modern complex organizations. It occurs frequently and steadily in academic systems. Everyone possibly can get more, as sociologists and anthropologists found out when they gave up joint departments and went separate ways.

Even within departments, subgroups use their specialization as protection against domination by others and to reduce conflict over unified courses of action. This is most noticeable in departments likely to be conflict-ridden because of low consensus on paradigms, e.g., history or political science. Conflict is increased by efforts to hammer out agreements on first principles, required courses, central and peripheral subjects. Conflict is averted by recognizing the bona fide different specialties and giving each a piece of the departmental turf. As reported in research on departmental organization, "the political science department studied here averted conflict by avoiding the coordination of individual activities through structuring of the curriculum," i.e., a structured course sequence. The need to reduce conflict encouraged senatorial courtesy: "the group tended to approve anything about which a single member felt strongly. Course assignments were made, as much as possible, to suit individuals."[37] It remains no mystery why "curricula are like huge beanbags that keep on being added to, bean by bean," since "each new faculty member brings new courses with him or her. . . . The most important impact of all is steady accretion, since little is ever subtracted."[38] Old courses never die, but simply fade away when supporters change their interests or leave.

Arthur L. Stinchcombe has developed a powerful argument on the persistence of types of organizations, seeking a way to explain systematically but historically why a particular mosaic of organizational types exists at a particular time, with the parts in effect "deposited" into the present out of different periods of the past.[39] Persistence has three possible explanations. One is apparent effectiveness: a particular form persists—for example, the American liberal arts college—because it is a more efficient tool than its competing alternatives. A second explanation is that persistence stems from lack of competition: the form in question never has to battle against other forms that may be equally or more effective because it has developed a protected niche within a domain of units. Third, persistence may follow largely from sheer institutionalization, that is, all the sociological tendencies that turn an organizational form into an end in itself. Central to the institutionalization is the vesting of interest in the form. Participants work to perpetuate a form that serves and protects them, in which they develop rights seen as legitimate by others, and around which they develop ideologies that justify perpetuation and control.

The third possibility can readily dominate the first two. A vested form often has a protected niche, even an unquestioned one. It is also generally not asked to compete, at least not to the extent of proving that it is more effective than actual or possible alternatives. This basic pattern of a vested form located in a protective, noncompetitive niche occurs frequently in academic systems. Even under general conditions of institutional competition, as in the American system, such forms as the secular and religious small college are strongly guarded by structurally entrenched practitioners richly equipped with ideologies that justify traditional practice and legitimate group rights. Oh, how they sing the praises of religious values and/or liberal education!—and some outsiders believe them to the point of paying their fees for the privilege of sending sons and daughters. Under market conditions, the carving out of protected niches for individual universities and colleges is virtually a necessary act. Under state control, the vesting of interest is an even more stubborn source of persistence, with government often granting monopoly position and virtually ruling out competition and comparison. There is no more secure niche for the survival of a college or university, a faculty or an institute, a teaching budget or a research allocation, than to be a long-standing part of a national budget, fixed in perpetuity in a bygone day and so much unconsciously accepted as a part of things that no one asks why, or does so only by way of idle speculation.

Thus, once created and made valuable to a group, often to an alliance of groups, academic forms persist. Out of successive historical periods come additional forms, with birthrate greatly exceeding the death rate. Differentiation is then an accumulation of historical deposits.

Following Durkheim, we can state the principle that differentiation is a means of group protection. Alas, for easy generalizing, *de*differentiation can also be a means of protection. We have noted at several points the widespread occurrence of academic drift: forms become more alike as lower-status enterprises pursue their own welfare by evolving toward more prestigious and rewarding forms. Therefore, which way do groups go as they seek to protect and enhance self-interest? It depends on the legitimacy of institutional roles. Where plural roles have been made acceptable—to student clienteles, external supporters, and primarily the faculty and administration of each segment—legitimacy is an anchor for differentiation, holding it in place and stabilizing new segments as they emerge. When only a single role is acceptable, then legitimacy of form encourages *de*differentiation.

The point is clearest in the case of major institutional sectors. To stabilize a role, a sector must have a separate set of tasks in which its personnel believe. Believing comes from doctrines that spell out the importance of the tasks and the value of committing one's career to them. Without the anchor of such ideology, a sector will move toward the roles of others that are strongly legitimated. As we have seen, such drift occurs in both planned and unplanned systems. For example, the California system of higher education, under its well-known 1960 master plan, attempted to stabilize a tripartite structure of community college, state college, and state university. The community college role became legitimated and increasingly institutionalized, but the state college role was not accepted by the personnel of the colleges and did not become well anchored. As a result, these colleges have evolved, de facto and de jure, toward the university role.

In general, the chief form of academic drift in American higher education over the last three to four decades has been that of public four-year colleges moving away from the unwanted role of teaching teachers and otherwise concentrating on bachelor's-level career preparation, and toward the standing of a university. Numerous institutions have moved along a path from normal school to teachers' college, to state college, to state university. In Britain, planned and unplanned differentiation has been diminished over many decades by the drift of institutional types upward in the academic pecking order toward university status and, particularly, toward features characteristic of Oxford and Cambridge.[40] Technical colleges in particular have been subject to drift, developing aspirations for university status as they matured. As they do so, they shun the work and most of the types of students for which they were set up, e.g., part-time students and ones studying for diplomas or certificates rather than degrees. At the same time, the British Open University was given a task "which was not directly competitive with that of any existing university and polytechnics" and, around clearly different activities, it deliberately developed a separate set of values.[41]

Academic drift has also been strong in Australia, where a "second-best" sector converges with a more prestigious university sector.[42] The displacement of colleges from an unwanted role may occur repeatedly in a single location, each time leaving a vacuum of attention to a needed task that brings another institution into the unoccupied territory, soon itself to move on to apparently higher rewards. Thus, in Manchester, England, the less-desirable role has been filled and then vacated successively by Owen's College, Manchester Technical College, and the Royal Technical College, Salford, all moving on to university status, leaving as the latest in line the John Dalton College of Technology, now perhaps somewhat stabilized as part of Manchester Polytechnic.[43]

Distinctive sector roles may be legitimated in various ways. In tightly administered systems, governmental fiat may establish and maintain a differentiation of sectors. In loosely administered systems, different bureaus may serve as the supporters and protectors of different sectors, isolating their "own" schools from the pressures of uniformity within a single encompassing ministry. In market systems, competing sets of institutions may find protective niches of attracted funds, personnel, and clientele, differentiating themselves as they differentiate locations in the general market. The conditions of competition generate some entrepreneurial search for advantage in being different. One can find combinations of these forms of legitimacy. For example, in Yugoslavia, despite the extreme localization of authority in the university sector previously described, the state managed to bring into existence in the 1950s and 1960s a nonuniversity sector of *više škole*, two-year institutions that were later judged in a 1976 international comparison (by the Organisation for Economic Cooperation and Development) to fulfill the aims of short-cycle higher education more effectively than the British polytechnics or the French IUTs.[44] This sector draws its students mainly from the homes of manual workers and trains middle-level staff for local industry. Working at a lower level of instruction than that of the faculties, the *više škole* appeared to have developed a role that is accepted within and without. They have not vacated that role in order to emulate the faculties, and local legitimating belief has helped to stabilize the separation set of activities originally initiated by the state authorities.

At the institutional level, individual universities and colleges face the fateful decision of whether to strive for greater distinctiveness, and hence to differentiate oneself more from peers, or to find protection in similarity. In recent European reforms, new Norwegian regional colleges and the French IUTs seem to have taken the first path to a large extent, whereas the new German comprehensive universities have moved in the second direction. Self-differentiation can be highly rewarding, but it is hard and even risky work. A special staff must be recruited and oriented and a particular clientele attracted. A singular ideology has to be worked out, one embodied in the core programs and internalized by faculty and students. Such efforts call for uncommon leadership, generally in short supply. If an individualized role thereby becomes legitimated, the rewards are great: a protected niche in the marketplace of consumer choice and a special hold on personnel that motivates them and retains their loyalties against offers to go elsewhere.[45] But the risks are considerable: the rugged individualist has few allies to help in times of trouble; the one who raises his head above the crowd can become envied and made a target of distinctive opposition; and excessive self-differentiation can produce rigidity in character that is dysfunctional when changing conditions call for modified response.

At the discipline level, we have noted that some would-be disciplines find a niche and become readily institutionalized within the university; others are either blocked at the door or heavily attenuated in a few years' time, and in this way kept from adding to the extant division of fields. The new fields nearly always need some powerful friends among the old disciplines. In general, they must be perceived as fitting within the current definition of academic fields, working with bodies of knowledge or analytical approaches that others in bordering fields see as appropriately academic. Behind the emerging power of new fields lies their emerging legitimacy.

The interest-group perspective can be applied to specific innovations.[46] For example, in the late 1960s, the New York system of higher education began an effort to turn the University of Buffalo, formerly a private institution, into a first-line state university—a Berkeley of the east—and to do so by means of a host of internal colleges that would divide the large, amorphous undergraduate student population commonly found in the American state university into much smaller clusters organized around broad subjects, such as technology and society, literature and film.[47] A vigorous and promising president, Martin Meyerson, was brought in, a person who had been chancellor of the Berkeley campus and hence knew well its good and bad features. Meyerson was also closely tuned to the research literature and scholarly criticism of the day that emphasized the importance of small membership units, as opposed to just departments, in the large university. Six colleges were initiated in a first wave, ten more in a second. Innovative professors and administrators were appointed as college masters. Control was decentralized so that each master could plan the substance of his college and pursue his own direction. In 1966, conditions were highly favorable; everything seemed possible.

By 1970, all had gone sour. State funding declined; the campus as a whole became intensely politicized from student unrest and reaction to it; all the new colleges became suspect by people on and off campus as publicity concentrated on the radical ways of the more deviant and controversial colleges; Meyerson resigned and left for another presidency. Most important, the balance of power shifted in the early 1970s away from the supporters of the colleges to those in the administration and faculty who wanted to bring the colleges in line with the reemerging and reconsolidated values of the central faculty. A few of the colleges were terminated or chose to go out of existence; the great majority, after much review and rechartering, were "resocialized."

To make some conceptual sense of this case, Arthur Levine developed a continuum of outcomes of innovative efforts that extends from full institutionalization to termination.[48] Four modes that range along that continuum are: diffusion, where the ways of the innovative part spread through the host organization; enclaving, where the innovative unit maintains its ways but in an isolated position within the larger organization; resocialization, where the innovators fall back in line with traditional values and practices; and termination, where the innovation is eliminated. Failure is a relative matter and can be seen as a shift down the continuum, away from the most expanding mode and toward the most contracting. And group power largely determines the outcome. Two or more groups of relevant actors define their own interests in relation to the innovation. Self-defined interests place the relevant groups along a support-nonsupport continuum, from total support to complete opposition. What effects the various groups have on the implementation and outcome of the reforms is then largely a matter of the power they can bring to bear.

We depict the situation as a seesaw, a long board on which reform-supporting and reform-opposing groups sit at different points in relation to the center of balance, far out toward the end or close to the center according to the extremity of their views. If all the groups were equal in power, the seesaw's direction would depend on how many groups were located on either side of the balance, and particularly on the intensity of their commitment. Fanatics would outweigh moderates. But some groups are genuine heavies in terms of power whereas others are lightweight. Hence, they weigh differently in determining whether the innovation-supporting end of the seesaw will have its feet on solid ground or will be left dangling precariously in midair. New groups backing an innovation typically sit far out on the support end but are light in the weight of their power. Old groups that oppose the innovation typically start out sitting closer to the balance point, restrained by their commitment to the values of academic freedom and the philosophy of innocent until proven guilty, but are heavy in potential power. The innovative groups are also often aided at the outset by a temporary power imbalance and a sense of crisis and insecurity that restrains the older groups from applying normal judgments. But, as happened in the case of the German comprehensive-university reform, the nonsupportive and innovation-opposing groups shift their weight toward the end of the oppositional side when they decide some time later that the innocent have indeed proven themselves guilty and deserve to be hoisted.

When they seriously assert themselves, they can throw the weaker innovative groups off the seesaw, leave them dangling uncomfortably in midair, or force them to declare that the game is over.

If power finally makes the difference in the implementation of reform, there is no mystery why a new autonomous organization is a more promising setting for innovative action than an old organization. The autonomous setting cuts the "self-interest costs" of traditional groups by minimizing disturbance of prevailing practices and relations.[49] The established groups are then less likely to care enough to bring their power to bear. Innovating within an old organization, as in the Buffalo case, means that the interests of established groups are more directly stimulated and brought to bear as a counterforce. But the use of new organization also means a higher likelihood of innovation leading to an isolated enclave that can be ignored by the mainline institutions, as in the case of the University of Vincennes in France. So many individual American innovative colleges of different decades have been proud of their own success in being different, but have been dismayed that no one else would learn from them, let along replicate their style.

A straight interest-group approach emphasizes anew why centralized systems are likely to be less innovative than decentralized ones: the coercive comparisons brought to bear by powerful traditional groups are more decisive. Organizational theorists have noted, as general tendencies in complex systems, that centralization *and* formalization *and* the search for simplicity and efficiency reduce the rate of organizational change.[50] All operate to narrow the relevant interest groups and to concentrate the tools of control. There are fewer people making decisions in fewer decision-making areas; there are more rules and sanctions to enforce the rules.

Thus, higher education reforms in various countries are open to analysis from an interest-group perspective in which we use the metaphor of the seesaw of power. Innovations typically "fail" because the innovators cannot acquire enough power fully to protect their new ways. They are allowed to start, even to acquire a clientele, but unless they attach the interests of various groups to their own interests and persuade potential opponents at least to be moderate in their resistance, they can be tightly bounded—resocialized or terminated—as others raise their own level of concern, clarify their own self-interest with respect to the reform, and increase the bearing of their own weight.

Finally, success and failure in reform are relative matters heavily dependent on expectations. If reformers expect only isolated enclaves for their experiments, then they have not failed when the innovations do not infect host organizations or the general system. If innovators expect from the beginning to have their different forms made less different over time, as the innovating unit is resocialized by the host, then the fourth of the loaf they end up with is not failure. True expectations are nearly always difficult to identify, since they are masked by the rhetorics deployed in winning friends, enhancing morale, and otherwise building an institution. The stated purposes of reform are like all formal goals: they are to be assumed guilty of hiding the truth until proven innocent by congruence with operational patterns. Even then it is normal to reach for as much as possible and still be satisfied that one's grasp, falling far short, has made some difference.

INTERNATIONAL TRANSFER

As we seek a systematic picture of how change is determined, we soon come to the question of migration of academic forms among nations. Numerous higher education systems have acquired many of their basic characteristics by means of such over-the-border transference.[51] The initiation of major changes in the receiving country by this route takes two forms: external imposition and voluntary importation.

Imposition was widespread under colonial rule, of course, as the British, French, and Belgian models were carried into many of their nineteenth- and twentieth-century colonies, just as the Spanish model had been spread earlier throughout much of Latin America. The British transfer brought and left behind such features as institutional autonomy in appointing staff and selecting students and a commitment to general, even classical, education for future public administrators, whether in India or Jamaica or Canada or Ghana. The French imposition meant a nationalized and centralized academic system, equipped with a panoply of devices conducive to administratively integrated structure, such as a national ministry of education and civil service employment, whether in Thailand or Tunisia or Trinidad. Belgian colonialism went so far as to replicate in far-off countries the basic cultural and political splits of the metropole, including essentially Flemish and Wallonian universities.[52] The Mediterranean models from Spain and Portugal carried with them such crucial features as part-time employment of faculty, especially in medicine, law, and other professional fields, where it became understood that the academic staff was gainfully employed elsewhere and always had at least two major positions, of which university work was often the lesser.

Thus, throughout much of the Third World, the most fundamental change of all—the beginning of a modern system—came about through transplantation of forms under colonial rule. Africa is a continent of such cases: "Most African universities are recent European transplants, founded during the terminal colonial period with metropolitan capital and by metropolitan planners, and any Africans who were consulted were themselves the products of a colonial or metropolitan education."[53] Here the effects of international transfer run deep: forced imposition initiated a modern system, as modernity was defined in the advanced colonial power. The basic forms thereby put in place provided a division of work, a set of beliefs, and a structure of control that defined, with many unspoken assumptions, what higher education should accomplish and how it should be implemented. One or more other countries were deeply involved in laying down "the genetic imprint" of the emerging national system.[54]

The leading example of forced transfer in the last half-century has been the imposition of a Soviet Communist model on the many countries of Eastern Europe. Under heavy Soviet influence as well as that of the new "native" Communist regimes, the contemporary systems of the German Democratic Republic, Poland, Czechoslovakia, Hungary, Rumania, and Albania have added such features as the dual control of party apparatus and state administration, the explicit use of criteria of political loyalty, the separation of much research from the university into a separate academy of science, and a strong commitment to manpower planning and a correlated "rationalization" of the university for practical results. In such relatively developed societies, however, the new forms had to be grafted upon systems with deep historical roots and modern complexity.

For example, the universities already in place in East Germany in 1945 had centuries of development behind them, including a part in the nineteenth and twentieth-century evolution of the Humboldtian model in which research was assigned the central place and the chair-holding professor had achieved virtually unparalleled status and power. The genetic imprint was deeply embedded. Hence, the old structure was not entirely swept away by new forms, even though it was weakened in the previous fascist period. The result has been a hybrid of traditional German forms and new features imposed from the Soviet model. Firmer administrative pyramids have been constructed, laced together with ministerial controls and appointed rectors. Much research has flowed from the universities to separately funded research institutes. Government officials have planned and effected a differentiation in which nonuniversity sectors have been supported and strengthened. Yet senior professors have maintained much of their traditional status and, although challenged by criteria of state loyalty and party ideology, severely at times, they have undergone less erosion of their traditional power by internal "democratization" than their counterparts in the West. East European professors can remark, half-seriously, that their universities internally are the last stronghold of the Humboldtian tradition.

Voluntary importation has long been a fundamental means of academic change. The U.S. system is one great example, since it was influenced strongly not only by English understandings carried into a new territory by early settlers but also by Scottish-oriented reformers in the eighteenth and nineteenth centuries and, of course, by aspects of the German style brought back by U.S. scholars and observers who saw the German university in action in the late nineteenth and early twentieth centuries. Japan has been another major example. As Ikuo Amano puts it: "One must start from the fact that Japan created its higher educational system by using the Western universities as models."[55] Under a national commitment to modernization, beginning in the last quarter of the nineteenth century, a systematic effort was instituted to import foreign scholars, to send native scholars and students abroad, and to translate and disseminate materials written in other languages in other countries. In time, the foreign scholars were less needed, as nationals became experts and the universities thereby competently staffed.

The Japanese borrowing of forms was highly pragmatic: chair organization within the university was strongly influenced by the German model, but German provincial control was left aside, since the national government was the principal driving force behind modernization and turned to a national-ministry form of super-structure. One early state institution employed French professors and taught French law; another, initially staffed with faculty from Scotland, imitated a Swiss polytechnic; and in still another the basic idea of organization came from the American land grant college. Then, too, much Japanese importation was not state controlled. The government took a laissez-faire attitude toward private efforts, allowing a private sector to develop within which Christian liberal arts colleges, staffed in part by foreign missionaries, reflected British and particularly American sources. Out of all this came a hybrid structure in which "the state sector bore a close resemblance to the European, especially the German, system of higher education," but "in terms of its competitive nature, the private sector resembled the American college system."[56]

Forced importation is typically wholesale and broad in scope, since the agents of the dominating country have much power to enforce their understanding of how to organize higher learning. Then, too, they already have a complete idea of what an entire system could be like, even if they sense problems of fit in the new setting. Voluntary borrowing is typically more piecemeal, allowing various indigenous needs and expectations greater influence in determining what will be brought from abroad and applied experimentally toward creating an appropriate system.

In both cases, the most interesting aspect of the internation route of change is the adaptation of the foreign forms to native conditions and traditions. The greatest problems of adaptation are caused by the combination of (1) forced, wholesale transplantation and (2) countries differing radically in social structure and culture. This combination has appeared most often in the many poor countries of Africa and Asia that have emerged only in the mid-twentieth century from colonial rule. Here, the wholesale transplantation of European models, primarily English and French, served to establish universities that laid "great stress on the need for measuring up to the 'intellectual gold standard' as established in the West," thereby underestimating "the extent to which an institution of alien origin requires adaptation if it is to become an integral part of a society."[57] The universities were made exotic to their environments:

> [The African universities] were high-quality, high-cost institutions, somewhat aloof from the rest of the local educational system. They tended to accentuate the already serious cleavages in society by separating students from their social background, conditioning them to an alien life style, and leading them to expect that after they graduated they would be able to command salaries comparable with those in Western industrial countries. They also tended to regard research as the overriding criterion by which a scholar should be judged and to place inadequate stress on the quality of his teaching and his contribution to the immediate needs of his society. Moreover, their curricula followed metropolitan models so closely that, for example, Ibadan quickly developed a department of classics, but ten years after its foundation "no courses were offered in engineering, economics, law, geology, anthropology, sociology, public administration or Arabic and Islamic studies, and it had taken eight years to establish a department of education."[58]

With the metropolitan model deeply institutionalized in the new setting, the native regimes soon confront the issue of "cultural dependence": have we achieved political independence only to go on being dominated by alien cultural forms that are inappropriate to our condition and that tie us to international networks controlled by others? Efforts to achieve cultural independence then accentuate, as they have in Africa,

> the tension that exists everywhere between rival claimants for the allegiance of the professoriate: the territorial state and the universal profession. In each case [in Africa] the balance has shifted towards the state to a greater extent than in Western democracies such as Great Britain and the United States.[59]

The native regimes of the most underdeveloped countries are particularly prone to press their universities to become instruments of national development. As in many new African countries, the regime may stand back for awhile, busy with other more pressing problems, initially in awe of university intellectuals or confident that they will take up the necessary tasks. But impatience then sets in and the demands for relevance become more strident. As noted by James S. Coleman in the late 1970s, "the exhortation that an African university must be demonstrably relevant for and totally committed to national development has now become so incessant and all-engulfing that it saturates all speeches, studies, debates, and discussion of the raison d'être of the institution."[60] As regimes press hard in this direction, they risk emphasizing particularism at the expense of universality, seeking to leave the intellectual gold standard and live by a local intellectual currency.

The dilemma is acute, since to localize higher education is to risk becoming a permanent intellectual backwater, institutionalizing a parochial point of view, dampening the disciplinary and professional interests and contacts of the professors, and losing scarce talent to countries that provide more attractive conditions for research, scholarship, and teaching. "The developmental imperative," if effected and institutionalized, would leave its own genetic imprint on all that would follow.

The problems of adaptation are considerably less when transplantation is voluntary and piecemeal, since then, as in the United States and Japan, "alien" forms are tested for fit to native conditions and traditions and adopted and reshaped in bits and pieces. Such transplanting is made easiest when the receiving and sending countries are culturally similar, as in the case of Australia, New Zealand, and English-speaking Canada in relation to England and the United States. Knowledge and skills—and entire forms—may then be transferred and circulated with a minimum of nationalistic barriers and with few worries about cultural domination and dependence.

In the 1960s and early 1970s, Australian universities filled approximately forty percent of their openings with appointees trained in other countries, largely Britain and the United States, half of whom were returning Australians. Thus, the addition of foreigners was extensive, as was the cycling of Australians through foreign universities.[61] In Canada, the proportion of foreign-born academics in some disciplines, particularly the social sciences, exceeded fifty percent in the 1960s, a proportion so high as finally to stimulate resentment and heighten fears of cultural dependence on the United States. These borrowing countries were predisposed to adopt the intellectual gold standard, opting to be part of international networks through which academic talent flows. The movement of people brings a diffusion of forms and practices that range from how to organize a faculty and secure the job rights of academics to the necessity of assembling a good collection of port and sherry.

It is in the voluntary mode of international transplantation that we see the power of the historically central models of higher education: the British, the German, the French, and the American. The standards of these systems have flowed into an intellectual gold standard that acts as a magnet for the academics of internationally peripheral systems. As prestigious models, they set in motion a process of academic drift among nations, analogous to the voluntary convergence within systems identified earlier. But that process never goes uncontested, since countertrends are excited by the "local" interests of nations. The countertrends encourage country-by-country variation, an international diversity conditioned by the prior structures, educational traditions, and emerging needs of countries, new and old, large and small. Hence, intersystem change is subject to even more contradictory pulls than change stimulated largely from within a system, since the conditioning contexts are more varied across nations than within them.

What is the future of internation change? In higher education as in other institutional spheres, countries are in an age of increased voluntary learning from one another. For example, academics and academic officials in Western Europe are now in closer communication with one another across national boundaries than they were a quarter-century and a half-century ago, systematically linked by not only such general, international organizations as the European Economic Community and the Organisation for Economic Cooperation and Development (OECD) but also by multicountry disciplinary associations. Counterparts in Eastern Europe are also observant of one another's virtues and defects, successes and failures, as they attempt to operate systems of higher education within an Eastern bloc, variously fusing traditional ideas and forms with Communist doctrine and practices. The international organizations have an interest in offering lessons across national lines. And, as stressed earlier, increasing numbers of disciplines and professional fields reward academics for international contacts, leading them happily to internationalize higher education as they go about their duties. It requires no great effort to "whistle while you work" when making a trip to London or Paris or Rio de Janeiro.

Thus, as internation communication accelerates, so do the possibilities of internation learning, even if the observed lessons are ones to be avoided or counteracted. International transfer will not become an unimportant source of reforming ideas and unplanned flows, even if forced impositions are less numerous in the future and civil service restrictions on travel and employment more constraining. Reforming ideas drawn from other countries constitute part of the external demands pressed upon higher education systems, ideas that have to be interpreted for their bearing on local interests and then either rebuffed or revamped and adapted to the forms already in place.

KNOWLEDGE AND CHANGE

As modern society's main institution of knowledge creation and dissemination, the academic system is inherently multisided, diffuse, and bottom-heavy. Change is affected accordingly:

(1) Despite the belief of many observers that academic systems change significantly only when pressured by external forces, such systems increasingly exhibit innovation and adaptation among their bottom units. Invention and diffusion are institutionalized in the work of the departments and counterpart units that embody the disciplines and professions. Universities, and many nonuniversity units, move ahead in a somewhat self-propelled fashion in those areas of new thought that are perceived by academics as acceptable within general paradigms of academic knowledge. Such change is widely overlooked since it is not announced in master plans or ministerial bulletins and is not introduced on a global scale. It occurs in segments of the operating level that exchange with one another and is not characteristic of the larger entities. In a bottom-heavy

knowledge institution, grass-roots innovation is a crucial form of change.

(2) Much change that is instigated by influences external to specific academic enterprises comes about in largely unnoticed ways by means of boundary roles that are spread throughout the operating levels. Boundary roles are normally viewed as limited to managerial offices that specialize in contact with the environment, as in the case of admissions, public relations, and grant offices in universities. But members of professional schools reach outside to their respective professions, and members of the many disciplinary departments and clusters reach outside to other members of their fields, within and outside the system itself. Hence, boundary roles are spread throughout the professional understructure. Professors engage in activities defined as characteristic of such roles:[62] they scan and monitor external events; they engage in information gatekeeping; they transact with other groups; and they link and coordinate between the inside and outside. Thus, the bridges to the outside are numerous and widely dispersed, within the individual enterprise and the system as a whole. Changes creep across those bridges quietly and with little notice.

(3) Incremental adjustment is the pervasive and characteristic form of change. Since tasks and powers are so extensively divided, global change is ordinarily very difficult to effect. The more advanced the system, the more it is true that "anything that requires a coordinated effort of the organization in order to start is unlikely to be started. Anything that requires a coordinated effort of the organization in order to be stopped is unlikely to be stopped."[63] Especially in democracies, the leading false expectation in academic reform is that major results can be obtained by top-down manipulation. Such reforms are occasionally initiated and implemented, but more commonly small results follow from multiple efforts at the top, in the middle, or at the bottom that entail wrong experiments, false starts, and zigzag adjustments, a melange of actions out of which precipitate some flows of change. Dramatic examples of such flows are found in the evolutionary buildup of knowledge in first the physical sciences and then the biological sciences in the twentieth century, accompanied by an increasing dominance of these fields in resources and power within universities and national systems. Of

course, in less-developed systems under authoritarian rule, a less complicated and less bottom-heavy structure can be more readily manipulated from on high. But even in the most top-influenced systems, with such controls as those found in the Soviet Union, observers report that adaptation characteristically takes place "by small steps instead of far-reaching reform."[64] Small steps come with the territory.

(4) More than elsewhere, changes initiated at the top commonly need the support of interests residing at lower levels. Those at the top have to "carry the field" rather than command it, building internal constituencies and coalitions to support and implement their own desires. So many centrally announced reforms have no lasting deposit because internal constituencies are not effectively summoned to support them. When a system is bottom-heavy, groups at the grass-roots are key participants in implementing policies and reforms.

(5) Particularly in systems where tasks and powers are extensively divided and dispersed, change in structure is what fundamental change means. Structural change modifies who does what on a regular basis; *and* who decides regularly on who will do what. Another powerful reason why so many top-down reforms have no lasting deposits is that they do not alter the understructure of actual operations. Changes that proceed by altering the structure alter the fundamental biases of a system, changing the source of opinion and power expressed in the agendas of decision and in the procedures of daily operation.

(6) Much academic change is invisible. Knowledge is relatively invisible as a material and a product. Developing thoughts, as in research; transmitting thoughts, as in teaching; absorbing thoughts, as in learning—all are difficult to see and to evaluate directly at the time they occur. Reports on research provide some tracking of what occurred in research; but textbooks, examinations, and grades tangibly represent only in a partial way what is taking place in teaching and learning. Then, too, operations are particularly opaque when they are diverse, arcane, and shielded by layers of organization. In academic systems, it is difficult to perceive from on high or from the outside, or indeed from within, what is constant and especially what is changing.

Thus, innovation, reform, and change are not topics that can be divorced from the study of structure and tradition. The heavy hand of history is felt in contemporary structures and beliefs, and what is now in place conditions what will be. As internal structures acquire greater momentum, they thrust themselves powerfully into the future and snap back with considerable resilience after imposed changes seemingly alter their ways. Desired changes attenuate and fail unless they become a steady part of the structure of work, the web of belief, and the division of control. We begin to know the score in the study of academic change when we understand how the various current structures stack the deck.

III
Normative Theory

SEVEN

VALUES

In and around higher education, various groups press broad values upon the system. The claims come from all sides: business executives, union leaders, church officials, minority representatives, journalists and other stray observers, spokesmen for the family. The groups increasingly articulate the primary values through government, since government is *the* modern sponsor and hence the crucial part of the environment within which higher education resides. Vague societal values are brought down out of the clouds of free-floating rhetoric as they are defined in the chambers of the legislature, the meeting rooms of the political parties, the hallways of the executive branch, especially the department or ministry of education, and the offices of such bodies as the superior council of public instruction, the grants committee, and the national academy of science. We no longer need to guess about which values really count from among those presented in polls and in textbooks; nor do we need to turn to philosopher-kings for new statements on essence and eternal truth, for we observe the values expressed by powerful groups as they act out their interests in and around the system.

Cross-national comparisons help immensely in identifying basic values and their transformations into pressing interests, since we can thereby note underlying issues that key actors seem to face in common across many countries, even as they do so in different degrees and in situations that dictate dissimilar responses. Any given country may also understate a particular value, at least for a a time, thereby submerging what others more clearly project. Nations make major blunders in higher education as they ignore certain primary values and concentrate on others. They may swing in their efforts from one pole to another. An international view then supports normative postures that have some warrant in observed national experiences. We can advise the modern state, especially when its current commitments overlook what is obvious elsewhere.

THE BASIC VALUES

Three basic sets of values are inescapable in the expectations of attentive publics in the modern period, the interests of government officials themselves, and the attitudes of academic workers. One set may be denoted as justice, a second as competence, and a third as liberty. A fourth orientation, powerfully developed by government itself, we may call loyalty. Actions carried out on behalf of these values often clash, even contradict one another, necessitating accommodations that soften conflict and allow simultaneous expression.

SOCIAL JUSTICE

A national valuation of social justice—fair treatment for all—is pressed upon modern academic systems as a set of issues of equality and equity, first *for* students and second *by* faculty, other staff, enterprises, and sectors *for themselves*. With respect to students, equality is taken to consist, in ascending order of stringency, of equality of opportunity in the sense of access, equality of opportunity in the sense of treatment once admitted, and equality of outcome or reward. These broad conceptions of equality are variously defined, with significant effects. It is one thing to hold to a strict definition of equality of access whereby entry is determined by the academic qualification of the individual without regard to such "extraneous" characteristics as race, class, creed, or political affiliation, and quite another to define equality of access in a looser, more populist fashion as an open door for all, subordinating criteria of merit as defined by academic achievement.

Systems that profess open access but find only a third or less of their youth "qualified for higher education" clearly are using the first interpretation. The systems of Great Britain and nearly all of the European continent, and indeed most of the world, remain in this category, even as they expand manyfold from the time when only several percent of the population entered and even as an open-door concept becomes rhetoric and policy. "Open door" is taken to mean entry for all those who meet certain qualifications exacted by secondary schools, or the institutions of higher education, or both. In contrast, systems that let in anyone who wants to enter are clearly using the second interpretation.

Entry without particular academic merit is apparent in the U.S. system, where some students entering four-year colleges and universities are still reading at the eighth-grade level—products of automatic or social promotion in the lower grades—and some students entering the most modern and open of the community colleges, as in California, are illiterate in one language and sometimes in two. In lesser degree, this more open interpretation is found in the systems of countries as diverse as Japan, Canada, and Sweden— the latter, among the countries of Europe and Scandinavia, offering those who want to go to college the best chance to do so, regardless of academic background. This can be done by going to work for a few years, awaiting the twenty-fifth birthday, and then entering college under the 25-5 plan (later 25-4) established in 1977. Everywhere in democratic societies, equality of access is a strong and seemingly now-permanent value, and the trend in definition has been toward the looser form, under which virtually anyone can get in, in one way or another, at one time or another.[1] Even modern authoritarian and totalitarian regimes are hardly able permanently to ignore claims for equality of access: indeed, to the extent that these regimes promise greater fairness in society, as do the more socialist ones, they emphasize this value.

Beyond access, the interest in justice for students appears as a demand for uniform standards across a system so that students in given fields will be treated equally and will be given certificates of equal value. As noted in chapter 2, this point of view was institutionalized a long time ago in the university systems of such countries as France and Italy, in which the degree is issued by the national system as a whole and not by the individual institution, backed by the claim that training has been similar in programs throughout the nation. Ironically, although equal treatment is seen in modern reform as a more stringent definition of equality than is equal access, it developed in many systems at a time when access was sharply limited and decidedly unequal. For the few who were admitted, treatments—programs—were to be standardized, and rewards—

professional degrees—were to be similar across institutions. The nationalization of systems of higher education typically entails some movement in these directions. The demand for these forms of equality also typically strengthens as access widens, with various groups seeing them as the full flowering of a true democratization. After equal access, the refrain goes, the next steps are equal treatment while in the system and equal rewards upon leaving.

Personnel and whole enterprises also steadily pursue equitable treatment, as we have frequently noted, since "have-nots" have a driving and permanent interest in parity with the "haves." Uniformity is the seemingly obvious cure, in the eyes of many professors, institutional administrators, union leaders, and central officials alike. This form of equity is expressed in official insistence on fair shares for institutions and programs as well as for individuals. Bureaucracy and democracy here converge, as stressed by Susanne Hoeber Rudolph and Lloyd I. Rudolph in their study of Indian higher education:

> If bureaucratic uniformity is an important aspect of the genetic imprint that was impressed on the Indian education system, democracy has served to reinforce the propensity to uniformity. Andhra officials, like officials in other states, are likely to think uniformity a self-evident virtue. The union ministry of education, in establishing a national committee to formulate a "model act" for all universities, reflected India's educational heritage. The committee's charge contained bureaucratic notions that uniform rules might "neaten up" the confusion and conflict and perhaps "cure" the diseases that seemed to afflict academia. . . . Differences suggest the possibility of privilege and invite uniformity as a possible cure.[2]

The concept of fair share is so ubiquitous in public administration that evenhandedness, or balance, comes to mean that budget increases and decreases are to be shared as evenly as possible. As put by an observer of Japanese budget making: "Balancing represents avoidance of comparisons among programs and their merits by implying that simply because they are similar they should receive the same or equivalent budgets."[3] Equity is a natural concern of the bureaucrat. Thus, the claims of administrators and faculty in the

polytechnic colleges of the British system for salary levels and research support on a par with those of the universities found support
in the British government. In the United States, state colleges find
some support in the logic of state politics and administration in their
efforts not to be treated as second best; and the lesser campuses of
multicampus state universities can find support for parity with the
flagship campus. It is difficult for officials, elected or those under
civil service, to argue for differences in personnel treatment and
rewards across and within categories of institutions. They can find
legitimate reasons to support differences, but those reasons must
then come from such other values as competence.

Bureaucratic efforts to be orderly bring together the principle of
fair shares for everyone with a process of coercive comparison,
whereby unequal treatments are revealed, made invidious, and
leveraged by ideology and power. Norms of impartiality and objective treatment are brought into play, whether in Japan, the United
States, France, or Poland. And, what is critical, the placing of universities and colleges in larger systems highlights dissimilarities and
magnifies differences. If we are part of one system, how come *they*
are getting so much more than we? Such comparisons become
coercive as they become operationalized in the representation of
interest within the system and in the normal efforts of the various
parts to obtain more resources for their work. Lower administrators
and professors have a vested interest in knowing what other departments, faculties, and universities are getting, and then arguing
for parity whenever others get more. The have-nots have a more
coercive claim in the integrated system that they be brought up to
parity than they would if they were in a separate system or systems.
And, under bureaucratic norms, the higher levels of the system
are vulnerable to such internal demands, since fair administration means all hands should be treated equally without regard to
heritage, distinctive character, accumulated pride, and personal
opinion.

That administered systems are often explicitly dedicated to a
general equalizing of their many parts is made particularly clear
when a national system offers national degrees. Such degrees become ludicrous if the programs of study and the standards of passage are markedly dissimilar. "The state" is vouching for the preparation, certifying that the many graduates of the many institutions

have met common standards. The nationalized mode is one in which central administration works over decades to honor such commitments by spreading thousands of administrative categories across institutions.

COMPETENCE

A second powerful set of values emphasizes competence. So many social groups need a capable system of higher education, one effectively organized to produce, criticize, and distribute knowledge, one that can send forth, in a reliable stream, people well prepared for occupational performance and civil life. The state needs qualified people, preferably outstanding ones, as do the professions and private firms. Everywhere there is talk about improving or maintaining the quality of education overall, or at least in certain fields that appear deficient or are connected to a deepening national need (e.g., economic analysis or military preparation).

The true believers in "excellence" have no trouble in presenting dramatic arguments. When you are wheeled into the operating room, do you want an incompetent surgeon behind the knife? It is widely deemed inadvisable to become seriously ill in countries that have low-quality medical education. Or, if our planners must be tutored in the dismal science of economics, why should we allow them to receive admittedly mediocre instruction? If they got the best, the argument goes, we could at least reduce the probability of grand mistakes in national policy. Or, why is it necessary for our otherwise advanced nation to remain on the periphery in one scientific field after another—an argument heard even in technologically advanced Japan as critics castigate the country for a tradition of imitating rather than inventing and blame the academic system for not producing more Nobel Prize winners.[4] The preference for competence comes in so many sizes and shapes: the work of academic individuals and groups; the quality of students at entry and exit; the effectiveness of institutions and systems; general education; professional preparation; research; criticism—even competence in achieving social justice. As within any other broad set of values, internal contradictions will abound: to be very good at one thing means a concentration in it that courts weak capacity to do well in other endeavors.

Academics themselves often root their own individual and group
self-interest in quality of performance, since so many of them belong
to fields within which judgments on capability are made across the
borders of institutions and even, as we have seen, across national
systems. The more scientific the discipline the more those within it
judge virtue on the basis of international standards. The status-
award systems of most individual disciplines and professions use
quality as an important criterion to the point where perceived
competence dominates positional power: e.g., a brilliant assistant
professor is "better" than a mediocre full professor. A unified academic profession may also perform this way across much, if not all,
of a national system. Great Britain is the foremost case of quality
control by peer surveillance: the practice of external examiners
means that professors of different institutions test one another's
students and thereby indirectly but immediately evaluate the quality
of one another's performance. This procedure encourages critical
comment, much of it informal and oblique, about the teaching and
the research of others. The contrast is most noticeable with the U.S.
system, which, lacking similar peer surveillance of curricula and
student performance, has never been able to judge teaching across
institutions the way it does research. Perhaps the most important
way to improve teaching competence in large systems is to concentrate on practices that entail peer intrusion, lifting the veils that
normally shroud the teaching behavior of individual professors and
departments. Peer witnessing can enter where political and bureaucratic surveillance dare not, and ought not, tread, because it is
self-defeating.

Basic to competence is the robust fact that fields of study are
structures of knowledge that have to be mastered by those who teach
and those who learn. The general framework of education cannot
take any shape at all that will fit other values but must be constrained
by the relatively fixed forms constructed in the many fields as ways of
organizing knowledge.[5] There is science, mathematics, and languages; grammar, logic, induction, and deduction. So-called soft
subjects such as history are still complex, sufficiently pyramidal and
sequential that those who would be called competent must work
their way from lower to higher levels of understanding, from a
superficial to a genuine grasp. Mastery of subject matter and related
analytical skills is an inescapable aspect of formal learning, one not

likely to be overlooked by all observers all the time, even if some groups or states for awhile pretend otherwise. Nations that damp their interest in competence, through neglect or through attending to other values, are forced in time to turn around and face it. For example, China attempted to give low priority to academic competence during the period known as the Cultural Revolution, as reflected in the practice of forcing professors and students to spend large blocks of time in the rice fields or in some other way of participating in the work of the poorly educated masses.[6] But, at the end of the 1970s, with much fanfare, the public policies and some of the relevant practices of the central regime swung back toward a posture that would allow professors and students to concentrate on what they know most intimately and are able to do best.

It is possible to make the pursuit of excellence into a lethal habit, whether in research on human subjects, in the discovery of more ways of mass destruction, or in the emphasis on grades and credentials that leads to mental breakdown and suicide in young people. High concentration on competence in any one field, institution, or system has its costs. Perhaps most common now among the costs observed and heartily disliked by many is a certain lack of democracy. Whenever there are centers of excellence, a few are chosen and the many left out. The exclusion stimulates a counterargument that there should be a democratization of knowledge: if knowledge is power and it is concentrated, more effort should be made to scatter it. Then, too, the pursuit of self-interest on the part of competent specialist groups may or may not serve the general welfare. "Elite functions" are necessary, but they will always be in tension with mass participation and certain democratic ideals.

LIBERTY

A third set of values that plays upon systems of higher education links together choice, initiative, innovation, criticism, and variety. The central idea in this complex is liberty, connecting to traditional values expressed in Western political thought and emphasizing freedom of action as the basic condition for exercising choice, encouraging initiative, engaging in innovative behavior, sustaining criticism, and inducing variety. Liberties are sought by groups and institutions in higher education as well as by individuals. Departmental groups seek self-determination within the university; the university presses for autonomy from the state and from outside groups. The desired states of freedom are argued as a basis for wider choice in lines of action, more leeway in criticizing past and present policy, and so on, actions that in the aggregate extend variety. The subvalues of this complex interact: a variety of institutions extend the range of choice for students, teachers, and administrators alike; extension of choice on the demand side tends to lead to more innovation and variety on the supply side, as institutions respond differently to a wider set of demands and carve out different niches.

This set of values includes the powerful academic ideologies of freedom of research, freedom of teaching, and freedom of learning. Those who do research claim maximum freedom is necessary at work if they are to do their job properly and help science and scholarship to advance. Those who teach have long elaborated the notion that they must be free to say what they please without retribution if society is to benefit from self-criticism and wrongs are to be righted. Those who learn, in a variety of nations, assert individual choice in what they will study and even in what way and at what pace they will pursue learning. Freedom of the learner was given great dignity in the nineteenth-century German university, as the doctrine of *Lernfreiheit*—essentially, freedom to learn—was linked to and placed on a philosophical plane with the freedom to teach. The freedom of students to engage in social criticism and political action has had strong doctrinal support in Latin America since the 1920s, including the idea of the campus as a sanctuary for student expression. In general, freedom for one's own group is near the core of most group self-interest. Students have been no less influenced by this value than professors, even if they are less powerfully positioned in most systems to sustain a doctrine, press their claims, and effect their hopes.

Basic to this set of values is the desire for individual self-expression, not only among academics and intellectuals but among larger proportions of the general populace. Democratic values raise expectations of individuality—freedom, taken to mean more people allowed to do as they please. Economic progress lifts more people to a standard of living where time and resources are available for something beyond dawn-to-dusk labor. Rising educational levels encourage expectations about the enriched life that was formerly the province of the few. Consumers, then, come to education, especially higher education, with a variety of marginally differentiated hopes and desires that combine various aspects of self-development, such as increased autonomy, with occupational preparation and enhanced life chances; e.g., to be free and expert, therefore a computer consultant; to be altruistic but rich, therefore a lawyer who saves some time for helping the poor.

The demands of students upon nearly all advanced higher education systems clearly have multiplied tremendously, in part because of the more heterogeneous labor market into which they will later plunge, but also because the spreading valuation of individual self-expression argues against the "lockstep" of uniform programs and standard progression. Each individual literally can see higher education differently, come to it differently in preparation and personality, and ask for an individual arrangement. Linked to the desire for self-expression is a desire for variety and even for eccentricity. More people think that higher education can help them to be creative—and creative people, in myth and in fact, have long modeled to the world how richly rewarding it is to be inconsistent and eccentric.

LOYALTY

There is always a body of interests brought to bear in higher education that is centered in the operation of the state, a group of interests bound up in the survival of regimes and the identity of nations. "Loyalty" is perhaps the best name to apply to this complex that stretches from the limiting of criticism to the linking of the system to national integration. To overlook this set of values would be to avoid issues that are at the heart of the higher education question in one country or another.

Particularly poignant is the depth of the clash in values in many new underdeveloped nations that causes politicians and academics to collide head-on. As pointed out in chapter 6, the academics typically wish to pursue their work in line with their own adjustments of metropole models and international standards. But the national political and bureaucratic leaders seek to build a nation by promoting a singular symbolic identity, integrating diverse tribes and factions, constructing the infrastructure essential to nationhood (such as transportation and communication networks), and delivering on promises of a better life. In addition, they often are impatient with democratic forms—seeing them as dangerous to unity and slow in producing results—and prefer authoritative rule for a variety of reasons. Hence, they not only expect higher education to march shoulder-to-shoulder with other branches of government in the cause of nation building but also expect the university administrators and professors to follow the definition of nationhood, its ends and means, decided upon by the leader and his immediate staff. The relation between higher education and government, then, often tilts toward domination by government. Fealty to the state looms large. It is more difficult than in advanced nations to dissociate the tasks of the university from the tasks of the state.

This set of values, like the others, has its own contradictions. What the state wants from the higher education system may be at least three different types of relevance: socioeconomic relevance, defined in terms of practicality and professionalization; cultural relevance, referring to cultural revival and national identity; and political relevance, defined as good citizenship and commitment to political goals. The first means an emphasis on technology, natural science, and specific professional training. The second hinges on competence in the humanities and the social sciences, with a particular focus on one's own country, but allowing for freedom of inquiry and exposition in those fields. The imperative of political relevance places primacy upon conformity, uniformity, and discipline. As James A. Coleman notes in the case of African universities: "The ideology of relevance applied to frail new universities imposes upon them a heavy overload which is patently compounded when the demands upon them are so inherently contradictory."[7]

Basic to the state-university relationship everywhere are the boundaries established for outspoken criticism of state actions and societal conditions. The boundaries can indeed be very wide: fools have to be suffered gladly in British academic life by state officials because there is virtually no way to get rid of them. No direct orders can be given to block employment or disbar promotion or restrict salary. No leverage against the employing institution is available for its "mistaken" toleration. The boundaries can also vary markedly within a single system, in line with its diversity. In the United States, toleration varies by state—greater in New York than in Mississippi;

by level—greater in universities than in community colleges; by degree of public support—greater in private universities than in public; and by institutional quality—greater in excellent liberal arts colleges than in mediocre ones.

The limits on criticism can be especially wide also where sharp criticism of government and society has become a way of life in higher education institutions—the many countries, advanced and developing, where university and government exist virtually as two different cultures, and students expect both to be critical and to play out their personality development in politics. Criticizing and struggling against the government is a way of life in faculty and student subcultures in Italy and France, as it has been in such Latin American countries as Mexico, Chile, and Argentina whenever the government is something less than harshly authoritarian. In the many Latin countries, the posture of criticism, of course, is a dangerous game—often more persistent, more strident, more violent than that found elsewhere, but then subject to a crackdown by the state and a severe tightening of the limits of expression when a hostile regime comes to power, often by coup, or when under a benign regime state officials feel pushed too far.

Finally, the wide boundaries for criticism can contract sharply when authoritarian regimes come to power and act vigorously to stay the flow of critical comment. And narrow boundaries are institutionalized as one-party regimes remain in power and have the will and the means to define opposition as illegitimate and even illegal. Hence, in the worldwide picture, loyalty and subservience to the will of the state are primary values, even if they do not appear on the front of the stage in Sweden or Britain, Japan or the United States. They are prominent in most new nations in Asia and Africa and in authoritarian states everywhere.

CONFLICT AND ACCOMMODATION

Any sensible administrator asked to confront directly and to reconcile these four orientations would undoubtedly seek other employment. Fortunately for officials, the system, not particular individuals, does most of the work of reconciliation. System accommodation proceeds largely by indirection and delayed interaction—

by analogy, more in line with the urgings of Niccolò Machiavelli to temporize, temporize than with the injunctions of those management theorists who would have us clarify goals, order priorities, and implement objectives, all by five o'clock.[8] In higher education, any major enterprise is a compromise of conflicting values, and system organization is compromise written large. But some organizers are poor compromisers, more often for reasons of ideology than intelligence. System compromising can be badly done, as certain values become set in the concrete of position and power and then deny an adequate realization of other ends.

The conflicting values press behavior in contradictory directions and encourage antithetical forms and procedures. The value of social justice presses toward open-door admission, mass passage, and uniform graduation. But the interest in competence everywhere argues for selection at the outset, a willingness to fail and weed out, and for graded certification that will label some persons as more capable than others. The clash between equity and excellence on the issue of entry and certification has been widely noted in educational debate during the decades since World War II, especially in the 1960s and 1970s. The problem is found in Communist as well as democratic nations. Educational policy in the USSR has vacillated between emphasizing admission based on performance and admission based on social status, i.e., preference given to working-class and peasant youth. The result has been that "the quality of graduates has declined whenever social status has been the major criterion, but has increased whenever performance has been stressed." One value or the other had to give; or, a compromise might evolve.[9]

> The current situation may be seen as representing a compromise between ideological commitment to equality of opportunity and the necessity of meeting the skill needs of an increasingly complex economy. It is clear that in spite of recent reforms aimed at increasing the enrollment of working class and peasant youth in institutes and universities, the regime is very reluctant to give much weight to nonperformance criteria, and hence the overall impact of the reforms has been small. The manner in which the reforms have been implemented also indicates

that educators are themselves reluctant to forego universalistic criteria.

Similarly in the German Democratic Republic (East Germany): the
attempt to proletarianize DDR education has competed with the
desire

> to recruit the most gifted students wherever they are
> found and to train them so that they are able to serve
> DDR industry in the most productive way possible. . . . A
> victory of dogma over pragmatism . . . is apt to be brief
> and ineffectual.[10]

Less noted in both policy deliberations and research is how liberty
enters the fray, playing at times against both equity and competence.
For equity, fair shares is the name of the game and therefore
procedures must be set that apply across the board. The competence camp also presses for uniform arrangements, generally called
standards—well-constructed barriers to entry, required sequences
of courses and examinations for passage, and quality controls on
certification. But liberty is contrary to both, pressing away from both
fair shares and standardized forms and toward a maximizing of
choice and a celebration of variety.

U nder full sail, liberty means autonomous faculty individuals
acting with little regard for group norms and individual students
seeking individualized programs of study with little worry for common standards. Institutional liberty carries with it the likelihood that
institutions will vary all over the map in what they do, including the
marketing of shoddy goods to uninformed customers in the soft
underbelly of a diverse system. Those who want to ensure competence by measuring individuals against norms and standards ob-
struct such free choice and institutional self-determination. In turn,
liberties can clearly be diminished by equity-induced uniformities
despite the general hope that greater justice will bring more opportunity and choice. For example, a research assessment of widened
admission to higher education in Sweden by means of the much-
acclaimed 25-5 scheme pointed out that

> the strivings after fairness have resulted in its opposite:
> owing to excessively complicated rules and a gigantic
> central admission procedure the individual's possibility

> of asserting himself has suffered. Moreover, the system
> may disfavor applicants with unusual qualifications,
> social handicaps or the like.[11]

A generalized demand for fairness and equality in the Swedish case
has led to increased bureaucratization and centralization, which in
turn diminished individual choice. It also lessened the fairness that
comes from taking unusual qualifications or disadvantages into
account. Judging individuals by criteria plugged into a central computer, as was begun in the Federal Republic of Germany in the
1970s, cannot help but have mixed effects in areas of individual
choice and freedom to act.

Loyalty often conflicts straightaway with all three of the other
values, subordinating justice, competence, and liberty in the name
of a single higher good. When regimes are preoccupied with loyalty
of faculty and students, little heed is given to equal treatment or
competent training or freedom of choice.

Without doubt, the structure of a higher education system must
be full of contradictions, inconsistencies, and compromises if it is to
express effectively these four disparate primary values. As systems
modernize, as they move from less to more accessible education,
they widen and deepen their elemental strains and dilemmas by
having to attempt significantly to embody these values. Each system
must do so with forms and practices, institutionalized in earlier
decades, that are interlocked with one another as well as with various
structures in the larger society. Thus, post-1980, we need not wonder why modern systems of higher education should exhibit a bewildering mixture of the open and the closed, the elitist and the democratic, the flexible and the rigid, the traditional and the modern.

But all is not hopeless chaos. There are broad system arrangements that seem to reconcile these values better than others do. We
can assess how conflict among such fundamental interests is structurally abated. Although systematic inquiry into such matters has
hardly begun, six ideas deserve the light of day.

Idea One: Conflict among such basic values in higher education is
accommodated better by diverse than by simple structures. The
more diverse national systems are more capable of reconciliation
than the simple ones. Systems are pushed toward diversity by multiple values. A composite of *un*like segments and procedures (1) per-

mits better immediate response to different known demands; (2) allows varied later adjustment to the unknown and unantici- pated; and (3) provides a more ambiguous total space within which conflicting actions taken in the name of justice, competence, liberty, and loyalty can be played out. The sunk costs of each of the values are not so directly challenged since the true believers of each value get at least some territory of their own, are able to work their way around others, and find it difficult to determine who is doing what to whom. Those who are capable of holding several values in mind at the same time find some structural supports for each and maneuver by shifting priorities over time.

We have mapped the basic horizontal and vertical dimensions on which the needed differentiation occurs. Within their institutions, systems can and do generate more fields and programs side by side at any level of training and more levels arranged in a progression of increasingly advanced tiers. Among their institutions, systems can and do proliferate institutional types, arrange the types in func- tional and status hierarchies, and make permeable the boundaries between the sectors so that students can move from one to another in search of different types and levels of training. Diversification is the key to how higher education systems effect compromises among a plurality of insistent values. Simplicity demands confrontation among contradictory points of view.

Idea Two: In the service of competence, the most crucial form of diversification in modern advanced systems is vertical status differ- entiation among institutions. A moderate degree of hierarchy allows status to be awarded to institutions and sectors on grounds of perceived quality and encourages them to compete on this basis. One might immediately object and say that competence can be achieved better by administrative controls that seek to establish minimal standards and to reward for outstanding performance. But we have seen the complexity of tasks in higher education systems and the impelling need for the many parts to be at least semiauton- omous. It becomes virtually impossible, even self-defeating, to attempt to ensure competent effort in most of the system by top- down oversight, planning, and administration. Formal coordinators are in a steady state of frustration as critics demand that they move to improve the system and rulers send down commands from on high, but the levers of basic change remain remote if not hidden completely. The problem becomes sociological: namely, to find the ways to hook group and institutional self-interests to chariots of ambition. There must be something to be won by all those who man the understructure, working harder to be better. That something is higher status and its associated rewards.

Ralf Dahrendorf has argued effectively that both options and linkages ("ligatures") are necessary to enhance the life chances of individuals.[12] Options are possibilities of choice, the alternatives of action given in social structure. Linkages, no less important, are bonds that anchor persons and their actions and give meaning to choices. Those who are socially stitched together have some basis for judging where their choices will take them and what is worth doing. Without social links, choice becomes pointless; with ligatures, choice has coordinates. Further, undergirding both choice and linkage is hope, hope prodded not by utopian images but by realistic awareness that some individuals, groups, organizations, or countries possess what others aspire to. Thus, status inequality makes for hope, for both individuals and institutions. Institutional hope springs from institutional differences rather than from similarities.

The question of balance in hierarchical arrangements immediately occurs. The sharply peaked hierarchy that we noted in France, Britain, and Japan can isolate several institutions in elite positions and block out all others. The flat hierarchy noted as characteristic of the Italian system can block the incentives for enterprises to strive hard to better themselves. A middle ground provides the openness and the incentives, the grounds for hope. Institutions can compete for better personnel, and hence young scholars can flow from one institution to another in search of better conditions of work. Institutions can shift their clienteles toward the higher-quality inputs of their betters. There are many reasons to worry about academic drift, but competence as it is understood in the system and society at large is not one of them. Drift is toward "better"; it is a standards-serving process because it pursues status, and status is linked to perceived standards. This is a prime reason why status hierarchies are not as bad as they are normally viewed, through the modern perspectives of democracy. Where status hierarchies do not exist, there will be strong pressure to create them in order to guarantee a bottom-up search for competence.

The importance of institutional status hierarchies in promoting competence has been stressed by "best-science" advocates. Modern science at its best requires concentration of talent and resources. It can hardly be promoted by equalizing and thereby scattering talent and funds across institutions and programs. France in the West and the Communist nations in general have tried to assist "best science" by investing in a separate research structure—the national-academy approach. The Federal Republic of Germany has used the many institutes of the Max Planck shelter. But if best science, best scholarship more broadly, is to have protective and supportive locations within the higher education system itself, then there must be concentrations, some favorable treatment within and especially among institutions.[13]

The problem is to couple some hierarchy with some openness, pluralism, and peer review—a problem noted in classic form by Henry A. Rowland, an American scientist and exponent of best-science elitism who attempted to specify in the 1880s what needed to be done to improve the science of physics in the United States.[14] The existing system of 400 institutions he likened to a cloud of mosquitoes: hardly any could be compared with the "great academies" found in Europe, which provided "models of all that is considered excellent" and thereby stimulated physicists to their "highest effort." There had to be some concentration of talent in physics in a few first-class universities. Best science required an institutional pyramid, commanded at the heights by a best-science elite and open to talent at the bottom. All levels of the hierarchy would need to be pluralistic, with groups of physicists divided along lines of specialty, training, and geography and having access to many journals and granting agencies. The U.S. system, especially after World War II, did indeed evolve in the direction that Rowland had advocated.

In sum, institutional hierarchy can be and often is a form of quality control. It portions out status, respect, and rewards on grounds of perceived competence, utilizing both public opinion and peer assessment. It can and often does concentrate resources efficiently for the carrying out of expensive tasks, from the forming of bureaucratic elites to the manning of research laboratories. The problem is how thereby to preserve high standards and, at the same time, allow for institutional and individual mobility.

Idea Three: In the service of liberty, the most essential form of diversification is the creation and maintenance of different sectors and subsectors, down to the point of allowing institutions to be individually distinctive. Within the general system, enterprises need the freedom to initiate on their own and thereby choose a line of development. Much choice, we may note, can be made available within universities and colleges that are highly diverse in themselves, such as the "educational city" that we call the American state university. But there are limits to size and complexity of the individual enterprise that, when exceeded, cause severe problems of overload in work and management and confusion in organizational character. Institutions that try to do it all, replicating within their structures all that is found within the system at large—superinstitutions, we might call them—suffer some of the same problems of overload and characterological confusion as persons who try to be superwomen or supermen. What is critical is that certain bona fide group interests will be resisted or suppressed. No matter how extensive its internal diversity, an institution will still have some dominating points of view that will cause it to handle some activities badly, if not to prohibit them entirely.

The classic case in one country after another in recent years has been the resistance of university professors and administrators to short-cycle education and recurrent education. The resistance is motivated by a host of reasons that need not be explored here, but it has clearly weakened these forms of education. The groups that wish to carry the new values and work them up in operations need the freedom to choose for themselves. Increasingly it is necessary to divide up the work among institutions so that different units can wholeheartedly devote themselves to different tasks. Professional training at many levels, general education of different types and for different kinds of students, research of quite different complexities and ranging from the most basic to the heavily applied—all can be assumed by different structures of support and sorted out by planning or unplanned evolution or a combination of the two.[15] Separate institutions are typically less coupled than the parts of a single organization and hence can reap the benefits of flexibility that inhere in loose coupling.[16]

Thus, a prime reason why undifferentiated national systems cannot manage modern higher education very well is that they do not provide enough liberty for a range of ideas, activities, and supporting groups. Preeminently in academic systems, ideas have a right to be born, even at some inconvenience to system coordinators and their search for integration. Despite the confusion, duplication, and overlap thereby produced, a vast complex of institutional types and marginally differentiated institutions is the name of the game for liberty and innovation in modern higher education. But the problem is how to maintain a high level of institutional liberty and individual choice without limiting equality too severely and weakening standards too much. In this, permeable boundaries are crucial. Diversity becomes more acceptable to those with their eyes on equality if the diverse channels of participation are void of dead ends. Having second and third chances and the possibility of transferring from one sector to another, one institution to another, diminishes the disagreeable effects. Similarly, diversity and a high degree of individual choice become more acceptable to those with their eyes on competence and consumer protection if some academic surveillance, such as accreditation, operates across sectoral and institutional lines, maintaining some minimal standards and reigning in the roguish behavior on the part of institutions and their staffs that sometimes amounts to consumer fraud.

Idea Four: Justice in higher education is most effectively implemented if it is institutionally disaggregated instead of applied in a blanket fashion across a system. As we have seen, competence and liberty require sectors and hierarchies; merit and choice entail differences and rankings, unlike segments seen as relatively high and low, noble and less noble, even as systems strain to blur the perceptions of the differences. Hence, if these two values are to be served even modestly well, systemwide equal access, treatment, and outcome are not possible.

The idea of disaggregating justice is not a popular one, since equity issues loom large on the national agenda in many countries, attracting parents, students, politicians, and administrators alike to the promise that inequities can be wiped out by sweeping measures. But systemwide attacks on equity issues in higher education have great potential for boomerang effects as they try to flatten institutional differences and command a system to be unitary, thereby undercutting the grounds for competence and liberty. Since the system cannot be made operationally unitary and differences are maintained and enlarged, high expectations of equality are inevitably frustrated. Sooner or later, the vision of equity must center on fairness in segments of the whole and even, if possible, at the level of the individual institution.

Systems may thereby help contain the self-defeating tendency of the pursuit of equality. As Ralf Dahrendorf has noted, equality has a built-in frustration effect.[17] Behind the demand for equality is the wish to extend opportunity: how can more people come to enjoy more life chances? But many life chances defy continuous extension, since to increase them past a certain point is to destroy them. The acquisition of a degree increases one's chances in life as long as the degree has some special value in the eyes of others. To be valuable, it cannot be possessed by all. As soon as most persons can have it, it adds little or nothing to life chances. The declining value of the high school degree, the Associate in Arts degree, and the Bachelor's degree in the American system illustrates this point. It is a bitter irony for those who vigorously pursue the equalization of access, treatment, and outcome in higher education that the end results, if achieved, would be relatively worthless. Everyone would have the same thing but be worse off. A more sophisticated concept of extension of opportunity is required, one rooted in differentiation rather than integration, pluralities rather unities. Justice in academic systems must be varied and specific, attached to contexts that promote different competencies and, in their aggregate, widen the play of liberty.

Idea Five: State control of higher education works better by long-run rewards than by short-run sanctions. States can have intervention strategies that respect the peculiarities of institutions organized around multiple fields of knowledge, places where the values of justice, competence, and liberty must be exercised. But governments are inclined to reach for direct controls, rules that reduce day-to-day discretion. The model is: do this job in the following manner; do not deviate from this procedure; make sure every professor teaches twelve hours a week and reports periodically on how he spends his time. Negative sanctions are emphasized, eliciting defensive strategies from those to whom the sanctions are applied.[18] Then, too, when goals are not easily measured and compliance can at best be only partially evaluated, such sanctions soon lose effectiveness, frustrating those who try to apply them.

In contrast, governmental guidance can be effective over the long run where governments concentrate on setting broad directions of development, maintaining the quality of the professional personnel, and supervising the system in the mediated form, previously identified, in which the balance of control shifts from government to academics at successively lower levels. The key is the attractiveness of higher education as an area of employment—is talent attracted or repelled?—and the quality of professional socialization—are controls internalized in the individual academic and the operating group that make for responsible behavior? The state can have its "accountability" in the form of general oversight alone, if professional controls within the system hold academics accountable to one another and to general norms of objectivity and fairness. Enlightened oversight is the way to go, since no matter how precisely governmental officials attempt to define objectives, the outcome will largely depend upon the cooperation of those in the system.

Idea Six: Value ambivalence in higher education is mirrored in structural ambivalence. Modern complex higher education systems are mixed in character, rather than tending to one pole or the other, e.g., public or private, equity or excellence, liberty or loyalty. Like individuals, collectivities can be fanatical for a time, but the costs of pursuing only one set of values soon becomes too high and counter-reforms set in to restore the place of other values. The inherent contradictions of these systems in effecting basic social values lead to mixed structures.

We may learn from a similar situation in health care. After noting the virtues and vices of private, public, and mixed systems of health, Aaron Wildavsky concludes that "what life has joined together no abstraction may be able to put asunder. . . . By the next century, we may have learned that a mixed system is bad in every respect except one—it mirrors our ambivalence"[19]—ambivalence over extension of treatment, equal access, high quality, more choice, professional independence, responsiveness of doctors to patients' needs, personal control over personal costs, cost containment at the collective level, etc. No one likes mixed systems except the majority of those who participate. An all-private system makes sense on paper, especially on the note pads of economists; a fully public one is similarly an impressive theoretical model, particularly in the minds of governmental planners. But what we get in reality are ambivalent systems comprised of some of each, produced by the push and pull of contradictory values and interests. Likewise for the primary values considered here: only ambivalent structures can express the ambivalence contained in value opposition and contradiction.

Compromised systems also require modest expectations. We have seen that "failure" is often a shortfall against high expectations about how much will get done, how fast it will happen, and how superior will be the results. Many persons and groups, beginning with politicians, have a vested interest in promising large and quick results as they struggle competitively for favor in political and bureaucratic arenas. But systems that must interpret, embody, and implement a wide range of contradictory values need modest expectations on the possible realization of any single goal. Such realistic hope goes hand in hand with the growing uncertainty that attaches to policy and action. Organizational theory has come to emphasize the uncertainties produced within modern organizations by environments that change more rapidly than in the past. But it is not merely rapid change that is at work. It is also pressures, within and without, of heavily bearing values that have grown more numerous. Uncertainty comes from facing the challenges of equality *and* excellence *and* liberty *and* loyalty more fully than before. Modest expectations are an accommodation to this ambivalence of situation and response.

EIGHT

PREFERENCES

The compromise among conflicting values that allows their parallel realization may logically be effected by a single authority. It is not difficult to find theories that portray the individual political leader or senior administrator rationally choosing among a set of values, establishing priorities for all time or rearranging them from year to year. It can then be but a short step to the possibility that the powerful state can provide a workable resolution to the problems of multiple demands and conflicting values in each institutional sector that falls within its reach: simply put wise people in charge, an authoritative chief informed by expert staff. But we cannot depend on the wisdom of Leviathan, especially after witnessing so many lessons to the contrary in the twentieth century. And our analysis of the higher education system has shown one functional reason after another why all-powerful bodies prove particularly ineffectual in this sector. The task structure alone gives the modern system a low threshold in tolerating concentrated authority. More quickly than in other activities, the system becomes "overcentralized." Nations that run elementary and secondary education on a thoroughly national-ized basis, for example, right down to inspector generals visiting the classroom, are not able to operate higher education in a similar fashion.

But the large lessons of history almost seem beside the point as statesmen and politicians, administrators and professors and stu-dents, seeking solutions to pressing problems, generate responses that in the aggregate move to concentrate control. There are always ample reasons to centralize, since it is the central government that is best poised to make massive attacks on common problems. Issue by issue, various groups seek a central response to their will, and immediate effects are visible within the short-term perspective of governmental officials, elected or appointed, who need to show results. But the second-order effects, those that change the under-lying structures, are difficult to identify and, once identified, difficult to analyze. They are also beyond the horizon for those who are politically and administratively nearsighted, and thus are sys-tematically avoided. Furthermore, their constituency is small and confused.[1]

This phenomenon of unanticipated and undesired long-run effects of concentrated purposive action is clearly exacerbated in the higher education sector. The underlying characteristics of post-secondary activity are difficult to perceive and appreciate. They make any system peculiarly troublesome, recalcitrant to the central touch. But it is upon the characteristics highlighted in this study that realistic preferences for the organization of higher education need to be constructed. The preferences are most directly applicable to advanced systems in industrialized democracies, but they also bear on the evolution of other systems if they wish to do the work of modern higher education effectively. In its broadest dimensions, the case is three-sided: it is essential to divide power, support variety, and legitimate disorder. To link these preferences to the uniqueness of higher education is to end where we began the search.

THE DIVISION OF POWER

The previous three chapters demonstrated the value of perceiv-ing higher education as a power struggle. This approach builds on the Weberian legacy in classical sociological thought: modern soci-eties are replete with irreconcilable values; organized social life is then a power struggle, since it is power that ultimately determines whose values gain priority and who pays the costs. That necessary struggle has increasingly moved inside the webs of organization that constitute societal subsectors.[2] Thus, if a number of values and interests are each to have some emphasis in a higher education system, and respective supporters are to pay some of the costs, then organizational power must be divided in one way or another. Di-vided power permits partial expression of particular values in the sector overall, or full expression of each in some part of the system, or both.

Undivided power thereby becomes the greatest single danger in the operation of a system of higher education. Anything approaching a monopoly of power will express the concerns and perspectives of just a few groups, shutting out other interests. The history of higher education exhibits such effects. Students in some medieval Italian universities, through student guilds, could hire and fire professors and hence obtain favors from them. Senior faculty in some European and English universities during the last two centuries were answerable to no one and hence could sleep for decades. Dominating trustees in some early American colleges could and did fire presidents and professors for not knowing the number of angels dancing on the head of the ecclesiastical pin, or, in the twentieth century, for simply smoking cigarettes and drinking martinis. Autocratic presidents in some American institutions, especially teachers' colleges, have run campuses as personal possessions. State bureaucratic staffs and political persons in Europe and America, past and present, democratic and nondemocratic, have often been heavily dominant in ways, as we have seen, that retarded progress and limited the effectiveness of the system. Such concentrations of power have sometimes served well, protecting scholarship or helping to build distinctive enterprises, or even breaking open an immobilized system. But they do not work well for long, soon freezing organization around the points of view of just a few.

In the complex and turbulent settings of the last part of the twentieth century, no limited group can be wise enough to know the way, including the central staffs now most likely to evolve into near-monopolies of control. We have seen that state and party officials in East European countries have been forced to back off from total dominance, limiting the constraints of their manpower planning to allow, among other things, more room for the judgments of professors and the choices of students. And we have seen that various countries in Western Europe are attempting to reverse a long trend toward centralization in order to shift decision making out to the many segments of the periphery, closer to participants and to the realities of local operating conditions.

The underlying reason for all this is that organized systems of any complexity are increasingly replete with reciprocal ignorance. The expert in one activity will not know the time of day in another. Given the breadth of subjects they cover, such ignorance must be uncommonly high in developed systems of higher education. The chief state higher education officer may not even be able to do long division, let alone understand high-energy physics, whereas the professor of physics, able to understand Einstein, is incompetent in the everyday matters of system coordination. And, as earlier noted, business firms and government agencies have been driven to greater dependence on the judgment of authorities in different parts of the organization as their work becomes more rooted in expertise. The loosely woven texture of the effective university is a relevant model of how to function as those at the nominal top become more ignorant.

A central concentration of power also promotes a vicious circle of politicization, an excess of effort to influence action through political pressure. When the corridors of power are like a sharply tapered funnel, they become exceedingly crowded. All interested parties must push themselves forward in the limited space, encouraging a politico-administrative version of the war of all against all.

The classic political doctrine for advocating a division of power is federalism. James Madison and some of the other founding fathers who wrote the U.S. Constitution set out to devise a divided, balanced, and limited government that could steer between the mischief of fragmenting factions and the mischief of excessive control. The government overall should be pluralistic, promoting justice within a framework of diversity. Without monopoly, but with linkage, each branch or part could check the likely usurpations of the others.[3] The primary way to guarantee any major degree of democratic control through state regulation would be to use a federated structure that puts the regulation on a divided and piecemeal basis and forces parts of the system to check and balance one another. Madison spoke of a double security for the rights of individuals: two or more levels of government would control one another and, at the same time, the division of government into several interacting branches would cause each level to control itself.

This classic conception of divided and self-checking control can be applied to the internal composition of organizations and major sectors of society. The complex university in itself tends to become a federal system: semiautonomous departments and professional schools, chairs and faculties, act like small sovereign states as they pursue distinctive self-interests and stand over against the authority of the whole. After noting the growing importance of the department in the English university, produced partly as an unintended consequence of expansion, A. H. Halsey and M. A. Trow comment that

> it is not too fanciful to see the modern university as a federation of departments each facing outwards toward the research councils for research funds and towards schools and other universities for students and staff while at the same time living together on a campus with faculty boards and the Senate as mechanisms for negotiation and arbitration of their divergent interests.[4]

Graeme C. Moodie and Rowland Eustace also take note that in the English university "there is an important sense in which the 'higher' bodies seek validation from the 'lower.' Whatever the precise boundaries of departmental autonomy, its existence makes of every university a 'federal' structure rather than a strongly centralized system."[5] Federalism in higher education begins in the antithesis between discipline and enterprise noted at the beginning of our analysis of academic work.

But the problem is how to extend that principle to whole systems, particularly those that are formally unified. We need to apply the principle to the higher layers, emphasizing that control should look more like patchwork than cloth consistent in color and shape. We hardly need to worry about excessive patchwork, since the basic processes of the superstructure work to systematize, to tidy up. How then are checks and balances maintained? A middle ground has two essential features: the top levels of the system should themselves be pluralistic; and intermediate bodies should mediate between the central authorities and the many levels of the understructure, buffering one from the ungainly ways of the other.

Agency pluralism at the top of higher education systems is an important line of defense against the error of a monopoly of power. As we have seen, pluralism generally evolves from the natural pursuit of agency self-interest. Rare is the national system in which all matters of research and higher teaching are handled in a single ministry or department: even in relatively simple systems, ministries of agriculture, departments of defense, bureaus of mining, and institutes of health support universities, colleges, and research centers in whole or in part and have their own academic constituencies. Each headquarters office is then in part the representative of a particular set of operational interests, struggling for their welfare. Considering their typically intense need for highly trained experts, for the upgrading and retraining of professional personnel, *and* for the pleasing of constituencies, governmental agencies across the board can hardly stay away from higher education. Thus, agency conflict at the top is natural. It should be expected and encouraged. But there are strong inclinations to discourage it, even to seek to eliminate it. In the name of economy and efficiency, reform seeks to eliminate overlap and duplication. Conventional wisdom continues to view monopolies in the public sector as good, overlooking the need for pluralism within the governmental structure itself, in the governance of such a complicated and basic function as higher education.

Equally important is the buffering of control provided by intermediary bodies and forms. Levels of organization can and do check one another: when the Swedes inserted a regional level of governmental supervision during the 1970s, they created a possible counterforce to central direction as well as to university self-control. Different forms of authority also can and do balance one another: in the U.S. system, trusteeship, institutional bureaucracy, and faculty collegial control, individually and collectively, balance against state bureaucracy and legitimate political control. The central idea is to have forms that will offer different compositions of interest and expertise at successively higher or lower levels. In its golden age (1920–1965), the British University Grants Committee came close to the ideal. The processes of resource allocation at the top and the bottom were influenced by different mixtures of interests and expertise. Holding intermediate powers between the university people and the governmental officials, the UGC clearly protected one from the other. There were many informal features of trust and friendship, and common background among political, administrative, and academic elites, that helped make the committee work as well as it once did. But it is the form, the primary structure itself, that has been the most important invention in twentieth-century higher education in buffering central control by intermediate bodies.

The necessary division of power in academic systems should perhaps go by some other name than federalism, since the federal principle is so much attached to the U.S. experience and little valued and discussed in many countries. But one can take the long view and make the case, as has S. Rufus Davis, that the constitutional framework established in Philadelphia in 1787 was

> an evolutionary accident, as it were, brought into being out of the historical experience of all those who, from whatever motives, from whatever beliefs, for whatever purpose, or in whatever form, had ever sought the benefits of association without surrendering their identity as individuals.[6]

Thus, leaving aside the specifics of the American experience and form, the federalist principle is one appropriate for the internal constitution of major organized sectors of society. In higher education systems, individuals and groups, while strongly tempted to go their own way, must perforce seek "the benefits of association." But the need to preserve and strengthen individual and group identities is uncommonly high, for the good of the whole as well as in the service of self-interests. When freedom of research, freedom of teaching, and freedom of study are seriously curtailed, the system as a whole suffers. And such freedoms are protected to the extent that near-monopolies of power are restrained and a diffusion of power promoted.

Short-run thinking, affected so much by immediate problems, will cause systems to err in one direction or the other in seeking to rearrange the structure of power. If choice can be made, it is safer to err toward the mischief of multiple factions entailed in excessive fragmentation and minimal overall control; for to move in the other direction is to ease toward the mischief of monopoly entailed in excessive order and strong formal integration. The latter is much the greater error, the one that reduces sharply the structural flexibility required for later progress.

THE SUPPORT OF VARIETY

The case for a division of power is also a case for the support of variety. While monopoly tends toward narrowness, a multiplicity of authorities is likely to produce greater variety, even when subject to the effects of academic drift. Further, a direct case needs to be made for deliberate support of variation in institutional types and academic forms. As the values we wish to implement become numerous, more varied tools are needed to serve them. Then, too, growing complexity increases our uncertainty, leaving us more than ever unsure about facts and their interpretation as well as the policies and strategies to be derived from them. We are then best served by several approaches to major problems—different attacks on general education, different forms turned loose to promote short-cycle education, multiple types of research centers devoted to the cure of cancer or the reduction of air pollution. It also makes sense to have several universities or colleges doing virtually the same thing in the same locality, since conflict and struggle can promote their achievement. When such comparison is possible, errors in programs and institutional types may be caught and brought to light before they become entrenched. Error is also compensated for when one or more sets of institutions provide an alternative that serves as a bypass around the breakdown of another. Higher education may be the worst sector for putting all of one's eggs in one basket.

The observable need to support variety in the higher education system draws theoretical sustenance from the concept of rational redundancy. Martin Landau has convincingly argued the virtues of redundancy in administrative and social systems as well as in biological and physical ones.[7] An airplane is badly designed when it has only one way of putting down the wheels. Transportation in and out of cities works best when people have different ways of getting to work. The human body can recover from a heart attack when secondary muscles around the heart take over from damaged primary ones. In language, spoken or written, we repeat ourselves to increase reliability and to reduce errors of communication. Political systems are well designed when the whole is more reliable than any of its parts, because of a redundancy of structure, particularly of power centers. Auxiliary precautions are built in and compensating responses made possible that overcome weaknesses and failure in any number of different parts. Likewise for major organizations and their larger webs. They also need ways to allow rules to be broken and units to operate defectively without doing critical injury to the whole.

In the face of such an obvious need for redundancy, orthodox theory in public administration has long been wrong:

> For the public administration rationalist, the optimal organization consists of units that are wholly compatible, precisely connected, fully determined, and, therefore, perfectly reliable. The model which represents this dream is that of a linear organization in which everything is arrayed in tandem. It is as if the entire house is to be wired in series. . . . Organizational systems of this sort are a form of administrative *brinkmanship*. They are extraordinary gambles. When one bulb blows, everything goes. Ordering parts in series makes them so dependent upon each other that any single failure can break the system. It is the old story of "For want of a nail . . . the battle was lost [emphasis in original]."[8]

Thus, while conventional wisdom assigns to redundancy such meanings as needless, costly, excessive, and bad, it is preferable to emphasize its usefulness, its necessity, in considerable degree in modern organized systems.

The importance of variety in academic forms reverses the common sense assumption that coordination means to pull together. Instead, the most important coordination issue is differentiation. With the dominant pressures in the higher levels taking the form of standardization, integration can literally take care of itself. There is so much momentum behind it as to carry it too far. But the relative success of modern systems increasingly depends on a command structure that allows for myriad adaptations to specific contexts and local conditions. A unified system coordinated by a state bureaucracy, or by an interlocking network of bureaucratic and oligarchical controls, is not set up to work in this way. It resists differentiated and flexible approaches. Thus, the crisis of stalemated structure, as in France of the late-1960s that shakes the nation. Thus, the near-permanent crisis of a system, as in Italy of the 1960s and 1970s, possessed by a rigidity difficult to break. Coordination in these instances had so much settled down in particular narrow channels that it became out of phase with the organic understructure and the changes it would normally promote.

Hence, the central problem for coordinators becomes that of how best to anchor different roles for different institutions and groups in the system. *The* enemy of top coordinators should not be the messy, chaotic ways of students, faculties, and institutions, but the planned and unplanned convergence of the basic operating forms upon one another—the natural production of sameness that comes from status seeking in the field as well as from administration in headquarters. One can find insightful officials throughout the world who have grasped this point. A first level of awareness is shown in discussion of the need for "planned differentiation." A more penetrating awareness seeks diversity by creating conditions of autonomous action—planning for unplanned change, as it were—and giving legitimating help, by means of pronouncements and rewards, to those who accept and create limited niches. Thus, in the United States, some state chancellors have advocated that "statewide system leaders have a responsibility to *articulate* the virtues of institutional diversity, and to seek to distribute resources to reward institutions for doing well the more limited tasks associated with such diversity."[9] The basic work of legitimating an institutional role, or an ecological niche for a subsector, naturally falls to those on the spot. But those higher up the line can help or hinder. They can help create space and get obstacles out of the way. They can then bless those flowers that come up beautiful and hearty, and curse the weeds that foul the garden.

All those who advocate pluralism must admit to the vices of autonomous action, among which is the simple fact that the drift of the market can steadily undercut the crucial differentiation of institutions and sectors. Anchorage for the parts must develop—in budgets, rewards, and doctrines; coordinators need explicitly to encourage, against converging flows, distinct bases of support and authority that help to stabilize different roles. This requires a willingness to ride with a bothersome division of authority within the upper levels, since multiple sources of sponsorship and supervision will be the best guarantee of diversity. Multiple agencies protect multiple types, and a power market of competing agencies supplements the economic-and-status market of competing institutions and corrects for some of its failures.

Thus, in supporting variety, the central procedural concern is the relative and interacting contribution of planned and autonomous actions. Both are needed and both are operative everywhere, but in varying combinations that include radical imbalance. At this time in history, with current combinations tilting toward controlled action, support on the organic side is needed. The appropriate role for statesmen in higher education systems is to create and maintain broad frameworks that encourage constituents to generate changes that are creatively adaptive to a myriad of local contexts and, in the aggregate, thereby diversifying.

THE LEGITIMATION OF DISORDER

If educational powers are to be extensively divided and if coordinators are to take the support of diversity as central, then we need appropriate rationalizations—administrative doctrines and broader ideologies that tell officials they are doing all right when the system as a whole looks like a mess, nearly everyone in the system feels powerless, and no one can clearly identify who is doing what to whom. The doctrine of federalism, of pluralism, is a crucial part of the answer. But there is more that is needed: direct praise for ambiguity, two cheers for disorder.

An appropriate normative sense of the situation has been emerging at a rapid rate in efforts of the last several decades to understand the complexity of modern organizations and the decision making that ostensibly takes place within them. As discussed in chapter 5, Norton E. Long argued cleverly a quarter of a century ago that government could be and is coordinated by the play of political action in and around it rather than by top-down command in neat hierarchies. By the end of the 1950s, Charles E. Lindblom had presented his classic, persuasive case that muddling-through was a normal, rational, and effective means of decision making in complex organizations operating in complex settings. Astute government watchers among organizational theorists have portrayed in recent years the increasing ambiguity of governmental structure and action, within large agencies as well as in the government as a whole, as bureaus develop individual personalities and are taken over by professional groups. The highlighting of the functions of redundancy has obvious normative use. Aaron Wildavsky and his associates have shown the complexities of governmental action that defeat or greatly attenuate the implementation of policy. Other recent work has emphasized the point that so-called decisions, again in complex settings, are more the result of accretion than of clear, decisive judgment. The school of thought developed by James March and his colleagues during the 1970s, epitomized in the organized-anarchy metaphor, extended the growing awareness of complexity and related ambiguity to university organization.

The additional doctrine now needed for direct application to higher education systems as a whole is one that emphasizes and praises the benefits of disorder. Above all others, higher education systems need a disorder within which individuals and groups autonomously overexert themselves and consult informally and quasi-formally with one another, thereby achieving the effectiveness that formal controls are unable to produce. Given the tasks, beliefs, and authorities of the system, this is the only way over the long run. Systems are effective when they maximize their own possibilities, and maximizing what dozens of varied groups of professionals can do along the bottom side of the higher education system means the encouragement of their initiatives and choices.

At the top, the doctrine of disorder emphasizes redundancies among policy systems—never let one set of policy makers decide; and contingencies among policies—act tentatively, expressing policy through a series of experiments. In place of "adaptive specializations," such as more powerful planning units, high officials can seek "adaptive generalizations," such as multiple and overlapping policy systems and the flexible capacity to zig and zag, go forward and pull back on mistakes, that comes with a tentative approach.[10] If these arguments are too general, specific ones can be offered: e.g., do not write changes down in national laws, for then you will rigidify them, magnify their errors, and diminish future flexibility; do not put academic personnel into a general civil service if you can help it, for you will push rewards toward the serving of time and minimize the incentives for creativity.

Under the doctrines of disorder and mixed systems, central officials can restrain themselves in seeking consensus and contentment in the system as a whole.[11] Colleges and universities themselves do not need a great deal of consensus, since their structures and activities are only mildly interdependent. The larger systems are even less so. Higher education requires a fair amount of discontent so that people will speak up about what they think is going wrong, in a system where arcane knowledge can hide error from generalists.

Top officials can also seek to restrain consistency. Otherwise they
may be opting for revolution over evolution. If a system avoids the
zigs and zags of change in order to be consistent, its need for change
builds up and its capacity to accept change weakens. The drift is
then toward the revolutionary situation, the day when changes can
no longer be held off but the old regime has lost the capacity to
adapt. Fortunately, the low interdependence of units in any complex higher education system facilitates some experimentation with
an inconsistent variety of innovations and strategies. But central
officials and planners seldom believe this to be desirable and try to
move in the opposite direction. It is ironic that they should be so
involved in brinkmanship and the construction of revolutionary
situations as they seek to be rational and consistent and to offer
stability and happiness.

The Uniqueness of Higher Education

It does not make much sense to evaluate business firms according
to how much they act like universities, nor economic systems according to their resemblance to higher education systems. Neither does it
make any sense to do the reverse; yet it is built into current common-
sense and management theory that we do so. We persist in peering at
higher education through glasses that distort, producing images
that render more confusing a terrain that is naturally difficult. The
first source of trouble is in the borrowed assumptions that steer our
vision, assumptions that are no longer appropriate even in the first
instance. For good reasons, large business firms stray far from
idealized conceptions of economy and efficiency, and we have
learned to expect the economic system as a whole to be divided,
varied, and ambiguous. We now know that government departments, having a character of their own, will not behave according to
business models, and that "the political system" is a vast and opaque
web of conflicting tendencies. So, too, and more so, for the higher
education system. It may be smaller in scale than the economic or
political system, but it contains extended and unique complexities.
The imagery of "organization" and "system," the very terms themselves, lead us to expect simplicity—simplicity that must be there

and will be found if we are only intelligent enough. But if the higher education system was ever simple, it will not be again. We are looking at inordinate and uncommon complexity.

To understand that complexity much better than we currently do requires that we retreat somewhat from general theorizing across the major organized sectors of society and concentrate on analysis of particular realms. A sector is taken seriously when we seek its own ways of dividing work, promoting belief, and distributing authority, its own ways of changing and its own conflict of values. Once those ways are known, then features held in common with other societal subsystems appear readily enough. But to begin from the assumptions of other sectors is to misperceive and underestimate the unusual parts in the mixture of the common and the unique. In each case, the unique ways, we have cause to believe, center around the tasks of the system. For higher education, we have seen, the tasks are knowledge-centered. It is around the formidable array of specific subjects and their self-generating and autonomous tendencies that higher education becomes something unique, to be first understood in its own terms. Just one general effort alone, the creation of knowledge, remains poorly comprehended until we grasp the fact that "difference and plurality are part and parcel of the moral world of discovery and invention."[12] Field by field, the academic search for progress leads to alternative interpretations of the world. Uncertainty rather than the grail of truth characterizes the frontiers of knowledge, and mortals can offer only different and changing approximations of the truth. Knowledge will remain a divided and imperfect substance. In its fissions and faults we come closest to a root cause of the many odd ways of the higher education system.

NOTES

INTRODUCTION

1. Ralf Dahrendorf, *Life Chances*, p. 142.
2. For a powerful argument that all education has become a more autonomous system, see Thomas F. Green, *Predicting the Behavior of the Educational System*.
3. A. B. Cobban, *The Medieval Universities*, pp. 47, 38.
4. Charles Perrow, *Complex Organizations*, p. 246.
5. For an interest-group perspective on the study of American academic organization, see J. Victor Baldridge, *Power and Conflict in the University*; and J. Victor Baldridge et al., *Policy Making and Effective Leadership*.
6. Max Weber, *From Max Weber*, pp. 61–65.

1: KNOWLEDGE

1. Hastings Rashdall, *The Universities of Europe in the Middle Ages*; Charles Homer Haskins, *The Rise of Universities*; John W. Baldwin and Richard A. Goldthwaite, eds., *Universities in Politics*; A. B. Cobban, *The Medieval Universities*.
2. See Paul H. Hirst, *Knowledge and the Curriculum*.
3. See Fritz Machlup, *The Production and Distribution of Knowledge in the United States*; Daniel Bell, *The Coming of Post-Industrial Society*; Burkart Holzner and John H. Marx, *Knowledge Application*.
4. Jeanne Schmidt Binstock, "Design from Disunity," pp. 84–86.
5. Ioan Davies has noted that while education has such latent functions as selecting people for jobs, "its *manifest* function is the management of knowledge. Any comparative study which ignores this is in danger of trivializing the entire subject [emphasis in original]." See "The Management of Knowledge," p. 278.
6. Max Weber, *From Max Weber*, pp. 242–243.
7. Carnegie Foundation for the Advancement of Teaching, *Missions of the College Curriculum*, p. 11.
8. Robert H. Roy, *The Culture of Management*, p. 89
9. See James S. Coleman, "The University and Society's New Demands upon It," pp. 359–399, especially pp. 369–371, 387.
10. See Christopher J. Hurn, *The Limits and Possibilities of Schooling*, pp. 262–263.
11. John J. Corson, "Perspectives on the University Compared with Other Institutions," pp. 155–169; Stephen K. Bailey, "A Comparison of the University with a Government Bureau," pp. 121–136; Burton R. Clark, "Faculty Organization and Authority," pp. 236–250; Coleman, "University and Society's New Demands," pp. 359–399; John Millett, *The Academic Community*.
12. Corson, "Perspectives on the University," pp. 155–169; James C. March and

277

Johan P. Olsen, *Ambiguity and Choice in Organizations*; J. Victor Baldridge et al., *Policy Making and Effective Leadership*, pp. 20–21.

13. Graeme C. Moodie and Rowland Eustace, *Power and Authority in British Universities*, pp. 19–20. See also Eric Ashby, *The Academic Profession*, p. 10.

14. Carnegie Commission on Higher Education, *Purposes and the Performance of Higher Education in the United States*, p. 1.

15. Clark Kerr, "Goals for Higher Education," and "Appendix," in Clark Kerr et al., *12 Systems of Higher Education*. Quotation from p. 202.

16. Ibid., "Appendix."

17. Ibid., p. 195.

18. Michael D. Cohen and James G. March, *Leadership and Ambiguity*, p. 195.

19. Ibid., pp. 195–196.

20. Moodie and Eustace, *Power and Authority*, p. 20.

21. From a 1970 interview with Robert Maynard Hutchins, as reported in the *Chronicle of Higher Education* 4, 13 (1977). See also Hutchins's *The Learning Society*, chap. 8, "The University."

22. Cobban, *Medieval Universities*, p. 165.

23. Robert Ulich, *Abraham Flexner's Universities*.

24. John Henry Cardinal Newman, *The Idea of a University*; A. Dwight Culler, *The Imperial Intellect*.

25. The title of Wilhelm von Humboldt's classic memorandum on the outlines of the university to be founded in Berlin is translated as "On the Spirit and the Organizational Framework of Intellectual Institutions in Berlin." See bibliography.

26. Clark Kerr, *The Uses of the University*, pp. 2–4.

27. Ulich, *Flexner's Universities*, p. 317.

28. Margaret S. Archer, *Social Origins of Educational Systems*, p. 4.

29. Cohen and March, *Leadership and Ambiguity*, p. 223; March and Olsen, *Ambiguity and Choice in Organizations*.

30. Cohen and March, *Leadership and Ambiguity*, p. 211.

31. Charles Perrow, "The Analysis of Goals in Complex Organizations," pp. 854–866.

32. See Philip Selznick, *Leadership in Administration*; Lee S. Sproull, "Beliefs in Organizations," pp. 203–224.

33. John W. Meyer, "The Effects of Education as an Institution," pp. 55–77.

2: WORK

1. Burton R. Clark, *Academic Power in Italy*, chap. 1, "University."

2. Robert T. Blackburn et al., "Are Instructional Improvement Programs Off-Target?" pp. 32–48.

3. Norton E. Long, *The Polity*, p. 83.

4. Henry Mintzberg, *The Structuring of Organizations*, pp. 168–175; L. R. Sayles, "Matrix Organization," pp. 2–17.

5. See Derek de Solla Price, *Little Science, Big Science*; Warren Hagstrom, *The Scientific Community*; Diana Crane, *Invisible Colleges*; Jonathan R. Cole and Stephen Cole, *Social Stratification in Science*; Jerry Gaston, *Originality and Competition in Science*; Robert K. Merton, *The Sociology of Science*.

6. See Logan Wilson, *The Academic Man*; Paul Lazarsfeld and Wagner Thielens, *The Academic Mind*; Theodore Caplow and Reece C. McGee, *The Academic Marketplace*; A. H. Halsey and M. A. Trow, *The British Academics*; Pier Paolo Giglioli, *L'Università italiana tra patrimonialismo e burocrazia*; Philip G. Altbach, ed., *Comparative Perspectives on the Academic Profession*.

7. Harold Perkin, *Key Profession*; Harland G. Bloland, *Higher Education Associations in a Decentralized Education System*; Harland G. Bloland and Sue M. Bloland, *American Learned Societies in Transition*.

8. Barbro Berg and Bertil Östergren, *Innovations and Innovation Processes in Higher Education*, p. 102.

9. On the resilience of the core units in the face of institutional pressure, see Tony Becher and Maurice Kogan, *Process and Structure in Higher Education*, chap. 6, "Basic Units."

10. Burkart Holzner and John H. Marx, *Knowledge Application*, p. 199.

11. Graeme C. Moodie and Rowland Eustace, *Power and Authority in British Universities*, p. 61.

12. Bloland, *Higher Education Associations*, pp. 176–183; Bloland and Bloland, *American Learned Societies in Transition*.

13. Gaston, *Originality and Competition in Science*, p. 160.

14. Earlier versions of this typology appeared in Burton R. Clark, "Problems of Access in the Context of Academic Structures," in *Access, Systems, Youth and Employment*, ed. Barbara B. Burn; idem, "Academic Differentiation in National Systems of Higher Education."

15. See Janice B. Lodahl and Gerald Gordon, "The Structure of Scientific Fields and the Functioning of University Graduate Departments," pp. 57–72; Anthony Biglan, "Relationships between Subject Matter Characteristics and the Structure and Output of University Departments," pp. 204–213; Judith Adkison, "The Structure of Knowledge and Departmental Social Organization," pp. 41–53.

16. Lodahl and Gordon, "Structure of Scientific Fields," p. 58.

17. Ibid., p. 70.

18. Ibid., p. 71.

19. Ibid.

20. Biglan, "Subject Matter Characteristics," p. 213.

21. James D. Thompson, *Organizations in Action*.

22. Clark Kerr, *The Uses of the University*, chap. 2, "The Realities of the Federal Grant University."

23. Joseph Ben-David. *Centers of Learning*, chap. 4, "General Higher Education."

24. Roger L. Geiger, *A Retrospective View of the Second-Cycle Reform in France*.

25. Geoffrey Giles, *Higher Education in Yugoslavia*.

26. See Joseph Ben-David, *American Higher Education*; Peter M. Blau, *The Organization of Academic Work*; E. D. Duryea, "Evolution of University Organization," in *The University as an Organization*, ed. James A. Perkins, pp. 15–37; Talcott Parsons and Gerald M. Platt, *The American University*; Burton R. Clark and Ted I. K. Youn, *Academic Power in the United States*; John H. Van de Graaff et al., *Academic Power*.

27. For an analysis of traditional and modern forms of academic guild organization, see Clark, *Academic Power in Italy*, chap. 5, "Guild."

28. John W. Baldwin, "Introduction," to John W. Baldwin and Richard A. Goldthwaite, eds., *Universities in Politics*, pp. 8, 19.

29. Marjorie Reeves speaks of the development of the guild form of organization from the medieval period "right down to the present age" and comments: "The astonishing thing is that the medieval-guild model has served the Western universities so long and has shaped so powerfully the thinking of so many academic generations," in comparison with "the industrial-plant concept" and other modern models. Marjorie Reeves, "The European University from Medieval Times," in *Higher Education*, ed. W. R. Niblett, p. 64.

30. John H. Van de Graaff, "Federal Republic of Germany," in Van de Graaff et al., *Academic Power*, p. 16. See also R. Steven Turner, "The Growth of Professorial Research in Prussia 1818 to 1848," pp. 137–182.

31. Ivan P. Hall, "Organizational Paralysis," in *Modern Japanese Organization and Decision-Making*, ed. Ezra F. Vogel, p. 311.

32. Duryea, "Evolution of University Organization," pp. 15–37.

33. In stressing the principle of sequence as one of the three primary characteristics of the education system, Thomas F. Green notes: "Perhaps the necessity of such a principle stems not from the nature of educational systems but from the more

primitive fact that there is always a definite sequence in what is to be learned or a definite sequence in human growth and development." See *Predicting the Behavior of the Educational System*, p. 8.

34. Ben-David has made the fascinating "counterfactual" point that *if* the United States had had a truly national system of higher education, under control of national law and regulation, a century ago, when support for the university swelled rapidly, there probably would have been a serious effort to reduce sharply by governmental edict the number of small liberal arts colleges, now "obviously" old-fashioned, redundant, and inefficient. The colleges were able to survive and prosper alongside the larger and more specialized universities, in part because "there were no central organizations (even to the extent that there were in England) to mastermind the changes and to pay out of public funds for services that might not have been in demand." See *Centers of Learning*, p. 81.

35. See Richard Hamilton and James Wright, "Coming of Age," pp. 335–349. Hamilton and Wright compared educational and training tracks in the United States and the Federal Republic of Germany, noting that the more ambiguous American structure seemed to contribute measurably to the anomic features of contemporary American society.

36. Ben-David, *Centers for Learning*, p. 83.

37. B. Clark, *Academic Power in Italy*, pp. 8–34. See also the statistical volumes prepared by the Organisation for Economic Co-operation and Development (OECD) in the late 1960s that compared the magnitude of university and "nonuniversity" sectors in a number of OECD countries. Organisation for Economic Co-operation and Development, *Development of Higher Education, 1950–1967. Statistical Survey*; *Development of Higher Education, 1950–1967. Analytical Report*.

38. Ninety percent by OECD computations, for the mid-1960s; eighty percent, according to Swedish researchers, for 1973. See OECD, *Development of Higher Education, 1950–1967. Analytical Report*. pp. 40–41; and Rune Premfors and Bertil Östergren, *Systems of Higher Education: Sweden*, pp. 32–33.

39. John H. Van de Graaff and Dorotea Furth, "France," in Van de Graaff et al., *Academic Power*.

40. S. Ketudat and W. Srisna-an, *Systems of Higher Education: Thailand*, pp. 1–23.

41. Ibid., p. 50.

42. Ibid., p. 53.

43. Abdol Hassein Samii, M. Reza Vaghefi, and Dariush Nowrasteh, *Systems of Higher Education: Iran*, pp. 1–16.

44. Ibid., pp. 6–8.

45. Jan Szczepanski, *Systems of Higher Education: Poland*, pp. 5–12. See also Aleksander Matejko, "Planning and Tradition in Polish Higher Education," pp. 621–648; Joseph R. Fiszman, *Revolution and Tradition in People's Poland*, pp. 57–71; Maurice David Simon, "Students, Politics, and Higher Education in Socialist Poland," pp. 32–49.

46. Detlef Glowka, "Soviet Higher Education between Government Policy and Self-Determination," pp. 175–185; Barbara B. Burn, *Higher Education in Nine Countries*, chap. 10, "Higher Education in the Soviet Union," pp. 277–315. For an analysis of Russian higher education before 1917, see James C. McClelland, *Autocrats and Academics*.

47. Barbara B. Burn and Peter Karmel, *Federal/State Responsibilities for Postsecondary Education*; Bruce Williams, *Systems of Higher Education: Australia*.

48. Edward Sheffield et al., *Systems of Higher Education: Canada*; Burn, *Higher Education in Nine Countries*, chap. 5, "Higher Education in Canada."

49. Halsey and Trow, *The British Academics*, chap. 2, "The Evolution of the British Universities"; Tony Becher, Jack Embling, and Maurice Kogan, *Systems of Higher Education: United Kingdom*; John H. Van de Graaff, "Great Britain," in Van de Graaff et al., *Academic Power*.

50. See Douglas Sloan, *The Scottish Enlightenment and the American College Ideal*.

51. Hansgert Peisert and Gerhild Framhein, *Systems of Higher Education: Federal Republic of Germany*, pp. 6–18; John H. Van de Graaff, "Federal Republic of Germany," in Van de Graaff et al., *Academic Power*.

52. Alfonso Rangel Guerra, *Systems of Higher Education: Mexico*.

53. Katsuya Narita, *Systems of Higher Education: Japan*, pp. 3–42; Donald F. Wheeler, "Japan," in Van de Graaff et al., *Academic Power*.

54. Morikazu Ushiogi, "The Japanese Student and the Labor Market," in *Changes in the Japanese University*, ed. William K. Cummings, Ikuo Amano, and Kazuyuki Kitamura, pp. 107–126.

55. Carnegie Council on Policy Studies in Higher Education, *A Classification of Institutions of Higher Education*; Alan Pifer et al., *Systems of Higher Education: United States*, pp. 19–49; Burton R. Clark, "United States," in Van de Graaff et al., *Academic Power*.

56. Carnegie Council, *Classification of Institutions of Higher Education*.

57. Oliver Fulton and Martin Trow, "Research Activity in American Higher Education," in *Teachers and Students*, ed. Martin Trow, pp. 39–83.

58. Daniel C. Levy, *The State and Higher Education in Latin America*.

59. Hence, such a medium of exchange is only a weak requirement of the higher education part of educational systems, found in most academic systems solely at the level of degrees that have shared meaning, but not in the form of transferable courses and degrees. This finding is at variance with Thomas F. Green's model of the educational system, in which a full-bodied medium of exchange is one of the three primary elements. An aggregation of educational institutions can be a system when the division of labor consists of parts that do not formally exchange credits. Cf. *Predicting the Behavior of the Educational System*, pp. 4–7.

60. See Akira Arimoto, *The Academic Structure in Japan*.

61. For an outstanding analysis of the French *grandes écoles* and their part in elite formation in French society, see Ezra N. Suleiman, *Elites in French Society*, chap. 1, 2, 3, 10. See also Alain Bienaymé, *Systems of Higher Education: France*, pp. 1–47; and Van de Graaff and Furth, "France," in Van de Graaff et al., *Academic Power*.

62. Harold Perkin, *British Society and Higher Education*; R. K. Kelsall, "Recruitment to the Higher Civil Service" and Frances Wakeford and John Wakeford, "Universities and the Study of Elites," in *Elites and Power in British Society*, ed. Philip Stanworth and Anthony Giddens, pp. 170–184, 185–197.

63. G. C. Allen, *The British Disease*.

64. Sheffield et al., *Systems of Higher Education: Canada*; Robert M. Pike, "Sociological Research on Higher Education in Canada 1970–1980."

65. B. Clark, *Academic Power in Italy*, chaps. 1, 2.

66. Peisert and Framhein, *Systems of Higher Education: Federal Republic of Germany*; Van de Graaff, "Federal Republic of Germany," in Van de Graaff et al., *Academic Power*.

67. Peisert and Framhein, *Systems of Higher Education: Germany*, p. 92.

68. Clark Kerr, "Higher Education," pp. 261–278.

69. Arimoto, "Academic Structure in Japan," p. 27.

70. Morikazu Ushiogi (personal communication), 1981.

71. Peisert and Framhein, *Systems of Higher Education: Germany*, pp. 12–15.

72. Rune Premfors, *Integrated Higher Education*.

73. For a useful analysis and guide to the classic literature on this point, see Dietrich Rueschemeyer, "Structural Differentiation, Efficiency, and Power," pp. 1–25.

3: BELIEF

1. C. P. Snow, *The Two Cultures and the Scientific Revolution*.

2. Everett Cherrington Hughes, *Students' Culture and Perspectives*, p. 28.

3. Ibid., p. 31.

4. Philip Selznick, *TVA and the Grass Roots*.

5. Reinhard Bendix, *Work and Authority in Industry*, p. ix.

6. Amitai Etzioni, *A Comparative Analysis of Complex Organizations*.

7. Herbert Kaufman, *The Limits of Organizational Change*, pp. 116–118.

8. John Meyer, "Environmental and Internal Origins of Symbolic Structure in Organizations."

9. See Ian I. Mitroff and Ralph H. Kilmann, "On Organizational Stories," in *The Management of Organizational Design*, vol. 1, ed. Ralph H. Kilmann, Louis R. Pondy, and Dennis P. Slevin, pp. 189–207; Andrew M. Pettigrew, *The Creation of Organisational Cultures*; Janice M. Beyer, "Ideologies, Values, and Decision Making in Organizations," in *Handbook of Organizational Design*, vol. 2, ed. Paul C. Nystrom and William H. Starbuck, pp. 166–202; Lee S. Sproull, "Beliefs in Organizations," in Nystrom and Starbuck, *Handbook of Organizational Design*, pp. 203–224.

10. Burton R. Clark, *The Distinctive College*; Burton R. Clark, "The Wesleyan Story," in *Academic Transformation*, ed. Verne A. Stadtman and David Riesman, pp. 367–381.

11. Frederick Rudolph, *The American College and University*, p. 210.

12. Robert H. Roy, *The Culture of Management*, chap. 6, "Academic and Other Organizations," especially p. 89.

13. Thomas S. Kuhn, *The Structure of Scientific Revolutions*, p. 176; Janice B. Lodahl and Gerald Gordon, "The Structure of Scientific Fields and the Functioning of University Graduate Departments," pp. 57–72.

14. S. M. Ulam, *Adventures of a Mathematician*, p. 274.

15. Tony Becher, "Physicists on Physics," pp. 3, 5, 6.

16. Bruce Kuklick, *The Rise of American Philosophy*, pp. 256–257.

17. Ibid., p. 257.

18. See Howard Becker et al., *Boys in White*.

19. B. Clark, *Distinctive College*, chap. 10, "The Making of an Organizational Saga"; Burton R. Clark, "The Organizational Saga in Higher Education," pp. 178–183.

20. Albert O. Hirschman, *Exit, Voice, and Loyalty*.

21. B. Clark, "Wesleyan Story," pp. 367–381.

22. See Philip Selznick, *Leadership in Administration*.

23. On the origin and development of intercollegiate athletics in the U.S. higher education system, see Frederick Rudolph, *The American College and University*.

24. Graham Little, *The University Experience*.

25. See Kenneth A. Feldman and Theodore M. Newcomb, *The Impact of College on Students*.

26. Burton R. Clark and Martin A. Trow, "The Organizational Context," in *College Peer Groups*, ed. Theodore M. Newcomb and Everett K. Wilson, pp. 17–70; Kaoru Yamamoto, ed., *The College Student and His Culture*.

27. Howard S. Becker, Blanche Geer, and Everett Hughes, *Making the Grade*.

28. Donald T. Roden, *Schooldays in Imperial Japan*.

29. See Martin Green, *Children of the Sun*.

30. Burton R. Clark, "Faculty Culture," in *The Study of Campus Cultures*, ed. Terry F. Lunsford, pp. 39–54.

31. Alvin W. Gouldner, "Locals and Cosmopolitans," pp. 281–306; 444–480.

32. T. R. McConnell and Stewart Edelstein, *Campus Governance at Berkeley*, pp. 4–5.

33. Terry F. Lunsford, "Authority and Ideology in the Administered University," in *The State of the University*, ed. Carlos E. Kruytbosch and Sheldon L. Messinger, pp. 91–92.

34. Ibid., p. 101. For an early statement of the general use of such myths, see Selznick, *TVA and the Grass Roots*, pp. 151–152.

35. Rune Premfors and Bertil Östergren, *Systems of Higher Education: Sweden*, pp. 23–25.

36. John Vaisey, "Higher Education Planning," in *Higher Education and the Current Crises*, ed. Barbara B. Burn, pp. 191−198.

37. Walter P. Metzger, "Academic Freedom and Scientific Freedom," p. 107.

38. Robert K. Merton, *Social Theory and Social Structure*, pp. 550−561.

39. The first comparative volume on the academic profession, reporting on eight countries or regions of the world, had little to say about the profession's more cultural aspects. See Philip G. Altbach, ed., *Comparative Perspectives on the Academic Profession*. On the values and attitudes, primarily political, of U.S. academics, see E. C. Ladd, Jr., and S. M. Lipset, *The Divided Academy*.

40. Max Weber, *From Max Weber*, pp. 61−65.

41. G. C. Allen, *The British Disease*.

42. Joseph Ben-David, *Centers of Learning*, pp. 106−107.

43. Loren R. Graham, *The Soviet Academy of Sciences and the Communist Party*, p. vii.

44. Ibid., p. 203.

45. See Max Weber's pragmatic conception of the relation of symbols to action, ideas to interests, using the switchmen metaphor. Weber, *From Max Weber*, pp. 61−65; Reinhard Bendix, *Max Weber*, pp. 64−70.

46. Thomas F. Green, *Predicting the Behavior of the Educational System*, p. 10. See also the argument of Christopher J. Hurn on the role of beliefs in the linkage between schooling and occupational status, in Christopher J. Hurn, *The Limits and Possibilities of Schooling*, pp. 260−262.

47. On the organizational marginality of adult education, see Burton R. Clark, *Adult Education in Transition*.

48. Jerry Gaston, *Originality and Competition in Science*, p. 172.

49. Emile Durkheim, *Emile Durkheim on Morality and Society*, chap. 4, "Individualism and the Intellectuals." Quotation from p. 49.

50. Tony Becher and Maurice Kogan, *Process and Structure in Higher Education*, p. 110.

4: AUTHORITY

1. E. E. Schattschneider, *The Semi-Sovereign People*, p. 71.

2. Peter Bachrach and Morton S. Baratz, "Two Faces of Power," pp. 947−952.

3. Graeme C. Moodie, "Authority, Charters and the Survival of Academic Rule," pp. 127−135.

4. Eric Ashby, *Adapting Universities to a Technological Society*, p. 59.

5. For a more extended discussion of these levels, and their application in analysis of seven national systems, see John H. Van de Graaff et al., *Academic Power*. An adaptation of the schema to the case of Mexico may be found in Daniel C. Levy, *Comparative Perspectives on Academic Governance in Mexico*. Levels analysis has also been prominently used by Tony Becher and Maurice Kogan in a study of British higher education in which they distinguish the four levels of individual, basic unit, institution, and system in order to analyze the relation between the normative and the operational aspects of organization within and across layers. See *Process and Structure in Higher Education*.

6. Howard E. Aldrich, *Organizations and Environments*, pp. 87−88.

7. Earlier formulations of these authority forms appeared in Burton R. Clark and Ted I. K. Youn, *Academic Power in the United States*; and Burton R. Clark, "Academic Power," in Van de Graaff et al., *Academic Power*, pp. 164−189.

8. See Guenther Roth, "Personal Rulership, Patrimonialism, and Empire-Building in the New States," pp. 194−206; and Max Weber, *The Theory of Social and Economic Organization*, pp. 346−354.

9. See Burton R. Clark, *Academic Power in Italy*, pp. 106−113.

10. On such outcomes in the traditional Latin American universities, particularly Brazil, see Darcy Ribeiro, "Universities and Social Development," in *Elites in Latin*

America, ed. Seymour Martin Lipset and Aldo Solari, pp. 343–381, especially pp. 358–368.

11. Weber, *Theory of Social and Economic Organization*, pp. 392–407.

12. Sylvia L. Thrupp, "Gilds," in *International Encyclopedia of the Social Sciences*, vol. 6, pp. 184–187; John W. Baldwin, "Introduction," in John W. Baldwin and Richard A. Goldthwaite, eds., *Universities in Politics*; Clark, *Academic Power in Italy*, chap. 5, "Guild."

13. See Thrupp, "Gilds"; and Max Weber, *General Economic History*, pp. 136–137.

14. In analysis of the executive branch of American government, Frederick Mosher has emphasized "professional hegemony," which reduces control by non-specialized authorities; Harold Seidman has portrayed agencies as self-governing professional guilds, with relations within and among them so balkanized around expertise and constituencies as to constitute a system of "cooperative feudalism" instead of cooperative federalism. Hugh Heclo and Aaron Wildavsky have viewed British government as a small society of civil servants analyzable in terms of the ties of nuclear family, village life, kinship, and culture. Frederick C. Mosher, *Democracy and the Public Service*; Harold Seidman, *Politics, Position, and Power*; and Hugh Heclo and Aaron Wildavsky, *The Private Government of Public Money*.

15. For a close account of personal and collegial rule in a Nigerian university, reflecting British antecedents, see Pierre L. Van den Berghe, *Power and Privilege at an African University*, especially pp. 127–144.

16. Karl Marx, *Pre-Capitalist Economic Formations*, pp. 109, 135.

17. Leon D. Epstein, *Governing the University*, chap. 6, "Professorialism."

18. Talcott Parsons, "Professions," in *International Encyclopedia of the Social Sciences*, vol. 12, pp. 536–547.

19. For revisionist thought in the sociology of professions, see Eliot Freidson, *Professional Dominance*; and Magali Sarfatti Larson, *The Rise of Professionalism*.

20. From the general laws of the Massachusetts Colony, as quoted in Hubert Park Beck, *Men Who Control Our Universities*, p. 28.

21. Graeme C. Moodie and Rowland Eustace, *Power and Authority in British Universities*, p. 30.

22. Epstein, *Governing the University*, p. 68.

23. Ibid.

24. For representative literature on American trustees, see Thorstein Veblen, *The Higher Learning in America*; Beck, *Men Who Control Our Universities*; Morton A. Rauh, *The Trusteeship of Colleges and Universities*; Rodney T. Hartnett, "College and University Trustees," in *The State of the University*, ed. Carlos E. Kruytbosch and Sheldon L. Messinger, pp. 47–71; Epstein, *Governing the University*, chap. 4, "Trusteeship."

25. On trusteeship in Latin America, old and new, public and private, see Daniel C. Levy, *University and Government in Mexico*, pp. 64–83; and Daniel C. Levy, *The State and Higher Education in Latin America*.

26. The classic study of the University Grants Committee is Robert O. Berdahl, *British Universities and the State*.

27. Michel Crozier, *The Bureaucratic Phenomenon*; Michel Crozier, *The Stalled Society*; and Ezra N. Suleiman, *Politics, Power, and Bureaucracy in France*.

28. Joseph LaPalombara, *Interest Groups in Italian Politics*; Henry W. Ehrmann, "Interest Groups and the Bureaucracy in Western Democracies," in *State and Society*, ed. Reinhard Bendix; Seidman, *Politics, Position, and Power*; Heclo and Wildavsky, *Private Government of Public Money*; Francis E. Rourke, *Bureaucracy, Politics, and Public Policy*.

29. Edward Shils, "Charisma," in *International Encyclopedia of the Social Sciences*, vol. 2, pp. 386–390; Weber, *Social and Economic Organization*, pp. 358–373, 386–392.

30. For a discussion of role elaboration and its outcomes in the case of Italian chair holders, see Clark, *Academic Power in Italy*, chap. 3, "Oligarchy." An insightful discussion of the rewards of "role accumulation" generally may be found in Sam D. Sieber,

"Toward a Theory of Role Accumulation," pp. 567–578.

31. See Burton R. Clark, *The Distinctive College*, especially pp. 237–245.

32. Rune Premfors has noted the role of personal influence in higher education policy making in Europe, pointing to the roles of Charles de Gaulle and Edgar Faure, Harold Wilson and Jennie Lee, and Olof Palme in reforms in the French, British, and Swedish systems, respectively. See *The Politics of Higher Education in a Comparative Perspective*, pp. 221–222.

33. Van de Graaff et al., *Academic Power*, chapters on Federal Republic of Germany, Italy, France, and Sweden. See also Barbara B. Burn, "Comparisons of Four Foreign Universities," in *The University as an Organization*, ed. James A. Perkins, pp. 79–103.

34. This happened in Prussia under a forceful minister of education, much to the dismay of Max Weber and his colleagues, even during years when the prestige and power of German professors was second to none in the world. See Max Weber, *Max Weber on Universities*.

35. Clark, *Academic Power in Italy*, chap. 3, "Oligarchy."

36. Lyman A. Glenny, ed., *Funding Higher Education*, p. 178.

37. Ibid., p. 3.

38. Van de Graaff, et al., *Academic Power*, chap. 6, "Great Britain."

39. Premfors, *Politics of Higher Education*.

40. Van de Graaff et al., *Academic Power*, chap. 7, "United States"; Clark and Youn, *Academic Power in the United States*.

41. Van de Graaff et al., *Academic Power*, chap. 8, "Japan"; William K. Cummings, Ikuo Amano, and Kazuyuki Kitamura, eds., *Changes in the Japanese University*; T. J. Pempel, *Patterns of Japanese Policymaking*.

42. Pempel, *Patterns of Japanese Policymaking*, p. 30.

43. Jan-Erik Lane, *Power in the University*, pp. 33–39.

44. Carol H. Weiss, "Knowledge Creep and Decision Accretion," pp. 381–404. Quotation from p. 392.

5: INTEGRATION

1. This dimension is adapted from the literature on interorganizational analysis that has focused on the problem of how organizations interact in making decisions. See Roland L. Warren, "The Interorganizational Field as a Focus for Investigation," pp. 396–419.

2. Edward C. Banfield, *Political Influence*, pp. 326–327.

3. Charles E. Lindblom, *Politics and Markets*, pp. 33–34.

4. See Masazo Ohkawa, "Government-Type and Market-Type Higher Education," pp. 16–32. Ohkawa divided his analysis into four types: "government-type," with the Soviet Union as the example; "quasi-government-type"—Great Britain; "incomplete market-type"—Japan; and "market-type"—the United States. Unfortunately, his discussion is marred by an economic rationality in which the types are fleshed out by reference to abstract principles of economic theory rather than to the realities of higher education.

5. Robert O. Berdahl, *Statewide Coordination of Higher Education*; Burton R. Clark, "United States," in John H. Van de Graaff et al., *Academic Power*, pp. 104–123.

6. Burton R. Clark, *Academic Power in Italy*, chap. 2, "Bureaucracy"; chap. 3, "Oligarchy."

7. Robert Gilpin, *France in the Age of the Scientific State*, especially pp. 112–123; Terry Nichols Clark, *Prophets and Patrons*; John H. Van de Graaff and Dorotea Furth, "France," in Van de Graaff et al., *Academic Power*.

8. John H. Van de Graaff, "Germany," in Van de Graaff et al., *Academic Power*.

9. Bruce Williams, *Systems of Higher Education: Australia*; Barbara B. Burn and Peter Karmel, *Federal/State Responsibilities for Postsecondary Education*; Grant Harman,

"Issues in the Co-ordination of Post-secondary Education."

10. Harman, "Co-ordination of Post-Secondary Education," p. 3.

11. See Loren R. Graham, *The Soviet Academy of Sciences and the Communist Party*; Barbara B. Burn, *Higher Education in Nine Countries*, chap. 10, "Higher Education in the Soviet Union"; Detlef Glowka, "Soviet Higher Education Between Government Policy and Self-determination," in *Higher Education in a Changing World*; Linda L. Lubrano and Susan Gross Solomon, eds., *The Social Context of Soviet Science*.

12. Tony Becher, Jack Embling, and Maurice Kogan, *Systems of Higher Education: United Kingdom*, p. 16.

13. Ibid., pp. 119–120.

14. Edward Sheffield et al., *System of Higher Education: Canada*, sections on Quebec and Alberta; Organisation for Economic Co-operation and Development, *Review of National Policies for Education: Canada*, p. 82.

15. Donald F. Wheeler, "Japan," in Van de Graaff et al., *Academic Power*.

16. Herbert Kaufman, *The Limits of Organizational Change*, pp. 76–77.

17. For outstanding empirical discussions of distortion of vertical communication in large organizations, see Herbert Kaufman, *The Forest Ranger*, pp. 66–73; and Jeffrey L. Pressman and Aaron B. Wildavsky, *Implementation*, chap. 5, "The Complexity of Joint Action."

18. Rune Premfors and Bertil Östergren, *Systems of Higher Education: Sweden*, p. 24.

19. John Vaisey, "Higher Education Planning," in *Higher Education and the Current Crises*, ed. Barbara B. Burn, pp. 191–198.

20. Rune Premfors, *The Politics of Higher Education in a Comparative Perspective*, pp. 30–32.

21. Terry F. Lunsford, "Authority and Ideology in the Administered University," in *The State of the University*, ed. Carlos E. Kruytbosch and Sheldon L. Messinger, pp. 87–107.

22. Graeme C. Moodie, "Authority, Charters and the Survival of Academic Rule," 127–135. Quotations from pp. 133–134.

23. B. Clark, *Academic Power in Italy*, p. 65.

24. Johan P. Olsen, "Integrated Organizational Participation in Government," in *Handbook of Organizational Design*, vol. 2, ed. Paul C. Nystrom and William H. Starbuck, pp. 492–516.

25. Premfors, *Politics of Higher Education*, chap. 2, "Higher Education in National Politics."

26. Graeme C. Moodie, "Academics and University Government," pp. 235–258.

27. On Poland, see Jan Szczepanski, *Systems of Higher Education: Poland*, "Management of the System of Higher Education," pp. 31–48. On the German Democratic Republic (East Germany), see Geoffrey J. Giles, *The Structure of Higher Education in the German Democratic Republic*.

28. See the section on "international transfer" in chapter 6.

29. See Van de Graaff et al., *Academic Power*.

30. Van de Graaff, "Germany," in Van de Graaff et al., *Academic Power*, pp. 25–26.

31. Ibid., p. 27.

32. See Clark, *Academic Power in Italy*, pp. 8–11, 154–158.

33. Alan B. Cobban, "Medieval Student Power," pp. 38–40, 44–45, 61–64.

34. Daniel C. Levy, *University and Government in Mexico*, pp. 92–94.

35. Levy, *University and Government in Mexico*; Larissa Lomnitz, "Conflict and Mediation in a Latin American University," pp. 315–338.

36. Lomnitz, "Conflict and Mediation," p. 319.

37. Ibid., pp. 319, 329.

38. Ibid., pp. 321–331, 332.

39. Premfors, *Politics of Higher Education*, chap. 2.

40. Chester E. Finn, Jr., *Education and the Presidency*, pp. 103–105.

41. A metaphor developed by F. G. Bailey, as discussed in Tony Becher and Maurice Kogan, *Process and Structure in Higher Education*, p. 71.

42. See Dietrich Goldschmidt, "Systems of Higher Education," in Van de Graaff et al., *Academic Power*, pp. 159–161; Becher and Kogan, *Process and Structure in Higher Education*, pp. 129–130.

43. Szczepanski, *Systems of Higher Education: Poland*; Giles, "German Democratic Republic."

44. Moodie, "Academics and University Government," p. 132.

45. Bertil Östergren, "Planning for Change in Higher Education," in *R & D for Higher Education*.

46. Becher, Embling, and Kogan, *Systems of Higher Education: United Kingdom*, pp. 22, 44–45.

47. Lindblom, *Politics and Markets*, p. 39.

48. Ibid., pp. 37–38.

49. For a major study of student consumerism and its power and effects in the U.S. system, see David Riesman, *On Higher Education*. For an insightful essay on government financing through students, see Larry L. Leslie, *The Trend toward Government Financing of Higher Education through Students*.

50. See Burton R. Clark, *Adult Education in Transition*, pp. 61–63.

51. Michael D. Cohen and James G. March, *Leadership and Ambiguity*, pp. 94–103. Quotation from p. 102.

52. Ibid., p. 102.

53. Levy, *University and Government in Mexico*.

54. Clark, *Academic Power in Italy*, pp. 82–85.

55. Akira Arimoto, *The Academic Structure in Japan*.

56. On the American academic labor market, see Theodore Caplow and Reece C. McGee, *The Academic Marketplace*; Allan M. Cartter, *Ph.D's and the Academic Labor Market*; and Neil J. Smelser and Robin Content, *The Changing Academic Market*.

57. Joseph Ben-David and Abraham Zloczower, "Universities and Academic Systems in Modern Societies," pp. 45–84.

58. Mario S. Brodersohn, "Public and Private Financing of Education in Latin America," p. 31.

59. On the use of the concepts of market failure and state failure in explaining the development of higher education, particularly as between the public and private sectors, see Daniel C. Levy, *The State and Higher Education in Latin America*.

60. See Ikuo Amano, "Stability and Change in Japanese Higher Education," in *Higher Education for the 1980s*, pp. 60–70.

61. Joseph S. Berliner, *The Innovation Decision in Soviet Industry*, pp. 17–18; see also Samuel Huntington, *Political Order in Changing Societies*, p. 138.

62. Neil Smelser, "Growth, Structural Change, and Conflict in California Public Higher Education, 1950–1970," in *Public Higher Education in California*, ed. Neil Smelser and Gabriel Almond, p. 129.

63. Rune Premfors, "New Patterns of Authority in Higher Education."

64. Olof Ruin, *External Control and Internal Participation*; Premfors and Östergren, *Systems of Higher Education: Sweden*.

65. Douglas M. Windham, *Economic Dimensions of Education*, p. 124.

66. Olsen, "Integrated Organizational Participation in Government."

67. Philippe C. Schmitter, "Still the Century of Corporatism?" pp. 85–131; Leo Panitch, "The Development of Corporatism in Liberal Democracies," pp. 61–90.

68. Quoted in Panitch, "The Development of Corporatism," pp. 63–64.

69. Premfors and Östergren, *Systems of Higher Education: Sweden*, p. 90; see also Ruin, *External Control and Internal Participation*, pp. 69–71.

70. See Harold Seidman's effort to distinguish and categorize several hundred major agencies of the U.S. government, most of which have a large number of important divisions within them. Harold Seidman, *Politics, Position, and Power*, chap. 7, "Administrative Agencies"; chap. 8, "Advisory and Intergovernmental Bodies."

71. B. Clark, *Academic Power in Italy*, chap. 5, "Guild."

72. See Barry Bozeman, "Governing the 'Republic of Science.'"

73. Ibid.

74. Ibid.

75. Guy Benveniste, *Bureaucracy and National Planning*, pp. 44–62; see also Levy, *University and Government in Mexico*, where the Mexican ministry is portrayed as a "loose coalition of fiefdoms," a case of "structural feudalism."

76. S. Ketudat and W. Srisa-an, *Systems of Higher Education*, pp. 6–10, 50–54.

77. Richard Kraus, William E. Maxwell, and Reeve D. Vanneman, "The Interests of Bureaucrats," pp. 135–155. Quotation from pp. 144–145.

78. Jean-Pierre Jallade, "Education and Development in Latin America."

79. Harman, "Issues in the Co-ordination of Post-secondary Education," p. 3.

80. Rune Premfors, *How Much Higher Education Is Enough?* p. 16.

81. Jack Hayward and Michael Watson, eds., *Planning, Politics and Public Policy*, p. 474.

82. Norton E. Long, "Power and Administration," pp. 257–264. Quotation from p. 262.

83. Lindblom, *Politics and Markets*, p. 32. See also Charles E. Lindblom, *The Intelligence of Democracy*.

84. See Barbro Berg and Bertil Östergren, *Innovations and Innovation Processes in Higher Education*.

85. Levy, *University and Government in Mexico*, pp. 28–40.

86. Daniel C. Levy, "Comparing Authoritarian Regimes in Latin America," pp. 31–52.

87. Graham, *Soviet Academy of Sciences*, pp. 204–209. Quotation from p. 208.

88. Szczepanski, *Systems of Higher Education: Poland*; Giles, *German Democratic Republic*.

89. Geoffrey Giles, *The Nazi Intelligentsia*.

90. Ibid.

91. Arye Carmon, "The Changeover of the University of Heidelberg under National Socialism," pp. 516–544. Quotation from p. 544.

92. Samuel A. Goudsmit, *Alsos*.

93. David Irving, *The German Atomic Bomb*, p. 303.

6: CHANGE

1. Theodore M. Hesburgh, C.S.C., "The Nature of the Challenge," in *The Task of Universities in a Changing World*, ed. Stephen D. Kertesz, pp. 2–11. Quotation from p. 3.

2. This distinction is the first building block in Margaret S. Archer's mammoth comparative and historical analysis of change in educational systems. Note the division of her volume into a first part devoted to the "emergence of state educational systems" and a second centered on "educational systems in action." See *Social Origins of Educational Systems*.

3. Tony Becher and Maurice Kogan, *Process and Structure in Higher Education*, pp. 146, 147.

4. Arthur Levine, *Why Innovation Fails*, p. 43.

5. Herbert Kaufman, *The Limits of Organizational Change*, p. 100.

6. Anthony Downs, *Inside Bureaucracy*, p. 20.

7. Archer, *Social Origins*, p. 3.

8. Martin Trow, "Problems in the Transition from Elite to Mass Higher Education," in *Policies for Higher Education*, pp. 51–101. Quotations from pp. 89–90.

9. Martin Trow, "Elite and Mass Higher Education," in *Research into Higher Education*, pp. 183–219. Quotations from p. 191.

10. Trow, "Elite and Mass Higher Education," p. 187.

11. Roger L. Geiger, *Two Paths to Mass Higher Education*. Quotations from pp. 22, 24.

12. Emile Durkheim, *The Evolution of Educational Thought*, p. 163.

13. Burton R. Clark, *Academic Power in Italy*, pp. 126–128.

14. John H. Van de Graaff, *Can Department Structures Replace a Chair System?*

15. Rune Premfors and Bertil Östergren, *Systems of Higher Education: Sweden*, pp. 36–37.

16. John H. Van de Graaff and Dorotea Furth, "France," in John H. Van de Graaff et al., *Academic Power*, pp. 57–58.

17. Geoffrey J. Giles, *The Structure of Higher Education in the German Democratic Republic*, p. 10.

18. Ibid., p. 12.

19. See Dean McHenry et al., *Academic Departments*.

20. Robert H. Wiebe, *The Search for Order, 1877–1920*, p. 121.

21. Becher and Kogan, *Process and Structure*, pp. 118–119.

22. Archer, *Social Origins*, chap. 8, "Structural Elaboration."

23. Ezra N. Suleiman, *Elites in French Society*.

24. Gerald Holton, "Striking Gold in Science," pp. 159–198.

25. See Hugh Hawkins, *Between Harvard and America*, chap. 2, "From College to University"; Robert A. McCaughey, "The Transformation of American Academic Life," pp. 239–332.

26. Joseph Ben-David, "The Universities and the Growth of Science in Germany and the United States," pp. 1–35. Quotation from pp. 26–27.

27. Ibid., p. 12.

28. Michel Crozier, *The Stalled Society*.

29. Arnold J. Heidenheimer, "The Politics of Educational Reform in Sweden and West Germany," in *The Dynamics of Public Policy*, ed. Richard Rose, pp. 81–111, especially pp. 93–94.

30. See Margaret S. Archer's separation of forces for change into external transactions, internal initiatives, and political manipulations, in *Social Origins*, pp. 775–784.

31. Ibid., p. 789. For analyses that use an interest-group perspective—a "political model"—in studying academic organization, see particularly J. Victor Baldridge, *Power and Conflict in the University*; and J. Victor Baldridge et al., *Policy Making and Effective Leadership*.

32. Dietrich Rueschemeyer, "Structural Differentiation, Efficiency, and Power," pp. 1–25. Quotation from p. 13.

33. Ibid., p. 13.

34. Warren Hagstrom, *The Scientific Community*, pp. 208–215.

35. See Emile Durkheim, *The Division of Labor in Society*; Rueschemeyer, "Structural Differentiation," p. 17.

36. Emile Durkheim, *Emile Durkheim*, ed. Anthony Giddens, pp. 153–154.

37. Judith Adkison, "The Structure of Knowledge and Departmental Social Organization," pp. 41–53. Quotations from pp. 52, 50.

38. Carnegie Foundation for the Advancement of Teaching, *Missions of the College Curriculum*, p. 8.

39. Arthur L. Stinchcombe, "Social Structure and Organizations," in *Handbook of Organizations*, ed. James G. March, pp. 142–193.

40. See John Pratt and Tyrell Burgess, *Polytechnics*; and Becher and Kogan, *Process and Structure*, pp. 37, 123–125.

41. Becher and Kogan, *Process and Structure*, pp. 124–125.

42. See Grant Harman, "Academic Staff and Academic Drift in Australian Colleges of Advanced Education," pp. 313–335.

43. Geoffrey Giles, "The Rise of the Polytechnics in Britain."

44. Geoffrey Giles, *Higher Education in Yugoslavia*.

45. As exemplified in leading U.S. liberal arts colleges. See Burton R. Clark, *The Distinctive College*.

46. Burton R. Clark, "Implementation of Higher Education Reforms in the

U.S.A.," in *Implementation of Higher Education Reforms*, ed. Ladislav Cerych and Paul Sabatier.

47. Levine, *Why Innovation Fails*.

48. Ibid.

49. On self-interest costs and other natural barriers to organizational change, see Kaufman, *Limits of Organizational Change*, chap. 1, "Why Organizations Tend Not to Change."

50. See the postulates of J. Hage and M. Aiken as summarized in Levine, *Why Innovation Fails*, pp. 170−173.

51. See Eric Ashby, *Universities: British, Indian, African*; Francis X. Sutton, "African Universities and the Process of Change in Middle Africa," in *The Task of Universities in a Changing World*, ed. Stephen D. Kertesz, pp. 383−404; Susanne Hoeber Rudolph and Lloyd I. Rudolph, eds., *Education and Politics in India*.

52. Francis X. Sutton, "The International Liaison of Universities: History, Hazards and Opportunities" (Keynote Address to Invitational Seminar of the Overseas Liaison Committee, American Council on Education, April 1979).

53. Leonard Thompson, "Some Problems of Southern African Universities," in *The Future of the University in Southern Africa*, ed. Hendrik W. Van der Merwe and David Welsh, pp. 280−296. Quotation from p. 282.

54. "The origins of educational institutions impress upon them certain forms and traditions that function rather like a genetic imprint, which dictates the further evolution of their institutional arrangement, not with the exactitude it exercises in a biological organism, but with a certain dependability." Rudolph and Rudolph, *Education and Politics in India*, p. 13.

55. Ikuo Amano, "Continuity and Change in the Structure of Japanese Higher Education," in *Changes in the Japanese University*, ed. William K. Cummings, Ikuo Amano, and Kazuyuki Kitamura, pp. 10−39. Quotation from p. 11.

56. Ibid., p. 17.

57. Thompson, "Some Problems of Southern African Universities," p. 282.

58. Ibid.

59. Ibid., pp. 292−293.

60. James S. Coleman, "The Academic Freedom and Responsibilities of Foreign Scholars in African Universities," pp. 14−33.

61. Lawrence J. Saha and Alden S. Klovdahl, "International Networks and Flows of Academic Talent," pp. 55−68.

62. See Robert H. Miles, *Macro Organizational Behavior*, chap. 11.

63. Michael D. Cohen and James G. March, *Leadership and Ambiguity*, p. 206.

64. Detlef Glowka, "Soviet Higher Education between Government Policy and Self-determination," p. 182.

7: VALUES

1. See Dorotea Furth, "Selection and Equity," pp. 259−277.

2. Susanne Hoeber Rudolph and Lloyd I. Rudolph, *Education and Politics in India*, p. 171.

3. John Creighton Campbell, "Japanese Budget *Baransu*," in *Modern Japanese Organization and Decision-Making*, ed. Ezra F. Vogel, pp. 71−100.

4. See Michio Nagai, *Higher Education in Japan*, chap. 3, "The Tasks of the University."

5. Noël Annan, "Equality in the Schools," in *Whatever Happened to Equality?*" ed. John Vaisey, pp. 89−102, especially pp. 101−102.

6. John Shea, "Background Paper," in *Observations on the Relations between Education and Work in the People's Republic of China*, pp. 33−47.

7. James S. Coleman, "The State and the University in the Republic of Zaire," Quotation from p. 29.

8. Machiavelli on reform: "I say, then, that inasmuch as it is difficult to know these evils at their first origin, owing to an illusion which all new things are apt to produce, the wiser course is to temporize with such evils when they are recognized, instead of violently attacking them; for by temporizing with them they will either die out of themselves, or at least their worst results will be long deferred." Niccolò Machiavelli, *The Prince and the Discourses*, chap. 33, *Discourses*, p. 200. Machiavelli's point of view comes closer to the attitudes appropriate for reform in modern public administration than those that propose sweeping reform as a way of reconstructing a system from the top to the bottom.

9. T. Anthony Jones, "Modernization and Education in the U.S.S.R.," pp. 522–546. Quotations from pp. 536, 544.

10. Thomas A. Baylis, *The Technical Intelligentsia and the East German Elite*, p. 51.

11. Lillemor Kim, "Widened Admission to Higher Education in Sweden (the 25/4 Scheme)," in *Implementation of Higher Education Reforms*, ed. Ladislav Cerych and Paul Sabatier, p. 60.

12. Ralf Dahrendorf, *Life Chances*, chap. 6, "Inequality, Hope, and Progress."

13. On the need for "elite" components within "mass" universities and colleges, and modern systems generally, see Martin Trow, "Elite Higher Education," pp. 355–376; and Clark Kerr, "Higher Education," pp. 261–278.

14. Daniel J. Kevles, *The Physicists*, pp. 43–44, 375.

15. See Joseph Ben-David, *Centers for Learning*, especially pp. 165–169, 180–182. Ben-David concludes that "the feeling of crisis and anomie that prevails in many academic circles . . . derives mainly from internal causes, namely, the difficulties of systems of higher education to accommodate within their existing structures their new and extended functions" (pp. 180–181).

16. For outstanding discussions of loose coupling, see Karl Weick, "Educational Organizations as Loosely Coupled Systems," pp. 1–19; and Howard E. Aldrich. *Organizations and Environments*, pp. 76–86.

17. Dahrendorf, *Life Chances*, p. 94, 118.

18. Guy Benveniste, "Implementation and Intervention Strategies: The Case of PL 94-142," mimeograph (Stanford-Berkeley Seminar on Law, Governance and Education, October 1980).

19. Aaron Wildavsky, "Doing Better and Feeling Worse," pp. 105–123. Quotation from p. 122.

8: PREFERENCES

1. See James Douglas and Aaron Wildavsky, "Introduction," in *Russell Sage Foundation, the Future and the Past*, pp. 50–51.

2. See Kenneth McNeil, "Understanding Organizational Power," pp. 65–90.

3. James Madison, in *Federalist Papers* number 10, 47, 48 and 51, argues that (1) factions are the price as well as the product of liberty; (2) the many necessary factions should be able to represent and express themselves, rather than be suppressed by a dominant faction or centralized state; (3) toward that end, formal powers should be divided between several levels of government; and (4) central government should be composed of separate and distinct branches that are able to check and balance one another. Madison concluded that security for the rights of the people is not found in charters or in appeals to humanity but in "the multiplicity of interests" that characterize a free society. See *The Federalist Papers*.

4. A. H. Halsey and M. A. Trow, *The British Academics*, pp. 111–112.

5. Graeme C. Moodie and Rowland Eustace, *Power and Authority in British Universities*, p. 61.

6. S. Rufus Davis, *The Federal Principle*, chap. 4, "The United States Model, 1787." Quotation from pp. 119–120.

7. Martin Landau, "Redundancy, Rationality, and the Problem of Duplication and

Overlap," pp. 346–358.

8. Ibid., p. 354.

9. R. E. Lieuallen, "The Ecological Frame of Mind," in *The Monday Morning Imagination*, ed. Martin Kaplan, p. 152.

10. Hugh Heclo, "Policy Dynamics," in *The Dynamics of Public Policy*, ed. Richard Rose, pp. 237–266.

11. See Bo L. T. Hedberg, Paul C. Nystrom, and William H. Starbuck, "Camping on Seesaws," pp. 41–65; and George Ecker, "Administration in Higher Education," pp. 23–31.

12. Ralf Dahrendorf, *Life Chances*, p. 157.

BIBLIOGRAPHY

Adkison, Judith. "The Structure of Knowledge and Departmental Social Organization." *Higher Education* 8 (1979):41–53.

Aldrich, Howard E. *Organizations and Environments.* Englewood Cliffs, N.J.: Prentice-Hall, 1979.

Allen, G. C. *The British Disease.* Hobart Paper 67. 2d ed. London: Institute of Economic Affairs, 1979.

Altbach, Philip G., ed. *Comparative Perspectives on the Academic Profession,* New York: Praeger, 1977.

Amano, Ikuo. "Continuity and Change in the Structure of Japanese Higher Education." In *Changes in the Japanese University: A Comparative Perspective,* edited by William K. Cummings, Ikuo Amano, and Kazuyuki Kitamura, pp. 10–39. New York: Praeger, 1979.

———. "Stability and Change in Japanese Higher Education." In *Higher Education for the 1980s,* pp. 60–70. Report of the Hiroshima International Seminar on Higher Education. Hiroshima: Research Institute for Higher Education, Hiroshima University, 1980.

Annan, Noël. "Equality in the Schools." In *Whatever Happened to Equality?* edited by John Vaisey, pp. 89–102. London: British Broadcasting Corporation, 1975.

Archer, Margaret S. *Social Origins of Educational Systems.* London: Sage Publications, 1979.

Arimoto, Akira. *The Academic Structure in Japan: Institutional Hierarchy and Academic Mobility.* Higher Education Research Group Working Paper, no. 27. New Haven, Conn.: Yale University, 1978.

Ashby, Eric. *Universities: British, Indian, African.* Cambridge, Mass.: Harvard University Press, 1966.

———. *The Academic Profession.* Oxford: Oxford University Press, 1969.

———. *Adapting Universities to a Technological Society.* San Francisco: Jossey-Bass, 1974.

Bachrach, Peter, and Baratz, Morton S. "Two Faces of Power." *American Political Science Review* 56 (1962):947–952.

Bailey, Stephen K. "A Comparison of the University with a Government Bureau." In *The University as an Organization,* edited by James A. Perkins. New York: McGraw-Hill, 1973.

Baldridge, J. Victor. *Power and Conflict in the University.* New York: John Wiley, 1971.

Baldridge, J. Victor; Curtis, David V.; Ecker, George; and Riley, Gary L. *Policy Making and Effective Leadership.* San Francisco: Jossey-Bass, 1978.

Baldwin, John W., and Goldthwaite, Richard A., eds. *Universities in Politics: Case Studies from the Late Middle Ages and Early Modern Period.* Baltimore: Johns Hopkins University Press, 1972.

Banfield, Edward C. *Political Influence.* New York: Free Press, 1961.

Baylis, Thomas A. *The Technical Intelligentsia and the East German Elite.* Berkeley, Los Angeles, London: University of California Press, 1974.

Becher, Tony. "Physicists on Physics: The Aristocracy of the Intellect." Mimeographed. University of Sussex (United Kingdom), 1981.

Becher, Tony; Embling, Jack; and Kogan, Maurice. *Systems of Higher Education: United Kingdom.* New York: International Council for Educational Development, 1977.

Becher, Tony, and Kogan, Maurice. *Process and Structure in Higher Education.* London: Heinemann, 1980.

Beck, Hubert Park. *Men Who Control Our Universities.* New York: King's Crown Press, 1947.

Becker, Howard; Geer, Blanche; Hughes, Everett C.; and Strauss, Anselm L. *Boys in White: Student Culture in Medical School.* Chicago: University of Chicago Press, 1961.

Becker, Howard S.; Geer, Blanche; and Hughes, Everett. *Making the Grade: The Academic Side of College Life.* New York: John Wiley, 1968.

Bell, Daniel. *The Coming of Post-Industrial Society.* New York: Basic Books, 1973.

Ben-David, Joseph. "The Universities and the Growth of Science in Germany and the United States." *Minerva* 7 (1968–69):1–35.

———. *American Higher Education.* New York: McGraw-Hill, 1972.

———. *Centers of Learning: Britain, France, Germany, United States.* An essay prepared for the Carnegie Commission on Higher Education. New York: McGraw-Hill, 1977.

Ben-David, Joseph, and Zloczower, Abraham. "Universities and Academic Systems in Modern Societies." *European Journal of Sociology* 3 (1962): 45–84.

Bendix, Reinhard. *Work and Authority in Industry: Ideologies of Management in the Course of Industrialization.* New York: John Wiley, 1956.

———. *Max Weber: An Intellectual Portrait.* Garden City, N.Y.: Doubleday, 1960.

Benveniste, Guy. *Bureaucracy and National Planning: A Sociological Case Study in Mexico.* New York: Praeger, 1970.

Berdahl, Robert O. *British Universities and the State.* Berkeley and Los Angeles: University of California Press, 1959.

———. *Statewide Coordination of Higher Education.* Washington, D.C.: American Council on Education, 1971.

Berg, Barbro, and Östergren, Bertil. *Innovations and Innovation Processes in Higher Education.* Stockholm: National Board of Universities and Colleges, 1977.

Berliner, Joseph S. *The Innovation Decision in Soviet Industry.* Cambridge, Mass.: MIT Press, 1976.

Beyer, Janice M. "Ideologies, Values, and Decision Making in Organizations." In *Handbook of Organizational Design: Remodeling Organizations and*

Their Environments. Vol. 2, edited by Paul C. Nystrom and William H. Starbuck, pp. 166–202. Oxford: Oxford University Press, 1981.

Bienaymé, Alain. *Systems of Higher Education: France.* New York: International Council for Educational Development, 1978.

Biglan, Anthony. "Relationships between Subject Matter Characteristics and the Structure and Output of University Departments." *Journal of Applied Psychology* 57 (1973):204–213.

Binstock, Jeanne Schmidt. "Design from Disunity: The Tasks and Methods of American Colleges." Ph.D. dissertation, Brandeis University, 1970.

Blackburn, Robert T.; Pellino, Glenn R.; Boberg, Alice; and O'Connell, Colman. "Are Instructional Improvement Programs Off-Target?" *Current Issues in Higher Education* 1 (1980):32–48.

Blau, Peter M. *The Organization of Academic Work.* New York: John Wiley, 1973.

Bloland, Harland G. *Higher Education Associations in a Decentralized Education System.* Berkeley: Center for Research and Development in Higher Education, University of California, Berkeley, 1969.

Bloland, Harland G., and Bloland, Sue M. *American Learned Societies in Transition.* A Carnegie Commission Report. New York: McGraw-Hill, 1974.

Bozeman, Barry. "Governing the 'Republic of Science': An Analysis of National Science Foundation Officials' Attitudes about Managed Science." Paper read at the Annual Meeting of the Society for Social Studies of Science, Indiana University, Bloomington, 1978.

Brodersohn, Mario S. "Public and Private Financing of Education in Latin America." Paper read at the Seminar on the Financing of Education in Latin America: Jointly sponsored by the Inter-American Development Bank and the Department of Public Education of Mexico. Mexico City, 1978.

Burn, Barbara B. *Higher Education in Nine Countries.* A General Report prepared for the Carnegie Commission on Higher Education. New York: McGraw-Hill, 1971.

———. "Comparisons of Four Foreign Universities." In *The University as an Organization,* edited by James A. Perkins. New York: McGraw-Hill, 1973.

Burn, Barbara B., and Karmel, Peter. *Federal/State Responsibilities for Postsecondary Education: Australia and the United States.* New York: International Council for Educational Development, 1977.

Campbell, John Creighton. "Japanese Budget *Baransu.*" In *Modern Japanese Organization and Decision-Making,* edited by Ezra F. Vogel, pp. 71–100. Berkeley, Los Angeles, London: University of California Press, 1975.

Caplow, Theodore, and McGee, Reece C. *The Academic Marketplace.* New York: Basic Books, 1958.

Carmon, Arye. "The Changeover of the University of Heidelberg under National Socialism." *Minerva* 16 (Winter 1978):516–544.

Carnegie Commission on Higher Education. *Purposes and the Performance of Higher Education in the United States.* New York: McGraw-Hill, 1973.

Carnegie Council on Policy Studies in Higher Education. *A Classification of Institutions of Higher Education.* Rev. ed. Berkeley, Calif., 1976.

Carnegie Foundation for the Advancement of Teaching. *Missions of the College Curriculum.* San Francisco: Jossey-Bass, 1977.

Cartter, Allan M. *Ph.D.'s and the Academic Labor Market.* New York: McGraw-Hill, 1972.

Clark, Burton R. *Adult Education in Transition: A Study of Institutional Insecurity.* 1956. Reprint. New York: Arno Press, 1980.

——. "Faculty Culture." In *The Study of Campus Cultures*, edited by Terry F. Lunsford. Boulder, Colo.: Western Interstate Commission for Higher Education, 1963.

——. *The Distinctive College: Antioch, Reed and Swarthmore.* Chicago: Aldine, 1970.

——. "Faculty Organization and Authority." In *Academic Governance*, edited by J. Victor Baldridge, pp. 236–250. Berkeley, Calif.: McCutchan, 1971.

——. "The Organizational Saga in Higher Education." *Administrative Science Quarterly* 17 (1972):178–183.

——. "The Wesleyan Story: The Importance of Moral Capital." In *Academic Transformation: Seventeen Institutions under Pressure*, edited by Verne A. Stadtman and David Riesman, pp. 367–381. New York: McGraw-Hill, 1973.

——. *Academic Power in Italy: Bureaucracy and Oligarchy in a National University System.* Chicago: University of Chicago Press, 1977.

——. "Problems of Access in the Context of Academic Structures." In *Access, Systems, Youth and Employment*, edited by Barbara B. Burn, pp. 39–52. New York: International Council for Educational Development, 1977.

——. "Academic Differentiation in National Systems of Higher Education." *Comparative Education Review* 22 (June 1978):242–258.

——. "Implementation of Higher Education Reforms in the U.S.A.: A Comparison with European Experience." In *Implementation of Higher Education Reforms*, edited by Ladislav Cerych and Paul Sabatier. Paris: Institute of Education, European Cultural Foundation. Unpublished.

Clark, Burton R., and Trow, Martin A. "The Organizational Context." In *College Peer Groups*, edited by Theodore M. Newcomb and Everett K. Wilson. Chicago: Aldine, 1966.

Clark, Burton R., and Youn, Ted I. K. *Academic Power in the United States: Comparative, Historical, and Structural Perspectives.* ERIC/Higher Education Research Report, no. 3. Washington, D.C.: American Association for Higher Education, 1976.

Clark, Terry Nichols. *Prophets and Patrons: The French University and the Emergence of the Social Sciences.* Cambridge, Mass.: Harvard University Press, 1973.

Cobban, Alan B. "Medieval Student Power." *Past and Present* 53 (1971): 38–40, 44–45, 61–64.

——. *The Medieval Universities: Their Development and Organization.* London: Methuen and Co., 1975.

Cohen, Michael D., and March, James G. *Leadership and Ambiguity: The American College President.* New York: McGraw-Hill, 1974.

Cole, Jonathan R., and Cole, Stephen. *Social Stratification in Science.* Chicago: University of Chicago Press, 1973.

Coleman, James S. "The University and Society's New Demands Upon It." In *Content and Context: Essays on College Education*, edited by Carl Kaysen.

New York: McGraw-Hill, 1973.

Coleman, James S. "The Academic Freedom and Responsibilities of Foreign Scholars in African Universities." *Issue* 7 (1977):14–33.

———. "The State and the University in the Republic of Zaire." Paper read at the Conference on Politics and Education, Western Regional Comparative and International Education Society, November 1981, University of California, Santa Barbara.

Corson, John J. "Perspectives on the University Compared with Other Institutions." In *The University as an Organization*, edited by James A. Perkins. New York: McGraw-Hill, 1973.

Crane, Diana. *Invisible Colleges: Diffusion of Knowledge in Scientific Communities*. Chicago: University of Chicago Press, 1972.

Crozier, Michel. *The Bureaucratic Phenomenon*. Chicago: University of Chicago Press, 1964.

———. *The Stalled Society*. New York: Viking, 1970.

Culler, A. Dwight. *The Imperial Intellect: A Study of Newman's Educational Ideal*. New Haven, Conn.: Yale University Press, 1955.

Cummings, William K.; Amano, Ikuo; and Kitamura, Kazuyuki, eds. *Changes in the Japanese University: A Comparative Perspective*. New York: Praeger, 1979.

Dahrendorf, Ralf. *Life Chances*. Chicago: University of Chicago Press, 1979.

Davies, Ioan. "The Management of Knowledge: A Critique of the Use of Typologies in the Sociology of Education." In *Knowledge and Control: New Directions for the Sociology of Education*, edited by Michael F. D. Young, pp. 267–288. London: Collier-Macmillan, 1971.

Davis, S. Rufus. *The Federal Principle*. Berkeley, Los Angeles, London: University of California Press, 1978.

Douglas, James, and Wildavsky, Aaron. "Introduction: The Knowledge Foundation in the Era of Big Government." In *Russell Sage Foundation: The Future and the Past*. New York: Russell Sage Foundation, 1979.

Downs, Anthony. *Inside Bureaucracy*. Boston: Little, Brown, 1967.

Durkheim, Emile. *The Division of Labor in Society*. New York: Free Press, 1947.

———. *Emile Durkheim: Selected Writings*. Edited by Anthony Giddens. Cambridge: Cambridge University Press, 1972.

———. *Emile Durkheim on Morality and Society*. Edited by Robert N. Bellah. Chicago: University of Chicago Press, 1973.

———. *The Evolution of Educational Thought*. London: Routledge and Kegan Paul, 1977.

Duryea, E. D. "Evolution of University Organization." In *The University as an Organization*, edited by James A. Perkins. New York: McGraw-Hill, 1973.

Ecker, George. "Administration in Higher Education: Making the Most of Ambiguity." *Review of Higher Education* 3 (Fall 1979):23–31.

Ehrmann, Henry W. "Interest Groups and the Bureaucracy in Western Democracies." In *State and Society*, edited by Reinhard Bendix, pp. 257–276. Boston: Little, Brown, 1968.

Epstein, Leon D. *Governing the University*. San Francisco: Jossey-Bass, 1974.

Etzioni, Amitai. *A Comparative Analysis of Complex Organizations*. New York: Free Press, 1961.

The Federalist Papers: Alexander Hamilton, James Madison, John Jay. New York:

New American Library, Mentor Books, 1961.

Feldman, Kenneth A., and Newcomb, Theodore M. *The Impact of College on Students*. San Francisco: Jossey-Bass, 1970.

Finn, Chester, E., Jr. *Education and the Presidency*. Lexington, Mass.: D.C. Heath, 1977.

Fiszman, Joseph R. *Revolution and Tradition in People's Poland: Education and Socialization*. Princeton, N.J.: Princeton University Press, 1972.

Freidson, Eliot. *Professional Dominance*. New York: Atherton Press, 1970.

Fulton, Oliver, and Trow, Martin. "Research Activity in American Higher Education." In *Teachers and Students*, edited by Martin Trow. New York: McGraw-Hill, 1975.

Furth, Dorotea. "Selection and Equity: An International Viewpoint." *Comparative Education Review* 22 (1978):259–277.

Gaston, Jerry. *Originality and Competition in Science: A Study of the British High Energy Physics Community*. Chicago: University of Chicago Press, 1973.

Geiger, Roger L. *A Retrospective View of the Second-Cycle Reform in France*. Higher Education Research Group Working Paper, no. 18. New Haven, Conn.: Yale University, 1977.

————. *Two Paths to Mass Higher Education: Issues and Outcomes in Belgium and France*. Higher Education Research Group Working Paper, no. 34. New Haven: Yale University, 1979.

Giglioli, Pier Paolo. *L'Università italiana tra patrimonialismo e burocrazia*. Bologna: Il Mulino, 1978.

Giles, Geoffrey J. *The Structure of Higher Education in the German Democratic Republic*. Higher Education Research Group Working Paper, no. 12. New Haven, Conn.: Yale University, 1976.

————. "The Rise of the Polytechnics in Britain." Mimeographed. New Haven, Conn.: Higher Education Research Group, Yale University, 1977.

————. *Higher Education in Yugoslavia*. Higher Education Research Group Working Paper, no. 39. New Haven, Conn.: Yale University, 1979.

————. *The Nazi Intelligentsia: Students and Professors at the University of Hamburg, 1919–1945*. Forthcoming.

Gilpin, Robert. *France in the Age of the Scientific State*. Princeton, N.J.: Princeton University Press, 1968.

Glenny, Lyman A., ed. *Funding Higher Education: A Six-Nation Analysis*. New York: Praeger, 1979.

Glowka, Detlef. "Soviet Higher Education between Government Policy and Self-determination—A German View." In *Higher Education in a Changing World*. The World Year Book of Education 1971/72, pp. 175–185. London: Evans Brothers, 1971.

Goudsmit, Samuel A. *Alsos: The Failure of German Science*. London: Sigma Books, 1947.

Gouldner, Alvin W. "Locals and Cosmopolitans." *Administrative Science Quarterly* 1; 2 (1957):281–306; 444–480.

Graham, Loren R. *The Soviet Academy of Sciences and the Communist Party: 1927–1932*. Princeton, N.J.: Princeton University Press, 1967.

Green, Martin. *Children of the Sun: A Narrative of "Decadence" in England after 1918*. New York: Basic Books, 1976.

Green, Thomas F. *Predicting the Behavior of the Educational System*. Syracuse,

N.Y.: Syracuse University Press, 1980.

Guerra, Alfonso Rangel. *Systems of Higher Education: Mexico.* New York: International Council for Educational Development, 1978.

Hagstrom, Warren. *The Scientific Community.* New York: Basic Books, 1965.

Hall, Ivan P. "Organizational Paralysis: The Case of Todai." In *Modern Japanese Organization and Decision-Making,* edited by Ezra F. Vogel, Berkeley, Los Angeles, London: University of California Press, 1975.

Halsey, A. H., and Trow, M. A. *The British Academics.* Cambridge, Mass.: Harvard University Press, 1971.

Hamilton, Richard and Wright, James. "Coming of Age—A Comparison of the United States and the Federal Republic of Germany." *Zeitschrift für Sociologie* 4 (1975):335–349.

Harman, Grant. "Academic Staff and Academic Drift in Australian Colleges of Advanced Education." *Higher Education* 6 (1977):313–335.

———. "Issues in the Co-ordination of Post-secondary Education." Paper prepared for the Enquiry into Post-Secondary Education in South Australia, Education Research Unit, Australian National University, Canberra, 1977.

Hartnett, Rodney T. "College and University Trustees: Their Backgrounds, Roles, and Educational Attitudes." In *The State of the University: Authority and Change,* edited by Carlos E. Kruytbosch and Sheldon L. Messinger, pp. 47–71. Beverly Hills, Calif.: Sage Publications, 1970.

Haskins, Charles Homer. *The Rise of Universities.* Ithaca, N.Y.: Cornell University Press, 1957.

Hawkins, Hugh. *Between Harvard and America: The Educational Leadership of Charles W. Eliot.* New York: Oxford University Press, 1972.

Hayward, Jack, and Watson, Michael, eds. *Planing, Politics and Public Policy.* Cambridge: Cambridge University Press, 1975.

Heclo, Hugh. "Policy Dynamics." In *The Dynamics of Public Policy: A Comparative Analysis,* edited by Richard Rose, pp. 237–266. Beverly Hills, Calif.: Sage Publications, 1976.

Heclo, Hugh, and Wildavsky, Aaron. *The Private Government of Public Money: Community and Policy Inside British Politics.* Berkeley, Los Angeles, London: University of California Press, 1974.

Hedberg, Bo L. T.; Nystrom, Paul C.; and Starbuck, William H. "Camping on Seasaws: Prescriptions for a Self-Designing Organization." *Administrative Science Quarterly* 21 (1976):41–65.

Heidenheimer, Arnold J. "The Politics of Educational Reform in Sweden and West Germany." In *The Dynamics of Public Policy: A Comparative Analysis,* edited by Richard Rose, pp. 81–111. Beverly Hills, Calif.: Sage Publications, 1976.

Hesburgh, Theodore M., C.S.C. "The Nature of the Challenge: Traditional Organization and Attitude of Universities Toward Contemporary Realities." In *The Task of Universities in a Changing World,* edited by Stephen D. Kertesz, pp. 2–11. Notre Dame, Ind., University of Notre Dame Press, 1971.

Hirschman, Albert O. *Exit, Voice, and Loyalty: Responses to Decline in Firms, Organizations, and States.* Cambridge, Mass.: Harvard University Press, 1970.

Hirst, Paul H. *Knowledge and the Curriculum.* London: Routledge and Kegan

Paul, 1974.

Holton, Gerald. "Striking Gold in Science: Fermi's Group and the Recapture of Italy's Place in Physics." *Minerva* 12 (1974):159–198.

Holzner, Burkart, and Marx, John H. *Knowledge Application: The Knowledge System in Society.* Boston: Allyn and Bacon, 1979.

Hughes, Everett Cherrington. *Students' Culture and Perspectives: Lectures on Medical and General Education.* Lawrence: University of Kansas Press, 1961.

Huntington, Samuel. *Political Order in Changing Societies.* New Haven, Conn.: Yale University Press, 1968.

Hurn, Christopher J. *The Limits and Possibilities of Schooling.* Boston: Allyn and Bacon, 1978.

Hutchins, Robert Maynard. *The Learning Society.* New York: Praeger, 1968.

Irving, David. *The German Atomic Bomb: The History of Nuclear Research in Nazi Germany.* New York: Simon and Schuster, 1967.

Jallade, Jean-Pierre. "Education and Development in Latin America." Paper read at the Seminar on the Financing of Education in Latin America. Sponsored by the Inter-American Development Bank and the Department of Public Education, Mexico. Mexico City, 1978.

Jones, T. Anthony. "Modernization and Education in the U.S.S.R." *Social Forces* 57 (1978):522–546.

Kaufman, Herbert. *The Forest Ranger.* Baltimore: Johns Hopkins Press, 1960.

———. *The Limits of Organizational Change.* University: University of Alabama Press, 1971.

Kerr, Clark. *The Uses of the University.* Cambridge, Mass.: Harvard University Press, 1963.

———. "Higher Education: Paradise Lost?" *Higher Education* 7 (1978): 261–278.

Kerr, Clark; Millett, John; Clark, Burton; MacArthur, Brian; and Bowen, Howard. *12 Systems of Higher Education: 6 Decisive Issues.* New York: International Council for Educational Development, 1978.

Ketudat, S., and Srisa-an, W. *Systems of Higher Education: Thailand.* New York: International Council for Educational Development, 1978.

Kevles, Daniel J. *The Physicists: The History of a Scientific Community in Modern America.* New York: Vintage Books, 1979.

Kim, Lillemor. "Widened Admission to Higher Education in Sweden (the 25/4 Scheme)—A Study of the Implementation Process." In *Implementation of Higher Education Reforms,* edited by Ladislav Cerych and Paul Sabatier. Paris: Institute of Education, European Cultural Foundation. Unpublished.

Kraus, Richard; Maxwell, William E.; and Vanneman, Reeve D. "The Interests of Bureaucrats: Implications of the Asian Experience for Recent Theories of Development." *American Journal of Sociology* 85 (1979): 135–155.

Kuhn, Thomas S. *The Structure of Scientific Revolutions.* 2d ed. Chicago: University of Chicago Press, 1970.

Kuklick, Bruce. *The Rise of American Philosophy: Cambridge, Massachusetts, 1860–1930.* New Haven, Conn.: Yale University Press, 1977.

Ladd, E. C., Jr., and Lipset, S. M. *The Divided Academy: Professors and Politics.* New York: McGraw-Hill, 1975.

Landau, Martin. "Redundancy, Rationality, and the Problem of Duplication and Overlap." *Public Administration Review* 29 (1969):346—358.

Lane, Jan-Erik. *Power in the University*. Working Paper, no. 15. Umea, Sweden: Center for Administrative Studies, University of Umea, 1978.

LaPalombara, Joseph. *Interest Groups in Italian Politics*. Princeton, N.J.: Princeton University Press, 1964.

Larson, Magali Sarfatti. *The Rise of Professionalism*. Berkeley, Los Angeles, London: University of California Press, 1977.

Lazarsfeld, Paul, and Thielens, Wagner. *The Academic Mind*. Glencoe, Ill.: Free Press, 1958.

Leslie, Larry L. *The Trend toward Government Financing of Higher Education through Students: Can the Market Model Be Applied?* Center for the Study of Higher Education, Report no. 19. University Park: Pennsylvania State University, 1973.

Levine, Arthur. *Why Innovation Fails*. Albany: State University of New York Press, 1980.

Levy, Daniel C. *Comparative Perspectives on Academic Governance in Mexico*. Higher Education Research Group Working Paper, no. 28. New Haven, Conn.: Yale University, 1977.

————. *University and Government in Mexico: Autonomy in an Authoritarian System*. New York: Praeger, 1980.

————. "Comparing Authoritarian Regimes in Latin America: Insights from Higher Education Policy." *Comparative Politics* 14 (1981):31—52.

————. *The State and Higher Education in Latin America: Private-Public Patterns*. Forthcoming.

Lieuallen, R. E. "The Ecological Frame of Mind." In *The Monday Morning Imagination: Report from the Boyer Workshop on State University Systems*, edited by Martin Kaplan. New York: Praeger, 1977.

Lindblom, Charles E. *The Intelligence of Democracy: Decision Making through Mutual Adjustment*. New York: Free Press, 1965.

————. *Politics and Markets: The World's Political-Economic Systems*. New York: Basic Books, 1977.

Lipset, Seymour Martin, and Solari, Aldo, ed. *Elites in Latin America*. New York: Oxford University Press, 1967.

Little, Graham. *The University Experience: An Australian Study*. Carlton, Victoria: Melbourne University Press, 1970.

Lodahl, Janice B., and Gordon, Gerald. "The Structure of Scientific Fields and the Functioning of University Graduate Departments." *American Sociological Review* 37 (1972):57—72.

Lomnitz, Larissa. "Conflict and Mediation in a Latin America University." *Journal of Interamerican Studies and World Affairs* 19 (1977):315—338.

Long, Norton E. "Power and Administration." *Public Administration Review* 9 (1949):257—264.

————. *The Polity*. Chicago: Rand McNally, 1962.

Lubrano, Linda L., and Solomon, Susan Gross, eds. *The Social Context of Soviet Science*. Boulder, Colo.: Westview Press, 1980.

Lunsford, Terry F. "Authority and Ideology in the Administered University." In *The State of the University: Authority and Change*, edited by Carlos E. Kruytbosch and Sheldon L. Messinger. Beverly Hills, Calif.: Sage Publications, 1970.

Machiavelli, Niccolò. *The Prince and the Discourses*. New York: Modern Library, 1940.

Machlup, Fritz. *The Production and Distribution of Knowledge in the United States*. Princeton, N.J.: Princeton University Press, 1962.

March, James G., and Olsen, Johan P. *Ambiguity and Choice in Organizations*. Bergen, Norway: Universitetsforlaget, 1976.

Marx, Karl. *Pre-Capitalist Economic Formations*. New York: International Publishers, 1965.

Matejko, Aleksander. "Planning and Tradition in Polish Higher Education." *Minerva* 7 (1969):621–648.

McCaughey, Robert A. "The Transformation of American Academic Life: Harvard University 1821–1892." *Perspectives in American History* 8 (1974):239–332.

McClelland, James C. *Autocrats and Academics: Education, Culture, and Society in Tsarist Russia*. Chicago: University of Chicago Press, 1979.

McConnell, T. R., and Edelstein, Stewart. *Campus Governance at Berkeley: A Study in Jurisdictions*. Berkeley: Center for Research and Development in Higher Education, University of California, Berkeley, 1977.

McHenry, Dean E. and associates. *Academic Departments: Problems, Variations, and Alternatives*. San Francisco: Jossey-Bass, 1977.

McNeil, Kenneth. "Understanding Organizational Power: Building on the Weberian Legacy." *Administrative Science Quarterly* 23 (1978):65–90.

Merton, Robert K. *Social Theory and Social Structure*. Rev. ed. Glencoe, Ill.: Free Press, 1957.

———. *The Sociology of Science*. Chicago: University of Chicago Press, 1973.

Metzger, Walter P. "Academic Freedom and Scientific Freedom." *Daedalus* 107 (Spring 1978):93–114.

Meyer, John W. "The Effects of Education as an Institution." *American Journal of Sociology* 83 (1977):55–77.

———. "Environmental and Internal Origins of Symbolic Structure in Organizations." Paper read at the Seminar on Organizations as Ideological Systems. Arbetslivscentrum, Stockholm, June 1979.

Miles, Robert H. *Macro Organizational Behavior*. Santa Monica, Calif.: Goodyear, 1980.

Millett, John. *The Academic Community*. New York: McGraw-Hill, 1962.

Mintzberg, Henry. *The Structuring of Organizations*. Englewood Cliffs, N.J.: Prentice-Hall, 1979.

Mitroff, Ian I., and Kilmann, Ralph H. "On Organizational Stories: An Approach to the Design and Analysis of Organizations through Myths and Stories." In *The Management of Organizational Design*, vol. 1, edited by Ralph H. Kilmann, Louis R. Pondy, and Dennis P. Slevin, pp. 189–207. New York: Elsevier North-Holland, 1976.

Moodie, Graeme C. "Authority, Charters and the Survival of Academic Rule." *Studies in Higher Education* 1 (1976):127–135.

———. "Academics and University Government: Some Reflections on British Experience." Paper read in English at the Seminario "Políticas y Estructuras Universitarias: Antecedentes y Experiencias Internacionalies," Viña del Mar, Chile, 1979. Published, in Spanish, in *Universidad Contemporanea: Antecedentes y Experiencias Internacionalies*, edited by Ivan Lavados Montes, pp. 235–258. Santiago: Corporación de Promocion

Universitaria, 1980.

Moodie, Graeme C., and Eustace, Rowland. *Power and Authority in British Universities*. Montreal: McGill-Queen's University Press, 1974.

Mosher, Frederick C. *Democracy and the Public Service*. New York: Oxford University Press, 1968.

Nagai, Michio. *Higher Education in Japan: Its Take-Off and Crash*. Tokyo: University of Tokyo Press, 1971.

Narita, Katsuya. *Systems of Higher Education: Japan*. New York: International Council for Educational Development, 1978.

Newman, John Henry Cardinal. *The Idea of a University*. Garden City, N.Y.: Image Books, 1959.

Ohkawa, Masazo. "Government-Type and Market-Type Higher Education: A Comparative Survey of Financing Higher Education in the Soviet Union, Great Britain, the United States, and Japan." *Hitosubashi Journal of Economics* 19 (December 1978):16–32.

Olsen, Johan P. "Integrated Organizational Participation in Government." In *Handbook of Organizational Design: Remodeling Organizations and Their Environments*. Vol. 2. Edited by Paul C. Nystrom and William H. Starbuck, pp. 492–516. Oxford: Oxford University Press, 1981.

Organisation for Economic Co-operation and Development. *Development of Higher Education 1950–1967. Statistical Survey*. Paris, 1970.

———. *Development of Higher Education, 1950–1967. Analytical Report*. Paris, 1971.

———. *Review of National Policies for Education: Canada*. Paris, 1976.

Östergren, Bertil. "Planning for Change in Higher Education." Summary report of a project led by Bertil Östergren. In *R & D for Higher Education*, vol. 12. Stockholm: National Swedish Board of Universities and Colleges, 1977.

Panitch, Leo. "The Development of Corporatism in Liberal Democracies." *Comparative Political Studies* 10 (April 1977):61–90.

Parsons, Talcott. "Professions." In *International Encyclopedia of the Social Sciences*. Vol. 12. New York: Macmillan, Free Press, 1968.

Parsons, Talcott, and Platt, Gerald M. *The American University*. Cambridge, Mass.: Harvard University Press, 1973.

Peisert, Hansgert, and Framhein, Gerhild. *Systems of Higher Education: Federal Republic of Germany*. New York: International Council for Educational Development, 1978.

Pempel, T. J. *Patterns of Japanese Policymaking: Experiences from Higher Education*. Boulder, Colo.: Westview Press, 1978.

Perkin, Harold. *Key Profession: The History of the Association of University Teachers*. London: Routledge and Kegan Paul, 1969.

———. *British Society and Higher Education*. Higher Education Research Group Working Paper, no. 20. New Haven, Conn.: Yale University, 1977.

Perrow, Charles. "The Analysis of Goals in Complex Organizations." *American Sociological Review* 26 (1961):854–866.

———. *Complex Organizations*. 2d ed. Glenview, Ill.: Scott, Foresman, 1979.

Pettigrew, Andrew M. *The Creation of Organisational Cultures*. Working Paper 77-11. Coventry: School of Industrial and Business Studies, University of Warwick, 1977.

Pifer, Alan; Shea, John; Henry, David; and Glenny, Lyman, *Systems of Higher*

Education: United States. New York: International Council for Educational Development, 1978.

Pike, Robert M. "Sociological Research on Higher Education in Canada 1970–1980: A Review of Some Main Themes in the English Language Literature." Paper read at the Annual Meetings of the Canadian Society for the Study of Higher Education, Halifax, June 1981.

Pratt, John, and Burgess, Tyrell. *Polytechnics: A Report.* London: Pitman, 1974.

Premfors, Rune. *How Much Higher Education Is Enough? Public Policy in France, Sweden and the United Kingdom.* Higher Education Research Group Working Paper, no. 36. New Haven, Conn.: Yale University, 1979.

———. *The Politics of Higher Education in a Comparative Perspective: France, Sweden, United Kingdom.* Studies in Politics 15. Stockholm: University of Stockholm, 1980.

———. *Integrated Higher Education: The Swedish Experience.* Group for the Study of Higher Education and Research Policy, Report no. 14. Department of Political Science, University of Stockholm, 1981.

———. "New Patterns of Authority in Higher Education." Paper read at the Conference on Higher Education in the 1980s, Organisation for Economic Co-operation and Development (OECD). Paris, 1981.

Premfors, Rune, and Östergren, Bertil. *Systems of Higher Education: Sweden.* New York: International Council for Educational Development, 1978.

Pressman, Jeffrey L., and Wildavsky, Aaron B. *Implementation.* Berkeley, Los Angeles, London: University of California Press, 1973.

Price, Derek de Solla. *Little Science, Big Science.* New York: Columbia University Press, 1963.

Rashdall, Hastings. *The Universities of Europe in the Middle Ages.* Edited by F. M. Powicke and A. B. Emden. 1895. 2d ed. Oxford: Oxford University Press, 1936.

Rauh, Morton A. *The Trusteeship of Colleges and Universities.* New York: McGraw-Hill, 1969.

Reeves, Marjorie. "The European University from Medieval Times." In *Higher Education: Demand and Response,* edited by W. R. Niblett. San Francisco: Jossey-Bass, 1970.

Riesman, David. *On Higher Education.* San Francisco: Jossey-Bass, 1980.

Roden, Donald T. *Schooldays in Imperial Japan: A Study in the Culture of a Student Elite.* Berkeley, Los Angeles, London: University of California Press, 1980.

Roth, Guenther. "Personal Rulership, Patrimonialism, and Empire-Building in the New States." *World Politics* 20 (1968):194–206.

Rourke, Francis E. *Bureaucracy, Politics, and Public Policy.* 2d ed. Boston: Little, Brown, 1976.

Roy, Robert H. *The Culture of Management.* Baltimore: Johns Hopkins University Press, 1970.

Rudolph, Frederick. *The American College and University.* New York: Knopf, 1962.

Rudolph, Susanne Hoeber, and Rudolph, Lloyd I., eds. *Education and Politics in India: Studies in Organization, Science, and Policy.* Cambridge, Mass.: Harvard University Press, 1972.

Rueschemeyer, Dietrich. "Structural Differentiation, Efficiency, and Power." *American Journal of Sociology* 83 (1977):1–25.

Ruin, Olof. *External Control and Internal Participation.* Trends in the Politics and Policies of Swedish Higher Education. Group for the Study of Higher Education and Research Policy, Report no. 1. Stockholm: University of Stockholm, 1977.

Saha, Lawrence J., and Klovdahl, Alden S. "International Networks and Flows of Academic Talent: Overseas Recruitment in Australian Universities." *Higher Education* 8 (1979):55–68.

Samii, Abdol Hassein; Vaghefi, M. Reza; and Nowrasteh, Dariush. *Systems of Higher Education: Iran.* New York: International Council for Educational Development, 1978.

Sayles, L. R. "Matrix Organization: The Structure with a Future." *Organizational Dynamics* (Autumn 1976):2–17.

Schattschneider, E. E. *The Semi-Sovereign People.* New York: Holt, Rinehart and Winston, 1960.

Schmitter, Philippe C. "Still the Century of Corporatism?" *Review of Politics* 36 (January 1974):85–131.

Seidman, Harold. *Politics, Position, and Power: The Dynamics of Federal Organization.* New York: Oxford University Press, 1970.

Selznick, Philip. *TVA and the Grass Roots.* Berkeley and Los Angeles: University of California Press, 1949.

———. *Leadership in Administration.* Evanston, Ill.: Row, Peterson, 1957.

Shea, John. "Background Paper: Education in China." In *Observations on the Relations between Education and Work in the People's Republic of China.* Report of a Study Group (1978), pp. 33–47. Berkeley, Calif.: Carnegie Council on Policy Studies in Higher Education, 1978.

Sheffield, Edward; Campbell, Duncan D.; Holmes, Jeffrey; Kymlicka, B. B.; and Whitelaw, James H. *Systems of Higher Education: Canada.* New York: International Council for Educational Development, 1978.

Shils, Edward. "Charisma." In *International Encyclopedia of the Social Sciences.* Vol. 2. New York: Macmillan, Free Press, 1968.

Sieber, Sam D. "Toward a Theory of Role Accumulation." *American Sociological Review* 39 (1974):567–578.

Simon, Maurice David. "Students, Politics, and Higher Education in Socialist Poland." Ph.D. dissertation, Stanford University, 1972.

Sloan, Douglas. *The Scottish Enlightenment and the American College Ideal.* New York: Teachers College Press, Columbia University, 1971.

Smelser, Neil. "Growth, Structural Change, and Conflict in California Public Higher Education, 1950–1970." In *Public Higher Education in California*, edited by Neil Smelser and Gabriel Almond. Berkeley, Los Angeles, London: University of California Press, 1974.

Smelser, Neil J., and Content, Robin. *The Changing Academic Market.* Berkeley, Los Angeles, London: University of California Press, 1980.

Snow, C. P. *The Two Cultures and the Scientific Revolution.* Cambridge: Cambridge University Press, 1959.

Sproull, Lee S. "Beliefs in Organizations." In *Handbook of Organizational Design: Remodeling Organizations and Their Environments.* Vol. 2. Edited by Paul C. Nystrom and William H. Starbuck, pp. 203–224. Oxford: Oxford University Press, 1981.

Stanworth, Philip, and Giddens, Anthony, eds. *Elites and Power in British*

Society. Cambridge: Cambridge University Press, 1974.

Stinchcombe, Arthur L. "Social Structure and Organizations." In *Handbook of Organizations*, edited by James G. March, pp. 142–193. Chicago: Rand McNally, 1965.

Suleiman, Ezra N. *Politics, Power, and Bureaucracy in France: The Administrative Elite*. Princeton, N.J.: Princeton University Press, 1974.

———. *Elites in French Society: The Politics of Survival*. Princeton, N.J.: Princeton University Press, 1978.

Sutton, Francis X. "African Universities and the Process of Change in Middle Africa." In *The Task of Universities in a Changing World*, edited by Stephen D. Kertesz, pp. 383–404. Notre Dame, Ind.: University of Notre Dame Press, 1971.

Szczepanski, Jan. *Systems of Higher Education: Poland*. New York: International Council for Educational Development, 1978.

Thompson, James D. *Organizations in Action*. New York: McGraw-Hill, 1967.

Thompson, Leonard. "Some Problems of Southern African Universities." In *The Future of the University in Southern Africa*, edited by Hendrik W. Van der Merwe and David Welsh, pp. 280–296. Cape Town: David Philips, 1977.

Thrupp, Sylvia L. "Gilds." In *International Encyclopedia of the Social Sciences*. Vol. 6. New York: Macmillan, Free Press, 1968.

Trow, Martin. "Problems in the Transition from Elite to Mass Higher Education." In *Policies for Higher Education*, pp. 51–101. General Report of the Conference on Future Structure of Post-Secondary Education. Paris: Organisation for Economic Co-operation and Development, 1974.

———. " 'Elite Higher Education': An Endangered Species?" *Minerva* 14 (1976):355–376.

———. "Elite and Mass Higher Education: American Models and European Realities." In *Research into Higher Education: Processes and Structures*, pp. 183–219. Report from a conference in June 1978. Stockholm: National Board of Universities and Colleges, 1979.

Turner, R. Steven. "The Growth of Professorial Research in Prussia, 1818 to 1848—Causes and Context." *Historical Studies in the Physical Sciences* 3 (1971):137–182.

Ulam, S. M. *Adventures of a Mathematician*. New York: Charles Scribner's, 1976.

Ulich, Robert. *Abraham Flexner's Universities: American, English, German*. New York: Teachers College Press, Columbia University, 1967.

Ushiogi, Morikazu. "The Japanese Student and the Labor Market." In *Changes in the Japanese University: A Comparative Perspective*, edited by William K. Cummings, Ikuo Amano, and Kazuyuki Kitamura, pp. 107–126. New York: Praeger, 1979.

Vaisey, John. "Higher Education Planning." In *Higher Education and the Current Crises*, edited by Barbara B. Burn. New York: International Council for Educational Development, 1975.

Van de Graaff, John H. *Can Department Structures Replace a Chair System?: Comparative Perspectives*. Higher Education Research Group Working Paper, no. 46. New Haven, Conn.: Yale University, 1980.

Van de Graaff, John H.; Clark, Burton R.; Furth, Dorotea; Goldschmidt, Dietrich; and Wheeler, Donald. *Academic Power: Patterns of Authority in*

Seven National Systems. New York: Praeger, 1978.

Van den Berghe, Pierre L. *Power and Privilege at an African University*. Cambridge, Mass.: Schenkman, 1973.

Veblen, Thorstein. *The Higher Learning in America*. Stanford, Calif.: Academic Reprints, 1954.

Von Humboldt, Wilhelm. "On the Spirit and the Organizational Framework of Intellectual Institutions in Berlin." *Minerva* 8 (1970):242–250.

Warren, Roland L. "The Interorganizational Field as a Focus for Investigation." *Administrative Science Quarterly* 12 (1967):396–419.

Weber, Max. *From Max Weber: Essays in Sociology*. Translated, edited, and with an Introduction by H. H. Gerth and C. Wright Mills. New York: Oxford University Press, 1946.

———. *The Theory of Social and Economic Organization*. Translated by A. M. Henderson and Talcott Parsons. New York: Oxford University Press, 1947.

———. *General Economic History*. Translated by Frank H. Knight. Glencoe, Ill.: Free Press, 1950.

———. *Max Weber on Universities: The Power of the State and the Dignity of the Academic Calling in Imperial Germany*. Translated, edited, and with an introductory note by Edward Shils. Chicago: University of Chicago Press, 1974.

Weick, Karl. "Educational Organizations as Loosely Coupled Systems." *Administrative Science Quarterly* 21 (March 1976):1–19.

Weiss, Carol H. "Knowledge Creep and Decision Accretion." *Knowledge* 1 (1980):381–404.

Wiebe, Robert H. *The Search for Order, 1877–1920*. New York: Hill and Wang, 1967.

Wildavsky, Aaron. "Doing Better and Feeling Worse: The Political Pathology of Health Policy." *Daedalus* 106 (1977):105–123.

Williams, Bruce. *Systems of Higher Education: Australia*. New York: International Council for Educational Development, 1978.

Wilson, Logan. *The Academic Man*. New York: Oxford University Press, 1942.

Windham, Douglas M. *Economic Dimensions of Education*. Washington, D.C.: National Academy of Education, 1979.

Yamamoto, Kaoru, ed. *The College Student and His Culture: An Analysis*. Boston: Houghton Mifflin, 1968.

INDEX

Academic and scientific freedom, 92–95. *See also* Liberty

Academic beliefs, basic types of, 75–99

Academic drift, 221–222, 256, 289 n. 42

Academic forms, international transfer of, 227–234

Academic guilds: and chair organization, 46–48; in Continental mode of authority system, 125–127; as discipline-rooted authority system, 113–115; and interest-group control, 173–174; organization of, 279 nn. 27, 29. *See also* Academic oligarchy; Agencies, governmental

Academic oligarchy: as integrating force, 139–145; systemwide, 122–123. *See also* Integration, oligarchic

Academic profession: culture of, 91–95; fragmentation of, 34–36; values in, 240–262, 283 n. 39

Access, 38–40, 242; and belief, 95–96; and expansion and contraction, 100–102, 191–192; and tier structure, 51

Administration: effects of disciplines on, 40–41; multicampus, 109; specialization of, 148–149, 150; subcultures of, 89–91. *See also* Bureaucratic coordination

Adult and recurrent education, 67, 101–102, 258; marginality of, 283 n. 47

Africa, 48; adaptation of foreign forms in, 230–232; importation of educational forms in, 228; personal and collegial rule in, 284 n. 15; political relevance of education in, 250

Agencies, governmental: pluralism and power in, 267–268; as professional guilds, 284 n. 14; in U.S. government, 287 n. 70

Aldrich, Howard E., 291

Altbach, Philip, 283 n. 39

Amano, Ikuo, 229

American Association of University Professors, 34, 92

American Council on Education, 34

Anomie: in academia, 291 n. 15; and American structure of higher education, 280 n. 35

Antioch College, 82, 84

Archer, Margaret, 22, 184, 199, 217, 288 n. 2, 289 n. 30

Argentina, 251

Ashby, Eric, 108, 290 n. 51

Association of American Colleges, 34

Association of American Universities, 34

Associations: discipline-oriented, 34–35; professional, 80

Australia, 280, n. 47; academic mobility in, 165; adaptation of foreign academic forms in, 232; bureau balkanization in, 175; commissions in, 141; layering in, 146; sectors in, 57, 59; student subcultures in, 87

Austria: council of rectors in, 160; democratization in, 154

Authority in academic systems, 7, 107–134; bureaucratic (governmental), 119–122; bureaucratic (institutional), 118–119; charismatic, 123–124; distribution of national modes of 125–134; forms of, 110–125; guild, 113–115; and integration and adaptive capacity, 199–205; levels of, 108–110; multicampus administration and, 109; personal rulership as form of, 110–112; political, 120–122; professional, 115–116; state-sanctioned, and markets, 169–171; system-based,

309

education systems, 186–205; changes and reform in, 236, 237
Students: consumerism and, 287 n. 49; as a subculture, 87–88
Suleiman, Ezra N., 199
Sutton, Francis, 290 n. 52
Swarthmore College, 84
Sweden, 109, 118, 254, 268; access to higher education in, 242; administrative subculture in, 90; bureau balkanization in, 175; comprehensive universities in, 194; constraints upon change in, 214; corporatism in, 172, 202; democratization in, 154; discipline-centered units in, 33; evolution from chair to department system in, 188; personnel enlargment in, 148; political coordination and curricular change in, 202; politicization in, 153; professional authority in, 159; sectors in, 54, 69; state coordination in, 139; "U68" national commission in, 19
Switzerland, 160
Symbols, institutional, 72–75; bonding power of, 81–82
Szczepanski, Jan, 286 n. 27

Teaching. See Research, and teaching
Thailand: bureau isolation and competition in, 175; sectors in, 55
Tiers: and effects of change in academic systems, 190–193; and job market, 51–52; and research, 52–53; structure of, 49–53
Trow, Martin A., 185, 267, 291 n. 13
Trustees, 92, 265, 284 nn. 24, 25; authority of, 116–118

Undergraduate education. See Tiers, structure of
United States, 13, 17, 21, 24, 30, 38, 40, 59, 73, 95, 96, 97, 98, 112, 115, 118, 122, 124, 157; access in, 100–101; academic mobility in, 165; administrative subcultures in, 89–90; associational linkages in, 160; authority in, 129–130, 268, 269; belief systems in, 198; corporatism in, 172; decentralization in, 199; disciplinary associations in, 34–35; disciplinary cultures in, 81, 82–86; equality and equity in, 242; faculty subcultures in, 89; general or liberal education in, 44; hierarchy effects and changes in, 195, 196; importation of academic forms to, 229; interest groups and innovation in, 224; layering in, 146–147;

market conditions and adaptation in, 204; market linkage in, 139; oligarchic control in, 144–145; private sector employment in, 97; professional and graduate schools in, 37; scientific freedom in, 92–93; sectors in, 60–64; status hierarchy in, 63–64, 65; student subculture in, 87; tiers in, 50–51, 190–193; trusteeship in, 92, 116–118
University Grants Committees (British), 119, 128, 129, 141, 143, 144, 147, 148, 151, 161, 177, 268, 284 n. 26
University Institutes of Technololgy (IUT), in France, 67, 223
University of Buffalo, 224–225, 226
University of California, 89–90, 109, 195, 287 n. 62
University of Chicago, 51
University of Kansas, 87
University of London, 58
University of Melbourne, 87
University of Vincennes, France, 226
USSR, 107, 236; Academy of Science in, 98, 283 n. 43; change in academic system in, 203; conflicting values in, 252; limits of state control in, 179; research belief in, 98–99; sectors in, 56; state coordination in, 142, 143; transfer of academic forms from, 228

Values, 9, 240–262
Van de Graaff, John, 283 n. 5
Van den Berghe, Pierre L., 284 n. 15
Von Humboldt, Wilhelm, 21, 278 n. 25

Weber, Max, 13, 99, 264–265, 283 n. 45, 285 n. 34
Weick, Karl, 291 n. 16
Wesleyan University, 84, 282 n. 10
Wiebe, Robert H., 190–191
Wildavsky, Aaron, 261, 273, 284 n. 14, 286 n. 17
Work, structure of: in academic organizations, 28–71; change in, 187–197; discipline and enterprise as units of, 28–34; as division of academic enterprises, 36–53; as division of academic systems, 53–63; loosely-webbed nature of, 69–71
Wright, James, 280 n. 35

Yale University, 51
Yugoslavia: faculty independence in, 45–46; short-cycle education in, 222

Zloczower, Abraham, 165